Faithful
SERVANT

The Life & Times of James McDowell Richards

Faithful SERVANT

The Life & Times of James McDowell Richards

JAMES DAVISON PHILIPS

Providence House Publishers
PROVIDENCE PUBLISHING CORPORATION
FRANKLIN, TENNESSEE

08   07   06   05   04   1   2   3   4   5

Library of Congress Control Number: 2004103316

ISBN: 1-55736-314-0

Cover design by Hope Seth

PROVIDENCE HOUSE PUBLISHERS
an imprint of
Providence Publishing Corporation
238 Seaboard Lane • Franklin, Tennessee 37067
www.providence-publishing.com
800-321-5692

To my wife, Kay Philips,
with appreciation for her encouragement
and support in this project

Contents

Acknowledgments   *ix*

Prologue   *xi*

Chapter One   *1*
   Person

Chapter Two   *31*
   President

Chapter Three   *78*
   Preacher

Chapter Four   *107*
   Pastor

Chapter Five   *136*
   Presbyter

Chapter Six   *157*
   Prophet

Epilogue   *185*

Notes   *191*

Selected Bibliography   *203*

Index   *205*

Acknowledgments

IN THE RESEARCH AND WRITING OF *FAITHFUL SERVANT*, Michelle Francis, the director of the Presbyterian Historical Society (Montreat), and her entire staff were most helpful. Julie Doyle Durway, John M. Walker III, and Diana Ruby Sanderson provided information essential to research in the important material in the Richards Papers. The facilities available for research and writing were ideal for scholars from the colleges and universities in the United States, Korea, and China. T. Erskine Clarke, professor of American church history at Columbia Theological Seminary, suggested materials describing the history of Columbia Theological Seminary in the southeastern United States during the period before and after the Civil War.

The scope of the letters, addresses, and sermons authored by James McDowell Richards goes back to his life as a student at Davidson College, and as a Rhodes Scholar at England's Oxford University. They continue to the last few months of his life. When Richards returned to the United States, he enrolled at Columbia Theological Seminary and received the bachelor of divinity degree. After five years of pastoral service in the mountains of North Georgia and Thomasville, Georgia, Richards reluctantly responded to a call to the presidency of Columbia Theological Seminary in 1932. While in North Georgia, Richards met his wife, Evelyn Narmore, who taught at Rabun Gap School for a few years until they married. For almost forty years, during good times and bad, Richards persevered in strengthening the institution and serving the Presbyterian Church (U.S.).

Essential to this project was the advice and counsel of Makemie Richards Nix. She provided information about her father and reviewed the manuscript. In doing so, she corrected false information and provided much material concerning the Richards family over three generations, and particularly family life in the president's home at Columbia Theological Seminary.

I'd also like to thank Mabel Query of Mt. Pleasant, South Carolina, for her generous support. My wife's Agnes Scott roommate, Mabel, and her late husband have been good friends for many years. I am also grateful to my daughter, June Philips Peel of Evans, Georgia, who gave many hours of typing the research material and manuscript.

Nancy Wise of Providence House Publishers has prepared the manuscript for publishing by thorough and constructive editing. I will always be grateful for her professional expertise and her patient counsel.

My wife, Katherine Wright Philips, encourgaged me in this project's lengthy period of research and writing. As a master of theological studies student at Columbia Theological Seminary in 1944–45, she experienced campus life firsthand under President James McDowell Richards. In the years of my own presidency from 1976 through 1986, Katherine served the seminary in countless ways, but particularly in hosting students, faculty, and guest lectureres in our home.

Finally, I am grateful for President Richards' impact on my own life and ministry. He recommended me to all the churches I served and gave me wise counsel during my presidency.

Prologue

AT ONE TIME OR ANOTHER," SAID JAMES KILPATRICK, THE well-known newspaper columnist, "most writers will take a crack at biography." He wrote:

> This could be in a term paper, a sermon, an obituary, or perhaps a speech introducing a visiting Elk. It's an art form worth examining. Anyone can write pedestrian biography: "Harlan Fiske Stone was born in New Hampshire in 1872 and was named to the Supreme Court by President Coolidge in 1925. He became chief justice in 1941 and served on the Court until his death in 1946. He wrote many notable opinions." Ho-Hum.
>
> What can we say of the subject that will make the person he was come alive? Did he captain the ping-pong team at Harvard? Was she best known for her quilts? Was he short, tall, red-haired, bald as a shaved egg, plump as a peach?

After admiring vivid phrases like these, Kilpatrick concluded: "Biography is an art form worth examining."[1]

That may be, but writing is still a difficult and demanding task. Jack Welch retired after a successful business career at General Electric. As one of America's most famous chief executives, he described his career in a biography entitled *Jack: Straight from the Gut*. It quickly became a best seller with an advance of $7.1 million from the publisher. Like so many writers, he described his year-long obsession with that memoir with authentic words, "It was a brutal job. I started writing at 8 o'clock A.M. in the morning and quit at midnight. Now I know why writers drink!"[2]

Writing is a brutal job. It takes a superb craftsman to shape images and events in a way that will reach a satisfactory level. One could say that James McDowell Richards was of average height, 5'8", with the body of an athlete and the mind of a scholar. His personality was reflected in his relationships on and off campus in respect for people of varying natures, views, and races. Those who knew him well knew him as an exceptional individual, with numerous roles. We will focus on the major ones.

In Kilpatrick's phrase, "this attempt to get out of the lapidarian rut" and see Richards as human, real, and as alive as any one I have ever known, is well worth the time and effort required. It will demand of author and readers a careful, lengthy look at a man devoted to his faith and to the mission of Jesus Christ. This produced a strong commitment to the Presbyterian Church. Both of these lifelong influences shaped his personality in important ways. He loved his family, whether among the generations flowing from Liberty Hill, South Carolina, or those closest to him. Though he rarely talked about it publicly the way some politicians do while running for office, it was especially true of his gratitude and love for his wife, Evelyn Knight Richards, and their children, McDowell, Makemie, and Charles.[3]

With the professional assistance of the staff of the Presbyterian Historical Society in Montreat, North Carolina, throughout research over a period of four years, Richards' correspondence, lectures, sermons, and articles were reviewed. Makemie Richards Nix provided other valuable materials, including many important family pictures. Three thick-bound books of letters of appreciation for him are reflections of a great ministry. Personal impressions created over years of observing and listening to him also helped in going beyond research to a gathering of memories and records from almost thirty years.

Dr. Richard T. Gillespie IV, Presbyterian minister and pastoral counselor, made available important papers of sermons, correspondence, and photographs from his grandfather, President Richard T. Gillespie II. As the immediate predecessor of President Richards, and the primary guide for the move of Columbia Theological Seminary from Columbia, South Carolina, to Decatur, Georgia, Gillespie no doubt shortened his life by working ceaselessly to secure financial support and save the threatened institution even after the relocation. While there were serious needs for faculty, students, and financial support in 1932, Richards inherited from Gillespie's leadership a great location and a splendid property for a theological seminary.

To rescue Richards from a "ho-hum" recital of events and places, we also observe him not in isolation, but in the light of significant political events, such as World War II. He supported those who fought the war, those who were left behind, and theological students who fled Europe to find sanctuary in the United States.

Since the Richards Papers in the archives of the Presbyterian Historical Society in Montreat, North Carolina, are the primary record of the life and work of J. McDowell Richards, they serve as the source of the biographical sketch developed here. Fortunately, most of the career and work of Richards as president of Columbia Theological Seminary is clearly presented in that record. He wrote letters, sermons, and articles that, after all these years, provide detailed information from both Richards' life and work and the setting in which he served. The papers present relevant data for serious reflection and analysis. I learned from him, worked with him, and counseled with him during thirty years of his presidency. This effort to listen and learn from Richards' complex life and work is valuable if admiration and gratitude do not distort reality. Those who read this effort to tell it like it was seen and felt can make that judgment.

Richards was capable of conciliatory letters and sermons. He often displayed that spirit in some of the most argumentative and combative days in the Church's history. He could make a point, though, with an unexpected phrase. In the last decade of his presidency, he wrote a report to the board on the process of electing faculty when everybody seemed to want to get into "the action."

> Should a professor name an associate professor or should a committee make a recommendation to the Board of Directors? In the light of our present policy on granting tenure, and in the light of original sin, should we not devise some means to evaluate each faculty member's work periodically? The "publish or perish" policy of many universities has caused extensive comment in the educational world. Yet, it has served as a procedure for evaluation in many instances. Can we devise a procedure that will take into account the whole role of the teacher, especially his contribution in the classroom? The purpose of the evaluation would be to enable the professor to work qualitatively at his maximum capacity.[4]

Earlier, as we shall see, Richards would have gathered the relevant data, consulted with the chairman of the Board of Directors, and made the decision personally. What is unique in Richards' use of theological language is the phrase in this context, "in the light of original sin." Thus, in his writing and preaching in the midst of his classical literary style there appears a surprising use of theological images and concepts. It was not so much a matter of what linguists would call slang or even "picture words," but a reflection of the way Richards' mind worked.

It is important also to see and recognize the development of Richards' theology and vocational patterns during his presidency. Even when he hesitated to change, he would eventually do so after careful thought and analysis. This was especially reflected in the last two decades of his service at Columbia.

The dual pressures of this changing world of the Church and the culture during the four decades of Richards' presidency represented his greatest challenge.

J. McDowell Richards, age 65.

All of this is to say that Richards never had an easy time at Columbia in light of economic depressions, wars, ecclesiastical crises, schism, and political revolution. He not only survived but also served valiantly to live up to his commitments and vows.

Was he perfect? Of course not, but who is? As Richards said, "after all, we live in the light of original sin." He was, however, "a good minister of Jesus Christ." As such, he faced many challenges and had to make tough choices during his ministry. He said it best in his sermon entitled "The Inevitable Choice":

Life is after all only a continual making of choices. There is never a day which does not offer two or more alternatives between which we must choose; there is hardly a situation which can arise but that we can meet it in at least two different ways. Some of these are made not for a day but for all the years we shall live upon the earth; there are some of them which are made not merely for time but for eternity. . . . Yes, life is a matter of making choices.[5]

Nurtured by faith and by family, and serving as president, preacher, pastor, presbyter, and prophet, Richards bore heavy burdens and fierce pressures beyond any reasonable expectation. The choices he made, whether for a day or for all time, were made as a servant of Christ called to His mission. Did he give the full measure of his mind, spirit, body, and life to the call of the Christ, the head of the Church? Indeed, he did.

CHAPTER ONE

Person

W<small>E CANNOT FULLY UNDERSTAND THE LIFE AND WORK</small>
of James McDowell Richards if all we ask is, "What did he do?" First and last,
and all through that remarkable life and work, Richards' character and personality shaped his thoughts and actions like a Michelangelo sculpting a "David."
We, therefore, ask first, "Who was he?"

What James McDowell Richards was as a person influenced his life's work
as a president, preacher, pastor, presbyter, and prophet. What he was also
formed what he did as a husband, father, and friend all through those tumul-
tuous four decades spanning 1932 to 1971. Even in retirement, Richards was "a
man for all seasons." What he did in all the chapters of his life and in all the
relationships with family, faculty, and friends was the product of the "person."
He was a person of faith, intelligence, conviction, and vision. That is where we
begin in an effort to listen and learn from his long and productive life.

John Wesley, the eighteenth-century British evangelist, once remarked to
a friend, "If I were to write the story of my own life, I should begin it before I
was born." We all could do so, for we are products of our past. Thus, in writing
the story of the remarkable life of James McDowell Richards, we must begin it
well before he was born, and continue throughout the eighty-three years of his
life. We remember it with respect and admiration.

As the Mississippi River emerges as a "mighty rolling stream" drawn from
springs and rivers hundreds of miles away, so James McDowell Richards' life
and work represents the product of family and community influences gathering strength from generation to generation. Naturally, from the letters and
papers of Richards, we know best those who were staunch Presbyterians,
scholarly professionals, and creative personalities.

The family includes civic leaders, educators, farmers, and ministers in the
broadest sense of those words. For much of its history, there have been

Richards and McDowells in the Liberty Hill Presbyterian Church, Liberty Hill, South Carolina. In a complete family history by Jane Leighton Richards, lineage is traced to England and Scotland, to both Presbyterian and Methodist ministers, and includes many other family names such as Smith, Makemie, Malone, and Righton. Though John G. Richards Jr., Richards' uncle, was governor of South Carolina from 1927 to 1930, he also served as clerk of the session and as a commissioner to the General Assembly of the Presbyterian Church, U.S. (PCUS). The number of ministers and missionaries produced by the families of that congregation is astonishing.

It is hard to find a more historic location in the Southeastern United States than this village where the Liberty Hill Church has served since 1851. Even before that, there were efforts to begin a church. The Presbyterians had to travel some distance to find a place of worship where there was not only the preaching of the Word, but most importantly, the celebration of the sacraments, also.

> This Liberty Hill Church and the others like it scattered throughout the up-country would be the backbone of Presbyterianism in South Carolina. Together with a few large urban churches, such as Second Presbyterian Church, Charleston, and similar churches in Georgia, they would be the ones to insist that a theological seminary be established for the education of Presbyterian ministers. The ethos of the up-country, modified by the more cosmopolitan perspectives of Charleston and Savannah, would thus shape to a large extent the nature and history of Columbia Theological Seminary.[1]

The men and women of Liberty Hill lived through five wars and survived numerous upheavals in society that were beyond all imagination. Through world crises symbolized in bayonets and bullets, atom and hydrogen bombs, and during the full range of economic changes, good and bad, they survived. Most impressive of all, many lived extraordinary lives.

Liberty Hill, South Carolina, was the center of life through many generations for the Richards family. Beginning with John Gardiner Richards, pastor of Liberty Hill Presbyterian Church from 1857 to 1887, the Richards clan multiplied and the descendents are now scattered across the world. James McDowell Richards claimed fifty-eight first cousins with Liberty Hill ties. Of the eleven ministers from the families of that historic church, four were from Richards' family: Richards (himself), John Gardiner Richards (grandfather), Charles Malone Richards (father), and John Edwards Richards.

It was this heritage of three generations of Presbyterian ministers who were deeply committed to Presbyterian Church government and their responsibilities to it that proved most important to Richards. His father, grandfather, and great-grandfather were all active in presbytery, synod, and General Assembly meetings of the Presbyterian Church. This sense of commitment and integrity certainly had a significant part in shaping Richards' life and work.

Equally important, this heritage of family also created a sense of responsibility. Not only did he reflect this in the rush of schedule and the pressure of multiple duties as a seminary president, he had twinges of remorse that he was neglecting his family. Once, out of feelings of neglect for the children, he took them to the circus.[2] Makemie Richards Nix, however, denies that she and her brothers felt any real sense of neglect.

The last letter to "Papa" in the collection among the Richards Papers expresses great satisfaction that each of his brothers and sisters joined in an endowed scholarship at Columbia Theological Seminary in honor of their parents, Charles Malone Richards and Jane Leighton McDowell Richards.

In addition, Richards' mother, Jane Leighton McDowell, also came from Liberty Hill. When Charles Malone Richards proposed to Jane Leighton McDowell, as the custom was, he wrote to her father, James McDowell, asking that he consent to the marriage. At the time, she was living with her father and caring for him in many ways. The poignant reply came back quickly on January 22, 1895:

Dear Mr. Richards,

I received your letter last week asking my consent to a union between yourself and my daughter, Janie, at sometime in the future. Of course, it is a very serious matter to give up a child, especially situated as I am. I would miss her loving services very greatly and I would miss her wise counsels in many matters respecting which I have learned to consult her more readily than I would others far beyond her years. If, however, it is Janie's desire to marry you I hereby give my consent, especially as I have so high a regard for you. I pray God that he will direct you both, and will bring about that which will be most for his glory and the happiness and welfare of you both.

With kind regards, I am yours very sincerely and truly,
James McDowell[3]

In describing the courtship and marriage of men and women at that time, Jane Leighton Wilson used an eloquent phrase for bride and groom, "for they loved each other and were married."

Other families with sons and grandsons in the ministry of the church were the Hays and Wardlaws. In 1951, Frances McDowell Perrin was the only woman in the list.

From the time Richards was welcomed at reunions as a newborn baby to the end of his earthly life at age eighty-three, he found Liberty Hill a highly valued place of family gatherings. These important experiences were more than brief superficial gatherings. They were very meaningful reunions. They regularly brought together several generations with grandparents, parents, children, aunts, uncles, cousins, and friends. For Richards, as a boy, it was never a matter of being dragged by his parents to a boring family meeting with strangers. It was, without question, a much-anticipated event in a much-loved place. Through all the seasons of life, Richards found in Liberty Hill an irresistible source of exciting and nourishing activities. There, worship and food and baseball games created a stream of valued experiences and positive influences. At the centennial celebration on August 12, 1951, the lead article of the *Camden News* began with this florid, but accurate sentence:

> The little white church in the wildwood whose clean-toned bell has been summoning Liberty Hill people of many generations to worship, opened wide its doors Sunday as many of its sons and daughters, grandsons and granddaughters returned to worship again in the little shrine where they worshipped as boys and girls, young men and young women.[4]

When he was finally persuaded to withdraw from the baseball games in his mid-fifties, Richards had moved from playing catcher, to being the pitcher and finally the right fielder. It is questionable if they were safer positions, but they did develop in him a kind of toughness essential to the presidency of a theological seminary. Reunions, then, included worship, feasting, visiting, talking, and his favorite sport, baseball. These, in important ways, helped form his personality and his sense of family. Liberty Hill was, beyond question, a place where others joined his parents in producing a direct and determinative influence on Richards' faith and life.

One act near the end of his presidency showed Richards continued to value and cherish Liberty Hill's experiences. In 1971 and 1972, letters were sent far and wide with fervent appeals for money to create a trust for the maintenance of the Liberty Hill Church and the cemetery that had served generations as a burial ground. Mary James Richards, a sister, left an endowment fund for the cemetery at her death on June 26, 1972. The church is still active today.

One of the most direct and lasting influences on Richards came from his father, Charles Malone Richards. His life spanned the years of February 1, 1871 to December 25, 1964. He was a unique and influential minister in the Presbyterian Church (U.S.), serving as pastor of churches in Statesville and Davidson, North Carolina. In the last chapter of his life, he became professor of Bible at Davidson College.[5]

In the centennial anniversary service at Liberty Hill Church on August 21, 1951, sons and daughters, grandsons and granddaughters, and a large company of other descendents of the original families worshipped together. Charles Malone Richards' sermon that day described the founders as lovers of liberty, beauty, learning, and, somewhat surprisingly, recreation. The residents built beautiful homes and gardens and valued music, art, literature, and the Presbyterian Church.

Davidson College students regarded professor Charles Malone Richards as something of a "character." As serious as he was about Presbyterian Church doctrine and government, he evidently had a unique sense of humor. How else can you explain the astonishment created when the dignified professor once umpired the student-faculty baseball game wearing a cowboy hat, a red bandana scarf, huge pants, and work shoes? On his shoulder he carried a squirrel gun to enforce his decisions.[6]

As an active presbyter, Charles Malone Richards attended General Assembly meetings regularly as a commissioner. It gave his son, James McDowell Richards, some satisfaction to learn from Richard T. Gillespie III that his father led the Assembly to decline an urgent request from Oglethorpe University that it be adopted by the General Assembly of 1917. Up until this point, numerous colleges and seminaries were limited to synods and presbyteries. There might have been advantages both ways, but it would have placed Oglethorpe University in a unique and favored position in receiving funds from the whole church when other colleges and seminaries could not. The latter, more equitable relationship has proven its wisdom well. Gillespie said: "It was your father's speech on the floor of the Assembly that turned the tide and the request was not approved." In Gillespie's view, "this was a very wise stand and one for which all of us who love the Church might well be grateful."[7]

More to the point, too, was the role of Charles Malone Richards as his son's valued listener and counselor. There is evidence that gives credence to the possibility that James McDowell Richards was dedicated to the ministry of the Church as an infant. In a strong lecture at Columbia Seminary in March of 1948, Charles Malone Richards made the case for such a practice. Much to his satisfaction, six members of the entering class that year indicated they had been so dedicated at baptism.

Communication in the first twenty years of Richards' presidency was usually done by mail. Letters full of important issues and events, therefore, went back and forth between father and son. True to mail service in those years, they were delivered the day after they were posted. (Now, of course, e-mail, telephone, and face-to-face conversations are the norm.) So, for the two Richards, in the 1930s and '40s, the issues of location and merger with the other three Presbyterian Church in the United States (PCUS) seminaries were fully and anxiously discussed, largely by mail, and with increasing fervor.

President and professor agreed on that decisive issue. The increasing talk of such a merger of the four institutions alarmed President Richards, and he confessed his feelings to his father. The Works Committee report, approved by the General Assembly in 1938, called for this action immediately. A thoughtful and unbiased letter probably did not reflect the true feelings of either son or father, but it did state the issue quite well. On September 12, 1942, McDowell, as his family called him, wrote to his "Papa:"[8]

> There are many things in the report which are worthy of careful consideration, particularly the reasoning with reference to the wisdom of some reduction in the number of our seminaries. On the other hand there are some criticisms, which appear to me to be groundless, and some proposals that are entirely too idealistic to meet with any success . . . In some respects, I think the report is unfair to Columbia Seminary. You will note that Louisville Seminary comes off decidedly best in this survey; that Austin Seminary met with no approval at all; and that Union Seminary is severely criticized for the graduate program. I shall be interested in the reaction of the Union Seminary faculty to that.[9]

Columbia's Board of Directors lost little time in expressing a negative response to these destructive recommendations. Richards reported to his father:

> As I anticipated, our directors did not feel that Columbia Seminary ought to be moved from its present location. They believe that this is the best location for a Seminary in our Church, and also that we have moral obligations here in view of the recent successful campaign which was supported fully on the understanding that Columbia would stay put.[10]

The themes of this flow of words and topics changed with the times, often abruptly. In the early years of World War II, citizens were urged to plant gardens, raise poultry, and keep a cow for milk. Thus, the "citizen Richards" reports to his father with some pride:

> My chickens seem to be getting on very nicely, and I have not lost any more of them. At times I wish very much that I could have the benefit of your expert advice on their care. The garden is also a subject on which we could well profit by your experience, but unfortunately it is a little difficult to do so at this distance. You will have to come down some time during the summer to see the important developments here in the field of agriculture and of poultry raising.[11]

The reports on such topics continued. With great pleasure, the farmer Richards reported in the fall:

> An outstanding development in our family circle was the laying of the first egg in our chicken house on last Sunday. At least four of our pullets have been laying with some regularity since that time . . . We have come just about to the end of our garden for the time being. After gathering a few more tomatoes and a few more butter beans, we shall have to wait for later fall crops. I spent the afternoon mowing my lawn in an effort to have it look fairly decent for the return of the students next week.[12]

There were also exchanges between father and son about preaching. On November 19, 1943, there was an expression of appreciation for birthday greetings, and for favorable comments on a sermon Professor Richards had examined. They were in agreement that the average printed sermon is a most insipid and uninteresting thing, and that there is seldom one that does not leave them wondering how it could have influenced anyone.

They also discussed the events in the life of the Church and the seminary. Criticism of Columbia's faculty and President Richards by Carl McIntire's *Christian Beacon* and, later, the *Southern Presbyterian Journal* was occasionally on their agenda. These publications, though critical, differed greatly in their purpose and spirit, and the *Journal* was far more influential in the Presbyterian Church (U.S.). Though surprised by these "very serious attacks," President Richards concluded: "Whatever may be said of the life of a seminary president, it is certainly never dull, and is always taking turns which one does not expect."[13]

The *Christian Beacon*, for example, blamed Richards' association with the Federal Council of Churches for "heresies" at Columbia Theological Seminary. So it must have been a relief to be weeding the garden or feeding chickens rather than reading such an angry diatribe.

Charles Malone Richards' death on Christmas Day, 1964, was a source of both rejoicing and grieving for immediate family members. Letters of condolences from many church leaders were a special source of comfort for James McDowell Richards. The usual mixed feelings were created by a sense of relief that his illness and hospitalization were over. In that mysterious experience of grief, however, Richards felt a very real sense of loss. Thus, the letters and calls were much appreciated. Dr. Robert Turner, the executive presbyter of the Synod of North Carolina put into words the feelings of many:

> Your father, Dr. Richards, in our estimation, was one of the great men of the church and rendered a service, the results of which shall carry forward in the years that lie ahead . . . Dr. Richards was one of the greatest influences in my life.

When I came to Davidson College he was the Professor of Bible and I sat at his feet in that capacity. He was also supplying the pulpit of the Davidson Church where we heard him preach . . . Dr. Richards examined me for ordination in English Bible. I considered him one of my good friends, and felt I always had the understanding and full support of Dr. Richards in the work which we tried to do. Therefore, I feel greatly indebted to him and I am most grateful for the opportunity I had of knowing him and studying under him and working with him.[14]

This letter went to all children of Professor Charles Malone Richards, including Mary Jane Richards, Jane Leighton Liston, Mrs. John C. Bailey Jr., and James McDowell Richards.

Wade P. Huie Jr., an alumnus and a young member of the Columbia Seminary faculty at the time, was quite pastoral in his letter to Richards. He spoke for many of the seminary community:

Writing a note of condolence seems a weak gesture, but I did want to assure you of my sympathy on this particular day, December 28, 1964. The death of your father has surely brought to mind many happy memories of the past and has certainly brought to mind your confidence that all is well with those who are "at home" with God. I remember hearing your father speak on covenant baptism at the Seminary. It was the only occasion I saw and heard him personally. However, I feel my life has been enriched by him as he has ministered through you. Thanks be to God for the many lives that enrich our lives! Thanks be to God for the One life through whom all this is made possible.

Sincerely,
Wade[15]

The significant thing about the obituary of Rev. Charles Malone Richards is that it included striking similarities to qualities in the life of his son, McDowell:

Dr. Richards had a winsome disposition, a strong sense of humor, a genial manner, and an understanding ear and heart. Yet, he was a stern follower of his uncompromising standards for the right and in his leadership for its promotion. An eloquent preacher of Biblical truth, a faithful pastor, and an able teacher, he was beloved by young and old in every walk of life. Many a Davidson man has declared that the influence of Dr. Richards in the pulpit, in the class room and on the athletic field was a powerful factor in determining his life.[16]

What are these similarities? Like father, like son, Professor Richards was an active presbyter, and a graduate of Davidson College and Columbia

Theological Seminary. Furthermore, he was, at one time, offered both the presidency and a professorship at Columbia Theological Seminary. Unlike his son, however, he accepted neither of these invitations. What is more, Richards, the son, was much more supportive of ecumenical relationships in the Federal Council of Churches and the World Presbyterian Alliance. In social issues such as racial justice, he was far more outspoken and active in seeking what he felt was God's justice for all people on the earth.

Dr. Walter L. Lingle, a classmate and longtime friend and president of Davidson College, paid this tribute: "A student vote, taken in November, 1891, concluded that 'the strongest moral character on the campus was C. M. Richards.' This is another proof that the boy is father to the man."[17]

Of paramount influence in Richards' life and ministry was his wife, Mary Evelyn Knight Richards. Her family provided her a home where the Presbyterian Church in Clearwater, Florida, was a strong influence. After two years at Agnes Scott College, Miss Knight's father died, and she took a teaching position in North Georgia. She remarked once, "I was glad to find it for it was the only one I could get in the depression years." There she met the newly ordained pastor of a group of mountain churches, fell in love, and married James McDowell Richards on December 31, 1929. A few months after the wedding, Richards became pastor of the First Presbyterian Church of Thomasville, Georgia, but after eleven months there, the desperate appeal of Columbia Seminary became a call that he could not refuse.

Three children survive, though a fourth, her namesake, Mary Evelyn, died shortly after birth in July 1936. The oldest, James McDowell Richards Jr., born July 26, 1931, is a psychologist living in Tucson, Arizona. Mary Makemie Nix, born December 12, 1938, had a distinguished twenty-six-year career of teaching children at the Westminster School in Atlanta. She continues today with a program preparing literature for children, which is widely used not only in Atlanta but also in Kenya. The youngest, Charles Malone Richards II, was born on April 10, 1946, and is an attorney in Atlanta. Both Makemie and Charles are active and useful members of their family's church, Central Presbyterian Church of Atlanta, Georgia. There are now seven grandchildren: Michael, Steven Malone, Thomas Makemie, Mary Evelyn, John Arthur Jr., Emily Malone, and Michael McDowell.

For years, Richards' letters concluded with family news. It was usually, "all are well" or occasionally, "some are sick with flu." However, an early letter with family news brought the announcement that:

McDowell's alligator and turtle, which he has named Bill and Juner are still alive and kicking. I am glad to say that we have not yet had to turn the bath tub over to them, however, as they seem to get along quite comfortably in the tub which was used for McDowell during his babyhood. For the past few days he has had them prominently displayed on a chair in the dining room and the two pets were dozing comfortably there when I left home a little while ago!

> With much love, your devoted brother,
> McDowell[18]

A sister, Mary Richards, of Davidson, North Carolina, was thanked profusely for a check for Columbia Seminary and presents for McDowell. It is difficult to tell whether the check or the presents pleased President Richards most. However, he reported:

McDowell is delighted with the present you sent him. He tried on the suit at once, and it is a good fit, but he is not permitted to wear it until Easter. He kept repeating at dinner on Saturday, "This has sure been a lucky day for me." Again, thanking you for your generous contribution to the Seminary and with a great deal of love for you all, I am, devotedly, your brother.

> McDowell[19]

All three children were enjoying the Christmas gift of a puppy from the John C. Baileys of Davidson. It obviously came early, for Richards wrote November 4, 1949, to his sister and her husband:

I want you to know that the Richards family greatly appreciates the Christmas present from the Bailey family and the present is getting along splendidly. The children really enjoy the puppy thoroughly and I do not think anything could have pleased them more. I wish you could see Charlie's face as he plays with the little dog throughout the day, but particularly in the morning. I do not know when I have seen him as happy over anything as he is over Mickey. . . . This is a real treasure and Kemie is also delighted with him. We have decided that there shall be joint ownership in this case and the two children both have a claim to the dog. There is a little conflict over him now and then, but in the main they get along satisfactorily. Incidentally, Evelyn, too, is really enjoying the puppy very much, and as you know, I have always been fond of dogs.[20]

Richards declined an invitation to help install Marshall Woodson as pastor of First Presbyterian Church, Thomasville, Georgia, in spite of his great appreciation and affection for that church where he had a brief pastorate. The reason? "We are expecting an addition to our family and I wish to stay near home at this time."[21]

Even occasional illness among the children was carefully reported to members of the Richards clan: "My own family is slightly under the weather at present as McDowell has the mumps and Mary Makemie has been suffering with a bad cough. Neither of them is really uncomfortable, however, and I think they will soon be all right."[22]

Three years later, the family report repeated that news: "Our house has been something of a hospital the past twenty four hours, since everyone but myself has been more or less under the weather yesterday."[23]

While there are reports on each family member, there was the exciting news that, "Little Charlie has been developing quite rapidly and has finally learned to get up to a sitting position any time he wants to, and he has immediately gone beyond that, and learned to pull himself up to a standing position by catching the side of the bed. He also does a great deal of talking."[24]

Richards obviously felt that having young children did much to help the family preserve a youthful outlook. This contradicts the estimate of one of his closest friends who will remain anonymous that, "Mac was born old!" He was mature and dignified, but there is evidence that he thoroughly enjoyed his days as a young student in all the places, programs, and years of study. He could easily be described as "a doting father." His delightful sense of humor helped in all the seasons of life.

As the years went on, this undiluted pleasure of having young children gave way to anxious moments with teenagers and college students. Grades and other measurements of academic work were increasingly important. He gave hints now and then of a feeling of having in some ways been away too much and having, thus, neglected his family. Richards responded to a form letter from Major General J. Binns, Camp Chaffee, Arkansas, where McDowell was a private. Since the general's letter mentioned the importance of good character in soldiers, the response of a parent was quite favorable: "We are glad our son is able to serve his country as a soldier and hope that he will prove himself a worthy man in doing so. We shall, of course, endeavor to keep in touch with him by correspondence as you suggested."[25]

Richards spoke and wrote of the children constantly. For example, a friend from Oxford days, A. A. Roberts, esquire, Cottingham, Yorkshire, England, received regular letters. Care packages were sent during the World War II crisis of shortages. These letters acknowledged correspondence, inquired about health and activities, and always reported family news. After dealing with world crises in Russia or China, Richards usually concluded: "My family are all well, and I am personally enjoying good health and spirits. There is really not a great deal that is new to report as life continues its ordinary routine."[26]

He added: "I hope to go with my family to Montreat in the mountains of Western, North Carolina for a vacation in August."

However, on December 21, 1955, he wrote A. A. Roberts, esq., that he was not sending his good Rhodes Scholar friend a care package that year since the economy had improved so much in Britain, and there were needs in the United States. The major portion of the letter deals with family. Richards wrote:

> The year which is ending has been an eventful one for my family in many ways, and has brought both its lights and shadows. Early last June I was elected Moderator of the General Assembly of the Presbyterian Church in the United States. Consequently, I have had a rather busy year. Naturally, the honor is one that I deeply appreciate and the experience I am having in visiting various parts of the Church is stimulating and enjoyable. At the same time it affords me a real opportunity for service.[27]

In a May 4, 1979, interview with Delores L. Donnelly, however, he strongly criticized the use of the moderator full time. At most, he served only half time in his 1955–56 moderatorial year.[28] At the maximum, Richards felt the moderator's duties should be largely carried out at the meeting of the General Assembly. He would be uncomfortable with the present situation that requires constant travel, meetings, sermons, and speeches.

Richards wrote in a letter to his Oxford friend, A. A. Roberts:

> I regret to say that my wife suffered a mild heart attack in June and that it was necessary for her to spend about four weeks in the hospital and to take things quietly after she came home. I am thankful for the fact that she seems to be greatly improved in health and that we have reason to hope for her full recovery.
>
> Our older son, McDowell, was drafted into the Army in September and is now stationed at Fort Ord, California. In light of the fact that he had taken advanced studies in psychology, the Army assigned him to Human Research Unit No. 2 and is using him in certain scientific investigations which will be of value to our armed forces. In that respect he is fortunate. Our daughter is in her senior year as a high school student and our younger boy is now in the fourth grade so we have varied interests. This Christmas for the first time one member of our family circle will be away from home since McDowell cannot come across the continent, but we look forward to a pleasant and peaceful time together.
>
> I still think with pleasure and often with nostalgia of my days in Britain and the friendships formed there.[29]

Montreat vacations were times that McDowell, Makemie, and Charles seemed to enjoy greatly. They grieved when the house there was sold.

The Richards celebrating their fiftieth wedding anniversary. Left to right: J. McDowell Richards, Evelyn Richards, Jane Leighton Richards Liston, and Robert T. L. Liston.

While troubled by heart disease as the years went on, Mrs. Richards maintained her flower garden at the president's home and is still remembered by those who knew her for her beautiful day lilies. She supported her husband in his ministry. According to Makemie Richards Nix, Mrs. Richards had said: "I have never known another man so deeply committed to doing the will of God."

One poignant moment for James McDowell Richards came in the last months of his residency in the Presbyterian Home in Summerville, South Carolina. Dr. Charles Robert Tapp, superintendent of Presbyterian Homes, talked with him once about his life and work. Richards mentioned his children. Dr. Tapp asked a powerful question, "Did you ever tell your children you loved them?" The reply, "I'm not sure, but they knew I did."

Mrs. Richards moved to the Presbyterian Home in Summerville, South Carolina, when Dr. Richards' health required such a facility. After his death, she returned to Atlanta to be with her children. She did confide in some special friends that there were too many Republicans in Summerville for her Democratic taste.

James McDowell Richards experienced change in his eighty-three years as persons had rarely seen it. The United States of America, as well as other nations, moved through those years of escalating transformation in the twentieth century with tremendous achievements and abysmal failures. The towns and villages Richards knew well had mushroomed into large cities with steadily expanding growth. Those mountain roads in North Georgia where he served his first pastorate became expressways and asphalt ribbons opening to the world. The scientific advances since his days as a student at Davidson, Princeton, Christ Church College, Oxford, and Columbia Theological Seminary were beyond anything he could have envisioned. Commerce, industry, television, and radio brought the world to our living rooms. Moreover, Richards changed as well.

What did not change was his commitment to Jesus Christ and to the Presbyterian Church (U.S.), as he knew it and longed for it to be. The Church itself became dramatically different and moved from a small collection of presbyteries and synods that Richards knew well to a national Church, with new leadership and programs. Travel and television opened windows to the world, offering glimpses of the planet earth and a vast and mysterious universe. In that complex context, Richards lived a life shaped by faith, hope, and love. Those powerful influences, exemplified by values found in generations of his family, helped to make him the person he was.

So who was Richards? We learn a great deal about a person by listening to what they say. We learn most by examining what a person does. Richards said many profound and significant words, but he showed the essence of his character by what he did.

First of all, he was faithful. The most formative influence in the mind and personhood of any human being is faith. It can be faith in everything from fact to fiction, and from good to evil. There are, among the people of the world, many faiths, true and false. The New Testament concept of faith as a deep and personal commitment to Jesus Christ was the focus early and throughout the life of Richards. It was not a temporary whim or a passing fancy of an adolescent, but the driving force of his lifetime. Nurtured in his childhood and youth in a family that valued such faith beyond all other values, and matured in his intellectual and scholarly pursuits, he was obviously driven to be "a good minister of Jesus Christ."[30] This description originates with the Apostle Paul and is used in several variations. In one of these, an emissary, Tychicus, was sent to the church at Colossae to tell of Paul's activities with this commendation: "He is a beloved brother and faithful minister, and fellow servant in the Lord."[31]

Richards' life, formed by his heritage and faith, was precisely that. The faith of a lifetime that created a decency and integrity in Richards' life is increasingly rare today. It is, without question, the key to unlocking the history of James McDowell Richards.

We saw in Richards a blend of kindness and strength. His kindness, however, in no way contradicted his strength. Two diverse individuals speak of this blend of apparent opposites. J. Phillips Noble, a Columbia Seminary graduate in the class of 1944, eloquently painted a portrait of him in these words:

In over thirty-five years of ministry, I have known and worked with many people. I have, however, never known a perfect person, but I have known some people who, as mature Christians have blessed my life a very great deal. They have blessed my life because they have inspired me to want to have in my life some of the wonderful qualities I have seen in them.

One such person whose name would be known to some of you is Dr. J. McDowell Richards. My entire ministry has been served as I have known, witnessed and observed him. As I have watched his work I have always known him to be extremely kind and fair, and yet strong in his commitment and direction.

I have seen him in another capacity also; that is his relationship to the church at large. Nobody could serve as the president of one of our church's institutions without having a great deal of involvement in the life of the institution as a whole. Over these long years I have seen him deal with problems in the denomination. I have seen him take stands on various controversial issues that have arisen. I have observed with a great deal of appreciation the fact that he arrives at his position with all the information that he can have at his command, and with as open and fair position as possible. . . . I saw him seek to make his contribution in this changing world and in the changing society, and do it from the standpoint of a deep commitment to the Christian faith. This was applied to the affairs in which he was involved, and in which his society was involved . . . I have observed him . . . as a father acting with gentleness and kindness and yet with strength. In these later years when his wife's health has become rather poor, his extreme devotion and commitment to her has been an inspiration.[32]

Mrs. J. Holmes Smith also wrote of this blend of kindness and strength as seen in the life of Richards. After the death of her husband, a well-known physician, Mrs. Smith left New Orleans, Louisiana, to become the director of Food Service at Columbia Theological Seminary. She never earned much salary and had a very limited budget for seminary meals. The move to Columbia Seminary brought her from a home in New Orleans to housing in Simons-Law Hall on the campus of Columbia Seminary, where she lived with two of her children in an apartment formed from dormitory rooms. But, as if it made much difference, she did have the title of "seminary hostess."

After a dinner honoring Richards, she expressed her appreciation of him in a gracious letter:

> My heart was overflowing with pride because of your fine useful life and accomplishments, and with gratitude because you are my friend. I am grateful to God for the privilege and many blessings that have come from working under such a great man. You are truly a "man of God," the finest Christian I have ever known.[33]

Such respect and appreciation from a staff member during difficult times is not only impressive, but magnificently illumines the quality of kindness and strength in Richards.

Again and again, that kindness was shown to students with problems and needs. To a surprising degree, this attitude was also reflected in his stance with those who differed with him in the governing bodies of the Church and in Columbia's constituency. The justice issues of the day and the ecumenical bodies he served were flash points of differences with ministers and elders. However, Richards always sought to unify, not divide, the Church.

Other seminary presidents were the recipients of kindness and respect from Richards. In a carefully considered stance, he maintained a courteous and supportive relationship with the other three Presbyterian (U.S.) seminaries. At times, their competition for students was felt very keenly, but no grudges were held. Even in the days when the territories were clearly marked in the ecclesiastical system of "ownership and control" by synods, Richards fought turf wars. Throughout the fifteen years of discussing the merger of the four Presbyterian seminaries, Richards was open and courteous to the proponents of this significant proposal. He began to lose confidence in the idea after the first two years of financial straits in 1932–33, but until the second decade of his presidency, he was open to any possibility that might remove his doubts. He fought no battles in the style of a lone ranger. Through discussions of the General Assembly action recommending merger and the subsequent negotiations, he always asked, "What is best for the Presbyterian Church (U.S.)?" The post–World War II boom in the population in the southern United States confirmed the need for all four PCUS institutions. The metropolitan area of Atlanta led the way for significant growth in the Presbyterian Church, U.S.

Greater numbers of Presbyterian ministers were needed, and returning veterans of World War II tripled enrollments at Columbia Seminary.

Richards' retirement brought him a steady stream of appreciation and affection. With all the accolades, tributes, honorary degrees, and two four-inch-thick books of grateful letters from all over the world, Richards was vulnerable to pride. However, it was difficult to thank him or praise him without receiving a sincere disclaimer.

He responded to flattering words with humility. The First Presbyterian Church of Winston-Salem, North Carolina, sent him one of a very few invitations given to a Southerner to speak in a special series of lectures. Usually, the ablest and best known ministers in the nation were invited. The Richards humility "kicked in" and he accepted with this response: "I am afraid I am stepping into company which is a little too fast for me in view of the names of other prospective preachers which you mention. Perhaps, however, the congregation will accept ordinary fare for one Sunday."[34]

Fifteen years after his graduation and ordination, a minister wrote to express great appreciation for his seminary experience. Richards' response was a mixture of gratitude and disclaimer.

> Your gracious letter of December 10 reached me by the morning mail and is one of the nicest things which has happened to me in a long time. I am all too conscious that I do not really deserve the kind things which you have said about me, but you may be sure that I have been touched by your confidence, and that I am deeply grateful for the spirit of friendship expressed in your letter.[35]

He proceeded to turn the compliment back on the writer by saying:

> The real joy and reward of my work here is observing the life and ministry of the sons of this institution who have gone out during the years I have been here. We are proud to claim you as one of these and I will continue to follow your career with deep interest and with the prayer that God will bless and use you increasingly in His service.

This quality of humility continued throughout Richards' presidency. Shortly before retirement, an appreciative letter went to Rev. Rex Salters of Waco, Texas. It went to thank Salters for his gift and his gratitude to Columbia for his education, but Richards' response follows a pattern of humility throughout a lifetime:

> Glad though I was to receive the gift for the Seminary, your letter meant even more to me by reason of the expressions which it contained concerning Columbia Theological Seminary. We are always conscious of deficiencies in our

work, and there are many times we are discouraged concerning it. For this reason it is most gratifying and encouraging to receive such an expression of appreciation as that contained in your letter. This has been a real source of encouragement to me. I am glad to know of your favorable evaluation of Columbia Seminary and its teachers, and I shall plan to share the sentiments of your letter with members of our faculty, particularly those you mentioned.[36]

In 1954, under the leadership of the president of the Alumni Association, Frank Alfred Mathes, an Oldsmobile automobile was presented to President Richards. The celebration of his presidency also involved many expressions of appreciation. The event produced tremendous feelings of gratitude in Richards:

> These expressions have warmed my heart, and as I said to Mrs. Richards this morning, they make me want to be a better man. Certainly I find in them a real sense of encouragement as I face the future and I hope that I shall be a better Christian and a more faithful servant of the Church by reason of what you did. I need not say that we are delighted with the beautiful Oldsmobile and there will be a warm sense of pleasure in our hearts each time we ride in it. Our children are filled with enthusiasm and wonder. After Charlie had examined each detail of the car with care, including the exhaust pipe, the glove compartment, the arm rests, and everything else, he remarked, "My this is tremenjous!" This is just the way Mrs. Richards and I feel about the car and about the whole thing planned on Thursday. This is "tremendous" and we are overwhelmed by it. I spent last night reading the Book of Remembrance from beginning to end and was both humbled and inspired by the experience.[37]

Every alumnus who sent a letter and a gift received a personal note of thanks.

In the most painful of his relationships, Richards reached out in humility, kindness, and a loving spirit. His presidency from the beginning to the end was hampered by a context of divided minds and convictions in the Church. It was particularly so in the synods related to Columbia Seminary. Even in the last year of his presidency, there was no lessening of the stormy seas in which he lived and served. They intensified, and the severing of the body of Christ through schism eventually occurred. Though persons of strong convictions could be found on both sides, Richards sought with diplomacy and tact to keep the denomination whole. Sadly, it was not to be.

A friend, the Rev. A. S. Moffatt, expressed with some anguish and irony his "concern" about a new association of ministers and elders called Concerned Presbyterians.[38] Richards responded:

> I appreciate your concern over the tactics and substance of the program which has been launched by the so called "Concerned Presbyterians." I trust that I am

also a concerned Presbyterian and I believe in many of the things so dear to those who have formed this organization. However, I cannot agree with the spirit and methods which too often characterize their activities, and I agree with you in feeling that they can cause a great deal of trouble for our Church.[39]

A small number of students once made accusations of heresy against Richards and the faculty. In such instances, his response was firm, but kind. At the height of campaigns against various faculty members, the chairman of the board, Patrick D. Miller, and the president gathered the accusers together and offered to transfer their credits to any institution they chose. Only a few accepted that offer. Most students were grateful for their experience at Columbia. However, in this, and in other things, a few ingrates poisoned the campus atmosphere.[40]

One cannot jump to the conclusion that such humility and modesty in his personality was a sign of weakness, or was even a pretense of some type. He appeared to feel, quite honestly, that he was "unworthy" of high praise. He was a Calvinist when it came to the concept of sinfulness. However conciliatory Richards might be, no one could ever describe him as a weak and vacillating president. Nor could he ever be described by the words of Winston Churchill in the heat of a political campaign against Clement Atlee: "Mr. Atlee, they say, is a humble man. True, for he has much to be humble about!"

An accurate, and indeed, eloquent description of Richards is that of journalist Delores L. Donnelly, who, after a long interview, produced a moving evaluation. In a comprehensive article, she used vivid images of poetry to describe him:

> An humble and modest man
> He clanged no cymbals
> Sounded no trumpets,
> Except for causes beyond himself.[41]

These powerful images followed a vivid analysis of Richards' courageous challenge to Governor Eugene L. Talmage of Georgia. Governor Talmage frequently spoke with scorn concerning the inferiority of African-Americans and angrily asserted his firm commitment to maintain "Segregation now, and Segregation forever." Richards strongly and publicly opposed Talmage with tremendous effect even while maintaining a respect for the office of governor of the state of Georgia.

However, Richards' kindness to friends, and especially to graduates and their families, is the focus of the major portion of Donnelly's ten-page article.[42]

Immediately after assuming the presidency, Richards faced the horrendous impact of the economic depression of the 1930s. However, in differing ways for the entire thirty-nine years of his presidency, the issue of financial needs of Columbia Theological Seminary and those who participated in its life remained. Families with children were involved. Faculty received minimal salaries. Students needed financial aid. Like a kind and concerned parent, Richards was there to help, and he made every attempt to do so. He did, moreover, expect occasional loans to be repaid. A graduate described Richards' compassionate concern:

> I brought little money with me to pay my tuition and fees. I worked at every job I could get for three years at Columbia Seminary. They included work scholarships in the dining hall and on campus. Most weekends, I preached in a small town in South Carolina. When my old car broke down, I rode buses and once hitchhiked to arrive on time for the Morning Service. Dr. Richards was always ready to listen and help me find a way to finish the three years. I will always be grateful to him.[43]

Richards maintained a pattern of formality and respect toward people of varied positions and views. It was a rare kind of dignity when today everything flows from a first-name culture. With Richards, it did not seem out of character to relate, courteously and warmly, to persons in all positions and status with an inoffensive formality. Perhaps it was an almost unconscious reflection of the life he had known as a student at McCallie School, Davidson College, Princeton University, Christ Church College, Oxford, and even at Columbia Theological Seminary. Unfailingly, he used formal titles, not just for faculty, but also for staff members and students. It was, for four decades, Professor McPheeters, Professor Green, Professor Gear, or Professor Cousar. For students, it was Mister Leith and Mister Ormond. Even for his closest associate, Miss Virginia Harrison, she was always Miss Harrison to Richards. In a way, his practice of those patterns made one feel as if one was important.

Miss Harrison was invaluable in her career of thirty-seven years at Columbia Theological Seminary. She, however, did not "suffer fools gladly" whether student or professor.

In the 1940s, an imaginative discussion by students took place seeking to identify the most reckless and outrageous approach possible toward President Richards. The winner, easily, was this suggested scenario: A student, in a sudden spasm of insanity, would stroll into the president's suite and, with reckless abandon, greet Miss Virginia Harrison, his administrative assistant, bookkeeper, and manager of the book store in these astonishing words, "Hi, Ginny, where's Mac?"

There is also an oral tradition that one student, a returning World War II hero, the Rev. Butterfly Hamilton, and his family spent the night with Dr. and Mrs. Richards, February 16, 1946. Richards reported with considerable astonishment that at the end Butterfly was calling Mrs. Richards, "Evelyn."

Even Richards didn't do that in public. She was "Mrs. Richards."

The one exception to this practice of formality goes back to Richards' college days. Sprinkled through personal correspondence with friends were many unique nicknames. They include "Ink," "Old Lady," and "Jas. A."

Richards could not possibly provide adequate salaries for faculty and staff in the depression of the 1930s. Gifts and grants steadily eroded. Endowment returns diminished to almost zero. During those frightening days, the faculty voluntarily agreed to a one-third reduction in salary. However, he showed strong support for them and reflected tenacious optimism in every report and every presentation to the Church. In occasional attacks upon a professor's theological integrity, he responded eloquently with a strong defense.

Tireless in carrying heavy burdens in his presidency, Richards came up the hill from the Inman Drive president's home to Campbell Hall to move heaven and earth to save and to strengthen Columbia. He traveled the highways and byways of the Southeast, and took overnight trains and ships at sea to meetings that were exhausting and challenging. He asked no one to do more than he himself was doing. Every invitation to preach was accepted if the dates were open in his schedule. He didn't hesitate when a minister scheduled for him three services and a talk to college students on a single Sunday. His host did offer to lessen the burden on that day, but concluded, "If this burden is too heavy, feel frank to say so. I believe in working a good horse when you find one!"

Richards had the rare capacity to relate to his occasional critics, whether they were a minister from Mississippi, a former student from Tennessee, or a lay trustee. Small in number, they wrote regularly about heresy in the Church and communism among the staff of the Federal Council of Churches. He may have disarmed them by courtesy in the governing bodies of the church, or with diplomatic letters which began: "You may be right, and I may wrong, but it is my deep conviction after prayerful analysis that these criticisms are unfounded to a very large degree."[44]

In the fierce and acrimonious debates in the presbyteries, synods, and General Assemblies of the Presbyterian Church, Richards rarely, if ever, answered humiliating accusations with eruptions of outrage. Rather, he sought a relationship with his adversaries with a disarming and kind respect for each critic. This often prevented a widening chasm between them at a personal level. This was most prevalent in debates on racial justice. He would begin with a simple expression of understanding the feelings expressed, and then proceed to discuss the issue in the light of God's will. This attitude was extended to diverse opinions of a flow of students passing through the educational and community life of Columbia Seminary.

Though he rarely, if ever, forfeited his convictions in the face of criticism, he weathered many a storm because of his calm and kind way of making his position crystal clear. Only toward the end of the fourth decade of his presidency did he grow weary of engaging in such confrontations.

One such example shows the qualities of both the president and a director. H. Lane Young, the director, was a prominent Atlanta banker, an elder in the First Presbyterian Church of Atlanta, and chairman of Columbia's Board of Directors for many years. He differed with Richards on issues such as the Federal Council of Churches and racial justice. Their relationship was never broken, however, even though it may have stretched like a rubber band at times. Two examples throw light on the way they worked together.

Once, J. Howard Pew and H. Lane Young were together for events involving them in a family wedding. Mr. Young was entertaining his friend in the den of his Atlanta home. After some conversation, Mr. Young raised the possibility of a gift from Mr. Pew to Columbia Seminary that he referred to as "my Seminary." He suggested that it was a very good investment. The conversation, as reported to Richards, went like this:

Mr. Young: "Howard, my seminary is a good one but needs money badly now. It turns out pretty good preachers. Can't you help us out?"

Mr. Pew: "Lane, how many communists do you have on your faculty?"

Mr. Young: "Not a damn one!"

Mr. Pew responded with a generous gift.

Richards was enormously appreciative of H. Lane Young's leadership in the work of the Board of Directors and, particularly, the Investment Committee. On December 20, 1960, he sent a warm and generous letter to his board chairman with gratitude for his friendship, counsel, and gifts to Columbia Theological Seminary. He wrote:

When help was asked, you answered gladly and wholeheartedly. Your friendship means all the more to me because I know that at times I have tried your patience sorely when I took positions with which you did not fully agree. I trust you know that I took these positions out of Christian conscience. I think that the real test of friendship is found in the ability of good friends to differ in matters which are not vital, and to remain loyal to one another and to the cause which is really vital in spite of these differences. It is because you have proven yourself this kind of friend that I appreciate you so much.

I am sure that I speak for all the faculty and the Directors of Columbia Theological Seminary, as I certainly do for myself, in thanking you again for all that you have meant to this institution and to wish you and your family a Christmas of deep spiritual blessing and a new year that is filled with all that is good.[45]

Unfortunately, there were also a few occasions of harsh and bitter attacks on Richards. One of a half dozen such letters came just before he retired, and drove him to a rather terse reply. The letter of October 11, 1969, from Horace J. Gault, of Cedartown, Georgia, was one of these:

After almost a half century of our Church going down, down to the very depths, I think I can see signs of a new day. You being one of the leaders who have carried it there, I am writing to ask that you repent and turn back to God and help us rebuild a Christian Church that we can be proud of and help support. Maybe, the best thing for the church that you could do would be to step down now and let us get a new start. It is a tragedy to the young men that have come to learn to preach and you have done to them what has been done. They found God at their mother's knee and maybe a Church Sunday School, but as soon as they go to any Seminary where God is forsaken, they forsake Him. You and your crowd are trying to start our children down the broad highway to Hell, which you think you destroyed by ignoring it and denying it from the pulpit. I can assure you that it is the same burning Hell as always and you will see that when you arrive there. I pray you to consider what you are doing for the Church that has done so much for you. Give us Christians a chance to change what you have done to the Synod. Let's have some Christian leadership.[46]

In a terse and rather untypical reply, Richards responded on October 14, 1969:

I regret very much to note the bitterness of spirit expressed in your letter and to note that it contains a number of untrue statements concerning the ministers of our church in general as well as with reference to myself. Both you and I will ultimately give account to God for "deeds done in the flesh." I am content to leave the issue in His hands and rejoice in the fact that He rather than any man is my judge.

Sincerely yours,
J. McDowell Richards[47]

No further correspondence appeared in the Richards Papers, but even this exchange does not alter the usual pattern of dialogue with critics that are more reasonable.

With a small but diverse faculty during the first fifteen years of his presidency, and a large but even more diverse faculty for the last twenty-four,

Richards was committed to all who taught at Columbia. While maintaining high expectations for their work and their scholarship, he regarded them as valued colleagues. What is consistent with that expectation, however, was a pattern of kindness and respect in personal relations. Richards showed strong support for them through various attacks upon their theological integrity. He may have defended a few incompetent ones too long, however. To the end of his presidency, he continued to defend the faculty and staff.

On August 25, 1970,[48] nearing retirement, he confessed a growing weariness with charges and countercharges against Columbia Seminary. These accusations were sent to numbers of prospective major donors to the campaign that year. He wrote to them with these words and in this spirit:

> These days of charges and countercharges in our Church, suspicion seems to exist everywhere. I feel that many unfair things have been said about Columbia Seminary and I am sure that some of these will have come to your attention. I know that the work which we are doing here is very imperfect and I am far from satisfied with it; yet I want you to know that we are trying to be faithful in training men to preach the unchanging Gospel of Christ as the only answer to the needs of the world.[49]

Fortunately, a longtime friend and trustee, Dr. U. S. Gordon, a pastor in Gainesville, Florida, wrote encouragingly three days before Richards learned of this attack: "As few of our leaders have, you have had the complete confidence and high regard of everyone in our Church."[50] Everyone? Probably not, but certainly a majority did support him.

By the last year of Richards' presidency, the conflicts had taken their toll. Impatience grew. Indeed, a student who had been critical of the faculty and particularly the New Testament scholar, James Torrance of Scotland, received a stern rebuke. Lecturing at Erskine Theological Seminary and at Columbia Theological Seminary, Torrance was greatly appreciated by the campus community and the Church at large. Richards wrote to the student saying:

> If I have been correctly informed as to your attitude, it would be wise for you to consider very seriously the question of transferring this year to some other theological seminary in which you would have confidence. It is not too late for you to make such a transfer and I would much prefer for you to do so than to return to this institution and be unhappy in this environment.[51]

Until the last years of his career, Richards participated personally in athletic events such as volleyball and softball. At Davidson, the younger Richards participated in football and his first love, baseball. Indeed, he probably would not have won a Rhodes Scholarship without significant abilities in scholarship, leadership, and athletic interests.

In the first two decades of his presidency, Richards ate an evening meal once a week with students in the refectory, and a volleyball game followed, weather permitting. At family reunions in Liberty Hill, South Carolina, games were played and hotly contested. Baseball was first on his list. It was played with a regulation baseball, not a softball. Family pictures show him as a catcher with a mask, chest protector, uniform, mitt, and spiked shoes. Family correspondence shows that he gave up catching in later years, but then wanted to pitch! In a game where all ages were represented he was able to hold his own. This well-known love of baseball motivated Richards' 1970 retirement committee to plan a series of memorable events and gifts. Among the gifts for Dr. and Mrs. Richards on that occasion were World Series tickets in New York, secured with great difficulty and through the influence of a deacon in Decatur Presbyterian Church, Ben Milton, and the famous baseball executive in Atlanta, Earl Mann. To the surprise of the committee, Richards called a few days later and rather hesitantly asked if the tickets could be exchanged for a color television set. His reasoning was consistent with his well-known frugal approach. Instead of a few World Series baseball games, the television set would enable him to view all the regular season games, and the World Series as well, for years to come.

Richards' correspondence with his father was unfailingly related in some way to athletic events because both were avid sports fans. A description of the

Shown above is the original Richards baseball team, with the exception of Stephen Richards, who was killed in World War I, as they appeared recently at Heath Springs for their game with the younger generation of Richards, which the elder generation won 4-3. In the first row are, (left to right): umpire, N. S. Richards, Sr.; centerfielder, James Richards; utility player, Dr. John Edwards Richards; pitcher, A. J. Richards, Sr.; right fielder, Dr. J. McDowell Richards; catcher, N. S. Richards, Jr.; and umpire, Dr. C. M. Richards. In the second row are: first baseman, J. P. Richards, Sr.; third baseman, J. G. Richards; second baseman, J. P. Richards, Jr.; left fielder, P. G. Richards; and shortstop, J. G. Richards, Jr. The team, organized in 1915, faced tough opposition, but never lost a game

The Richards family baseball team was organized in 1915 and never lost a game. This newspaper clipping shows the elder generation of players, which competed against a team of younger Richards' players, and beat them 4–3. J. McDowell Richards, third from right in the front row, played right field.

Duke-Georgia Tech game was so vivid as to cause a reader to conclude that Richards could have made a living as a sports writer or announcer.

> I had the good fortune to be invited as a guest to the Tech-Duke game on Saturday and enjoyed the contest very much. . . . The game was a sellout so I would not have gotten to go to it had it not been for the kindness of a friend in Atlanta. It rained hard all morning, but not at all during the game. Conditions were not bad from the spectators' point of view, but the field was muddy and the ball slippery. Duke took a little better advantage of its opportunities than did Tech and deserved to win.[52]

There is no question about Richards' love of baseball. In a full-page letter to his father dated October 4, 1945, he expressed "a disappointment in almost all respects" about the outcome of the first game of the World Series. He favored the Detroit Tigers because Paul Richards, their catcher, was once a popular player and manager for the Atlanta Crackers. His disappointment continued because the Cubs won, and what was most disturbing, he felt the brand of baseball was evidently far from brilliant. He concluded that this series would be Paul Richards' "climax of his career, as I thought he was a fairly old player when he was in Atlanta." His philosophy of the spirit of athletics is reflected in a prayer offered at the beginning of the Georgia Tech-Auburn football game on October 20, 1957. It was as follows:

> We thank thee today for the beauty around us; for strong young men, for courageous spirits, and for the love of play. We pray thy blessing upon the members of these teams and upon the institutions which they represent. Whether in victory or in defeat, teach us the lessons of fair play, of sportsmanship, and of loyalty to causes greater than ourselves. May thy blessing abide upon our country that increasingly ours may be a nation exalted by righteousness; that America may be a force for freedom, for justice, for mercy and for peace among all nations. Make us faithful as individuals in the performance of all the duties of free citizens, and use us for the accomplishment of thy purposes, we pray in Christ's name, Amen.[53]

Though few in number, there are elements of "righteous indignation" evident in Richards' personality in isolated instances. Several graduates, some students, and even a careless operator of an automobile were targets of honest irritation and, yes, anger.

En route to a Sunday appointment in Meridian, Mississippi, with students who were to assist in a weekend program, a minor accident prompted mild outrage, if there is such a thing. A driver drove through a stop sign into the path of the seminary car. It was a fender-bender of relatively limited damage, but

President Richards was quickly out of the car and, confronting the driver, asked, "What kind of driving do you call that?" The assurance of adequate insurance and the promise from police that it would all be taken care of calmed Richards. He drove on in a rental car until the emotion of the moment was overcome by intense and learned discussions about the presentations for the weekend.

Another one of the few occasions in which Richards showed genuine irritation involved a presbytery executive who reported that a small three-church field did not want to accept Richards' recommendation of a student. While not the most outstanding member of the senior class, he was a good and dedicated man, who, though limited in ability, would give everything he had to that ministry. In response, Richards was rather abrupt: "In my opinion it will be a misfortune both for the . . . churches and for your Presbytery if that group decides against this suggestion. But, it is perfectly all right with me and with him as there are various fields waiting!"[54]

Further, the stance of appreciation for his alma mater, the much loved Davidson College, was challenged by a report from a graduate who visited both Davidson and Southwestern at Memphis with minimal results in the recruitment of prospective students. Richards wrote in some frustration: "The attitude of these institutions is baffling to me. I hope I am incorrect in the matter but I have sometimes thought that there are those who deliberately fostered the idea that Columbia was simply a reactionary, fundamentalist seminary, when they actually know better."[55]

Richards' charitable nature ultimately took over, however, and he concluded: "We shall assume that it is a lack of full understanding rather than deliberate intent which lay back of what I believe has been real misrepresentation."[56]

Until air travel in the 1950s, there were time-consuming train trips from Florida to Canada. Indeed, appointments throughout the Southeast involved long and wearying hours by train or automobile, and sometimes by both. Voyages to Europe to the various ecumenical meetings took him away weeks at a time. The pace quickened even in the days of plane travel to meetings in New York and to preaching engagements throughout the Southeast. His appointment book was full while in residence with details of the total operation of the institution; buildings, grounds, finances, faculty, students, and staff were all his responsibility.

One small problem involved Richards' tendency to make the train departure at the last moment. Wade P. Huie, the Peter Marshall Professor of Homiletics, reported to Richards on his progress toward a Ph.D. at the University of Edinburgh in Scotland. Miss C. Virginia Harrison responded in the president's absence. Her letters to former students, especially those she liked, were long and full of campus news; and, as the years went on, these letters were increasingly reflections of Richards' literary style. In response, however, to the Huie letter, she had a mild complaint: "Dr. Richards is in

Left to right: Mary James Richards, J. McDowell Richards, and Mary Black during Oxford days.

Europe but I barely got him to the train on time. He is always cutting it short!"[57]

In Richards' personal value system, the one most often overlooked by others was his strong commitment to intellectual pursuits. From the position of a strong theological commitment to the Reformed theological traditions, he was convinced that God should be loved with our minds. Ignorance and obscurantism were grave flaws in any human being. In the degree programs Richards pursued at McCallie School, Davidson (Phi Beta Kappa, valedictorian), Princeton, Christ Church College, Oxford, or Columbia Seminary, he excelled. He read constantly, wrote clearly, and felt that it was his Christian duty to do so. One of his closest friends, Dr. Patrick Dwight Miller, who knew him well in college and seminary, once said, "Whatever Mac took one year, he could teach the next."[58]

The Millers and the Richards were close family friends, and often vacationed together in Montreat. In an exchange of Christmas gifts one year, Mrs. Richards received a tray, and Dr. Richards, a box of cigars. Miller enclosed a note saying, "I look forward to sitting on the porch in Montreat, and enjoying the good fellowship and good conversation which are always enhanced by Lady Nicotine!"[59]

An early influence in Richards' education, study as a Rhodes Scholar in Christ Church College, Oxford, comes alive in selections from his diary during that time. Among daily entries, these reflect the impact of both study and travel which remained with him throughout his life. A few entries are representative of many:

October 13, 1923: It is hard for me to tell what has not impressed. I feel overwhelmed by antiquity and the men who shaped the destinies of empires. The country is beautiful and the landscape a constant delight. The two Marys are good company.

October 14, 1923 (Sunday): I have experienced slowness in getting acquainted. I will try to overcome this tendency in my character.

October 17, 1923: The lectures are clear and interesting, but are lacking in the depth that I had expected. At the formal ceremony of inauguration, we were harangued in Latin by the Chancellor.

Letters arrived and were like water to a man perishing from thirst. The custom of tea in the afternoon was good and the conversation delightful. The Chaplain arranged for the Student Christian Fellowship to speak but my general impression was one of indifference. It reminded me of college boy antics at Davidson College.

Sunday afternoon, I had a pleasant walk through buildings and grounds which were impressive. Those of Magdalen College are the most beautiful I have yet seen.

November 6, 1923: My birthday passed in a quiet and unexciting manner. The bright spot were letters from home. I went to Communion which was not an inappropriate ceremony to enter my legal manhood and consecrate myself afresh.

November 7, 1923: I played golf at the University Club.

November 13, 1923: I am taking German. At the SCM meeting I heard a good quote from Ibsen: "Life is a mystery only an infinitely wiser mind can solve."

December 17, 1923: We are visiting Paris. French culture and cooking are a delightful surprise. How often our preconceived ideas and prejudices play us false. The girls are quite modest and unpretentious, and much prettier than I had been led to expect. By contrast, the tense and strained faces of the men and women crowded around the tables of roulette are pictures of anxiety, and sometimes of despair. Outside, the scenery was beautiful but they only had eyes for the wheel.

December 25, 1923: I was homesick for worship at home but cheered by beautiful music. The day after we found the cheapest and best lunch in our visit to Rome. Vesuvius and Pompeii were depressing. The pictures were of a depraved mind and they didn't even make lust appealing.

January 3, 1924: Michaelangelo's superbly colossal representation of the boy, David, with his sling held over one shoulder and his stones in the other hand is chiseled out of a block of marble thought spoiled. What a wonderful illustration of the way the Master Artist of the universe makes over and transforms the ruined lives of sinful men. [60]

After a three month's lapse in his diary, on March 26, 1924, Richards recorded a detailed description of a five-day visit in Bonn with the family of the Muezens. He laments his slow progress in learning German, which he calls "a thoroughly difficult language."

An entry dated March 28, 1924, indicated that he was impressed that the Germans had an intensely nationalistic feeling, but seemed disgusted by the war. He took the three daughters of the German family to the movies and wondered if men ever learn anything from the experience of the past. He also found opera with Wagner too heavy for pure enjoyment.[61]

Richards continued to be troubled by the poverty of Germany that followed World War I. A terrible consequence was no overcrowding in the schools. In addition, the daughter in the family where he boarded did not eat supper so the family could save money. He wrote in his diary, "What a terrible thing is war."

Richards was not only scholarly and, at times, brilliant, but adept at using these capacities in relating to persons of differing situations. They ranged from the much-loved mountain people of North Georgia, to the leaders of groups such as the Committee on a Just and Durable Peace, and the World Council of Churches in Europe. His was not the kind of disciplined intellect practiced by a recluse shut away from the world or the Church. Nor did he produce displays of flamboyant oratory. However, many of his addresses and sermons were quite thoughtful and even riveting. At times, they seem to be more powerful when read than when they were heard. His delivery was quiet, but his message was dynamic, and always appropriate to the occasion. Whether in the pulpit, class-room, or at the governing bodies of the Church, he had the power to inform, persuade, and influence. As important as his education was, the foundation for a disciplined use of the mind was laid in the environment of the family into which he was born and by whom he was nurtured. Education and intellectual pursuits were valued almost as much as worship, prayer, and the Church's nurture. A wasted mind was unthinkable and completely unacceptable.

One evaluation of Richards as a person is both eloquent and accurate:

> A serene, slow spoken, compact man radiated the confidence of a well-ordered, leisurely life. Dr. Richards received me readily enough in his big, sofa-lined living room designed for entertaining large groups. As we parted, he confessed that he had not looked forward to the interview.[62]

The only obvious flaw in these words is the use of "leisurely" in describing his life. He had a gift for seeming calm in a very stormy sea.

To know James McDowell Richards for almost fifty years, to listen to and read his sermons, addresses, lectures, correspondence, and conversations, is to be tremendously impressed. Those impressions include his intelligence, integrity, kindness, humility, tact, and respect for persons of diverse opinions and views. Beyond that, and, most of all, to know him is to know a person of firm commit-ment to Jesus Christ and to the Presbyterian Church. He was, to say the least, a faithful servant of Christ in all the changing seasons and situations of his life. Thus, the ultimate issue in understanding the person we see in James McDowell Richards is found in a simple question with a complex answer: "Who was he?"

CHAPTER TWO

President

*R*OBERT MERRILL HOLMES DREW A REALISTIC PICTURE of life in a university that he called, "The Academic Mysteryhouse." Writing at the end of Richards' presidency, Holmes contended that the world was caught up in the struggle between two diverse views of society, what it should not be and what it should be. Holmes pictured the university as a divided and struggling community. He described "a fundamental tension" between those who felt quite strongly that the eighth decade of the twentieth century called for new patterns of thinking, new modes of behavior, and new structures of society, and those who felt equally strongly that the need was to recapture something that had been lost out of the past. Holmes went on to speak approvingly of the Cambridge University scholar T. M. Cornfield and especially his view of life in the 1970s. Cornfield said:

> Nothing should be done for the first time. It is apparent, however, that in the decade into which we have now moved, more and more things are to be done for the first time. The old molds are largely broken and former blueprints are no longer adequate. Heretofore, commonly accepted living patterns are being questioned, and many traditional answers to current issues are being rejected.[1]

Cornfield's view suggests that what is said here about Richards' life and work during four decades at Columbia Theological Seminary is increasingly relevant to the present mission of such institutions. Moreover, what scholars say about the academic institutions and faculties of that time could be said about many of the ministers and churches during Richards' tenure at Columbia. This, more than anything, took its toll on Richards and increasingly influenced his presidency. Columbia Seminary was caught up in the changing church and the changing environment in which it served; so was he.

James McDowell Richards was president of Columbia Theological Seminary during thirty-nine ever changing and constantly challenging years. During those decades, he was scholar, administrator, counselor, preacher, and fund-raiser. The dominating influence of his life was that he was president of a small struggling Presbyterian seminary in Decatur, Georgia, during times of crisis when its existence was in doubt. He gave his life to the institution and the church that it served. During the difficult and demanding decades from 1932 to 1971, his ministry was absorbed in the leadership of a Presbyterian seminary with a useful past and an uncertain future. This venerable "school of the prophets" survived wars, economic disasters, and ecclesiastical upheavals led by Richards.

Columbia Theological Seminary began in Lexington, Georgia, in 1828, in the home of Dr. Thomas Goulding. The location was the result of twelve years' debate while the governing bodies of the Presbyterian Church (U.S.) could not agree on a location. Professor Goulding was the only teacher and there were five students. One year later, the seminary moved to Columbia, South Carolina, the center of the Presbyterian Church in the southeastern United States at that time. Columbia was one of four seminaries of the Presbyterian Church (U.S.) in the region stretching from Virginia to Texas. The other three were in Richmond, Virginia; Louisville, Kentucky; and Austin, Texas.

The Civil War was by far the worst and most destructive upheaval faced by Columbia. It left this school of the prophets bankrupt, caused not only by lack of students, but also because it had invested its endowment in Confederate States war bonds, which eventually were worthless. There were precarious times when Columbia Seminary closed during that war, and when it was seemingly on its deathbed at other periods.

Sixty-two years after the end of the Civil War, the institution once again faced closing. The still struggling institution moved to the oldest town in the Atlanta, Georgia, area, to the center of the rapidly changing southeastern United States, in Decatur, Georgia.[2] Columbia Seminary's fifty-three acres of former farmland had been a part of Atlanta and the southeast since 1927. With limited staff and resources, it focused on a challenging mission of educating pastors and teachers.[3] The location was within six miles of the center of metropolitan Atlanta, and was John Bulow Campbell's choice after searching all other possible alternatives. The fact that the land was a gift by leaders of Decatur Presbyterian Church probably significantly influenced the decision. A road was formed on the eastern side of the campus and named Columbia Drive.[4] To this day, there are those who think this seminary is named for the street, and not vice versa! The other streets around its property were given ecclesiastical names, such as Kirk Road and Missionary Drive. One was named Inman Drive for the chairman of the Board of Directors.

Indeed, even after the move to the Atlanta area, perceptive church leaders could hear an ominous death rattle in the institutional throat. For Richards, the thirty-nine years of his presidency, as we shall see, spanned four decades of dramatically escalating change in the Church and in the cultures affecting it.

Throughout his tenure, Richards identified with Douglas John Hall[5] in his concept of "Stewardship as a Missional Discipline." Hall presented a persuasive argument that ministry is in the persona of a steward:

> No one idea, metaphor, or doctrinal theme can contain the fullness of the gospel that is the "raison d'être" of the mission to which the disciples of Jesus Christ are bidden by the very grace that makes them disciples. The disciple community must always search for a language, a form, into which that gospel may in some partial expression of itself be poured ... I have proposed ... that stewardship—or better, the symbol of "the steward"—is one evocative and provocative linguistic form with which Christians may engage their context, especially this North American context.[6]

The one caveat in Hall's argument is that the concept of "the steward" cannot be used in the unfortunate captivity of stewardship to ecclesiastical self-preservation, nor can it be limited to keeping churches solvent and afloat. However, this symbol has the potential to keep the world afloat, or at least help to do so. It will be seen that ultimately President Richards kept the institution he served afloat in threatening, stormy seas, and led it to be much more. He viewed it as having a mission to open the church he loved and served to the preservation of God's beloved world.[7]

A grim situation confronted the new president when Richards arrived in 1932. Columbia Theological Seminary had survived for more than one hundred years, but it was clearly weak and struggling. In the move from Columbia, South Carolina, to Decatur, Georgia, in 1927, President Richard T. Gillespie Jr. brought a truckload of library books, a faculty of five, a worthy tradition of service to the Presbyterian Church in the Southeast, and a budget of $65,300. Even more ominous was an accumulated deficit of $12,673.01 from 1927, to be followed by another in 1928 of $17,992. President Gillespie, by all accounts, literally gave himself, mind and body, to an institution in crisis. He was bitterly disappointed that the churches and ministers who had urged and approved the move to Atlanta were unable or unwilling to fund it properly in the economic depression of 1928–31. He worked heroically to save Columbia Theological Seminary, but his health deteriorated so drastically that his physician forbad him to attend the 1928 commencement and centennial activities. The Board of Directors, alarmed by growing signs of eroding strength, gave Gillespie a year's leave of absence with full salary in the hopes of improving his health and vigor.

To the credit of all, no paralyzing panic immobilized the seminary leadership. During that year, the Board of Directors, under the chairmanship of J. T. Brantley, attempted to raise seventy-five thousand dollars by July 1929, to remove the accumulated deficit and balance the budget. Spurred on by an offer of a supporter to buy sixty thousand dollars of the bonds held by Columbia, they worked tirelessly to reach this goal, though it was not fully met. John Bulow Campbell, having been instrumental in the move from Columbia to the Atlanta area, once again went the extra mile in rescuing the institution. He gave the promised seventy-five thousand dollars, though the challenge conditions were not met in full.

Campbell's pledge was seventy-five thousand dollars, if the church contributed a like amount. Furthermore, he pledged to give five thousand dollars a year for five years, if the church gave a like amount. This pattern of challenge gifts has been as important a matter as the actual pledge itself.

President Gillespie returned to his duties in the fall of 1929, and was heartened by the numbers of students, but distraught over lack of support. A deficit for 1928–29 reached $23,785. What was particularly discouraging was the total lack of support from Alabama and Mississippi, with the exception of Meridian Presbytery. It seemed strange to him that the presbyteries of those states had strongly urged the move from Columbia, South Carolina, to Decatur, Georgia, but, for whatever reason, failed to support it. He died suddenly on May 31, 1930, while attending the General Assembly meeting of the Presbyterian Church (U.S.) in Charlottesville, Virginia. At a memorial service, Dr. J. Sprole Lyons, pastor of the First Presbyterian Church of Atlanta, eloquently summarized his leadership of Columbia Theological Seminary: "The crowning glory of his life and service was that he had no measure by which he gave himself to the task. He simply gave his entire self."[8]

The students and faculty of Candler School of Theology, in a much-appreciated act, gave the pulpit furniture and a communion table for Columbia's chapel in honor of President Gillespie. Without his untiring efforts, the institution would have collapsed into an ecclesiastical grave.

Columbia struggled through the next two years (1930–32), until the search committee called Richards to the presidency. One can analyze the years of Richards' presidency in various ways. For the purposes of this discussion, the analysis will reflect four quite different decades in his invaluable service to the Church, and to the institution that utilized most of his ministerial career.

The Decade of Survival
1932–1940

Few periods in the years of his presidency challenged Richards, as did the years from 1932 to 1940. He reluctantly came to this office of president on July 1, 1932, from a pastorate in First Presbyterian Church of Thomasville, Georgia. He resisted the call to become president for good reason. Less than a year had passed since the Richards family arrived with all the hopes and anxieties a new chapter in life brings. More importantly, Richards did not feel qualified in the essential responsibilities of fund-raising and administration. The prospect of moving his family after so few months in Thomasville seemed out of the question.

He reluctantly accepted the presidency when the search committee presented only one other alternative to his acceptance of the office. In a blunt analysis, they said, "We have approached twenty-three persons who refused the call, and we will close the Seminary, if you do not come."[9]

On May 10, 1932, therefore, James McDowell Richards accepted the call to serve as president of the institution that he, his father, and grandfather had attended, and which he loved and valued with untiring devotion. That strong church in Thomasville, Georgia, reluctantly but graciously respected his decision and accepted his resignation.

When he arrived at 701 Columbia Drive, Decatur, Georgia, on the edge of Atlanta, he found a small but devoted faculty; fifty students; indebtedness in loans; a bond issue of $166,000; two buildings valued at $277,117; four faculty homes costing $77,644; and additional land purchased for $21,395. The income of $32,200 still fell short of the expenses by $15,442. He also found Miss C. Virginia Harrison, who for thirty years served with Richards in invaluable ways as secretary, bursar, superintendent of buildings and grounds, and president's assistant.

The fifty students increased the expenses of Columbia because most were on financial assistance. Richards wrote:

> Students of the seminary had limited financial resources in the early days, but fortunately not much was required of them. For years it had been the custom at Columbia, as well as at other seminaries, to charge students no fees for tuition or room rent. Although the students did pay a modest amount for their board, most of them received scholarship aid to provide for that expense also. The theory behind this was that men being prepared for military service at West Point and Annapolis had all of their expenses paid by the United States government. It was thought to be no less appropriate that men preparing for the service of Christ in the ministry should be provided for in like fashion.[10]

Among the challenging and critical issues thrust upon the new president was the inability of churches to call graduates as pastors with a firm promise of a salary. Some had manses providing housing for their families. According to Bonneau H. Dickson, one of Columbia's most useful and loyal graduates, and a member of the class of 1933, none of his classmates went to a pastorate

with a "terms of the call" which included a specific salary. The churches promised to do what they could for them. They truly served as pastors "by faith,"
and were grateful for those parishioners who shared with them the produce of
gardens and even fish and game.

The inaugural address of President Richards went to the heart of concerns
for Columbia Seminary. The issues could be summarized in two questions:
"Shall Columbia continue to serve the expanding South?" If so, "What kind of
service will Columbia Theological Seminary render?"[11]

Both issues continued to press for authentic responses in various ways.
The answer to these questions, in President Richards' view, must have the
full support of the Church, the Board of Directors, the faculty, and the
students.

The basic pledge of the new president at his inauguration and for years
afterward included:

> A continual evaluation of the curriculum will be made, but the Bible will remain
> at the center of that curriculum. Further, it will proclaim clearly the Gospel, the
> truth on which it stands, even though it does so in an age of uncertainty and
> doubt. Columbia Seminary has a priceless heritage to project and a noble tradi-
> tion to be maintained. The truth for which it stands, and, God helping her, will
> continue to stand is the truth we find contained in the Scriptures of the old and
> new Testaments, the only infallible rule of faith and practice. Further, the truth
> of "redeeming love" for individuals and society in the whole world does not need
> to be defended. It needs to be proclaimed.[12]

This eloquent presentation of mission and purpose has just one goal, said
Richards, "That this may be an institution which shall ever be loyal to Christ as
its divine Lord and Redeemer and in which the spirit of Christ shall constantly
prevail."[13]

The first letter found in the Richards Papers was to key contributor John
Bulow Campbell, a devout member and elder of Central Presbyterian Church,
Atlanta. He was a self-made successful businessman whose company sold coal,
hardware, and building supplies. Campbell had been and continued until his
death in June, 1940, to be the person whose wisdom and philanthropy saved
Columbia Theological Seminary for the Church. This letter, unlike those that
followed, was an invitation to Campbell from President Richards to attend the
opening ceremonies of the seminary year in September 1932. It was more than
a courteous gesture. The procedure in calling faculty for the first fifteen years
of Richards' tenure was a matter of seeking advice from the chairman of the
board, and seldom, if ever, involved other faculty. Thus, when William T.
Riviere of Victoria, Texas, was being considered as professor of English Bible,

Richards felt the chairman of the Board of Directors should help him make "a personal estimate of Dr. Riviere's ability."[14]

It wasn't long, however, before Campbell was involved in financial matters. Indeed, he had "saved" the institution by moving it to Atlanta, the growing center of industry and population of the Southeast. In decisions both large and small, his advice was sought and followed in every aspect of seminary administration. One of the next letters from Columbia's new president contained a request for advice on spending fifty dollars for an advertisement in a special edition of the Atlanta *Journal-Constitution*. Campbell responded in his usual direct and careful way, "I agree that this expenditure should not be made. Not only could our limited funds be spent better elsewhere, but this would be little more than a contribution to the paper."[15]

Faculty appointments were brought into this cluster of early correspondence with the chairman, when an instructor was needed for a six-month term. However, one half of the letters to Campbell during the first six months of Richards' presidency were concerned with money. The value of endowments was relentlessly and frightenly eroding under the crush of the depression. Not all letters were answered by mail, for Campbell seemed to prefer the telephone. However, when the excitement of receiving a five-hundred-dollar gift was matched by Richards' caution in spending it, he turned to Campbell, his advisor and trustee. Richards sought advice on whether to use it for current expenses, as the pledge had earlier designated, or invest it in the very small endowment. Campbell's response was reflective of the economic decline in that year. His recommendation was clear and concise: "Safe investments are hard to come by, so use it now."[16]

Until June 1940, a constant stream of letters from Richards flowed into the second floor office of Campbell, in downtown Atlanta. Thus, President Richards wrote at Christmas, 1932, to say of John Bulow Campbell what he told him on numerous occasions: "Among those who have been friends of this institution since its removal to Atlanta, I can sincerely say that no one has occupied quite so high place as yourself."[17]

The economic situation grew steadily worse. The anxious new president became quite concerned, and rightly so. An analysis of the seminary's grim financial situation was painfully detailed. The congregations suffered from the depression as did the diminished resources of their most devoted members. The institutions supported by them shared in the impact of the collapsing economy. Instead of the thirty thousand dollars budgeted, President Richards concluded that there would not be available as much as twenty thousand dollars. Faculty and staff had voted to reduce their salaries by a third. Fortunately, the lowest paid staff were exempted from this severe cut. In the crisis of Richards first two years, however, the question went to Campbell:

Shall Columbia Seminary continue to operate? How shall we pay our debts and survive? Shall we send out a letter asking congregations to challenge their members to give 25 cents each to eliminate the deficit and pay some debts? Shall we approach General Assembly Committees for assistance? Can we collect on our Real Estate Loans?[18]

The reaction of the chairman of the board was direct and decisive. It contained simple but blunt advice. He wrote, "While greatly gratified over the improvement this year, a major effort must be made to finish the year without a deficit. I believe you can put it over, but it does mean hard work."[19]

Columbia Theological Seminary did survive by constant prayer and much hard work. Campbell not only gave very generously, but also urged others to give. His appeal is typified in a letter to Lindsey Hopkins of Courts and Company. He asked, "While Columbia Seminary is doing a great work in this section, there is an effort to consolidate it with Union Seminary in Richmond to solve many problems. However, the ministers of Atlanta and the Southeast are determined to raise $175,000. They lack $2000 of going over the top. Can't you figure out some way whereby you can take care of this $2000?"[20]

Richards continued to rely on Campbell for support and advice. They affirmed the need for Columbia Seminary and its graduates in service in the Presbyterian Church. They agreed that any approach to the General Assembly sources seeking funding would not be productive. However, individuals and churches related to the institution as a source for ministers would ultimately save the seminary for its essential mission. The real estate loans were probably worthless and uncollectable. So, Campbell encouraged Richards with this urgent advice: "Mr. Richards, go to the churches and tell the story. They will respond. Ask them for 25 cents per member."[21]

President Richards agreed to make such direct efforts. While extremely appreciative, however, he could not resist reminding the chairman of the board:

I am afraid that I am rather poorly fitted for the task of money-raiser, as there are few undertakings more uncongenial to me by nature. I considered this matter at the time that I accepted the Presidency of the institution. Had there been any prospect of anyone else accepting this position, I would have considered myself as unable to take it, because of the fact that I am so poorly fitted for this part of the task. Under the circumstances at that time, I felt there was nothing for me to do but to accept the work and go forward with it as best I could.[22]

He did precisely that, and the efforts paid off after several years of hard work and prayer. Things were slightly better by graduation in May 1933. He wrote to Campbell, "Let me at this time express a great deal of appreciation and pleasure for the delightful association I have had with you during this first year, and I am taking much courage in the future of Columbia Seminary based upon your lively interest in it."[23]

An affirming educational event in this decade took place on May 16, 1933, when Columbia Seminary was admitted to membership in the American Association of Theological Schools. It was one of forty-six institutions accepted as charter members with full accreditation.

The anguish of the first years of office began to give way to hope, slim though it was. Faculty and staff, with loyalty and with very real sacrifice, made contributions to Columbia's budget. John Bulow Campbell purchased securities from Columbia's endowment at a book value of $19,463.75, though their market value was almost zero. A man of exceptional integrity, he said that he had recommended them, and therefore felt obligated to recompense the institution. In 1934 and 1935, there were surpluses in Columbia's budget expenditures, but only in very small amounts such as $14.09. That there was any surplus was due to great sacrifices by donors and the faculty and staff of the institution they supported. President Richards continued to travel widely and plead fervently for gifts from the churches. There was a Florida tour for the first time in years in which he spoke in fourteen churches and traveled twenty-five hundred miles.

The decade of the 1930s brought new support for Columbia from the synods who "owned and controlled" Columbia Seminary. Indeed, a Columbia Theological Seminary Day was celebrated with widespread support early in Richards' presidency on February 4, 1934. Even in Columbia, South Carolina, the former home of the institution, churches gave it publicity and gifts.

The appeal to celebrate that day included a comment from Dr. Samuel Tenney on the tremendous influence of the graduates of this institution now in its second century: "On the basis of historical fact, it cannot be denied that Columbia Theological Seminary has influenced the life and thought of the Southern Presbyterian Church more than any other institution."[24]

As the decade passed, a faint moving of the tide of life and support for Columbia Seminary became a steady, though still too small, stream. On May 7, 1936, Atlanta Presbytery in a great leap of faith launched a two-hundred-thousand-dollar campaign with a challenge gift of one hundred thousand dollars to be given if it was successful. The discussion of merger with Union Theological Seminary in Richmond, Virginia, was not as vigorous, and it declined merger with Louisville Presbyterian Theological Seminary.

By November 17, 1936, Columbia Seminary still owed the banks of Atlanta $42,850 in loan payments, had a $15,000 mortgage, and thus a deficit of $57,850. As the years went on, due to strenuous efforts by Richards and all involved, deficits were avoided with extremely austere budgets and strenuous efforts to create all possible support.

In the Plan of Government developed in 1936, concepts appeared which defined the roles of the president, faculty, and Board of Directors. These roles, though couched in general terms, were clearly separated. The language used, however, contained clear and detailed descriptions of duties assigned to the directors by the Plan of Government and to the faculty for those duties remitted to the faculty by that plan:

> The President shall, for the board and faculty, exercise a general supervision over the institution, control its buildings and grounds, and maintain order and discipline. He shall possess the authority to employ such help as may be needed for the proper conduct of the seminary life and to discharge such other duties and responsibilities as are usual to the office.[25]

The Plan of Government has been through five major revisions since 1936, and has gradually moved Columbia Seminary toward a more collegial style of management. It is similar in philosophy to that of small institutions, but has no need to compartmentalize into sections found in large universities.[26]

The president's role included, and still does include, authority to represent the institution and to preside over faculty meetings and various events of seminary life. The president spoke for the seminary to the Church, and particularly the governing bodies in the region of the southeastern United States. The president made recommendations to the board of trustees concerning the appointment of staff and the election of faculty. The life of the seminary was carried on with appropriate committees including representatives from the board of trustees, the faculty, and the student government. It took vision, insight, and commitment from all concerned to make the system work effectively.[27]

By 1938, moreover, the urge to merge with Union Seminary in Richmond, Virginia, was dissipating. President Richards' position was clear: "I do believe that a strong seminary in Atlanta serves the purposes of the Church more truly than at any other center in our Church. Unless, however, the seminary in Atlanta is to be made and kept a really strong institution, it cannot serve effectively."

One of the unique additions to Columbia's curriculum in that era began with the first Rural Institute led by an authority on country churches, Dr. Henry Woods McLaughlin. In his fervent espousal of opportunities for effective ministry in small towns and rural areas, he was known on campus as "Country Church McLaughlin." Since the great majority of graduates served pastorates in such situations upon completing their degrees, it was an important element in the curriculum at that time.

Columbia established polices for sabbatical leave with a maximum of six months absence from campus. While this led to very real gaps in the courses offered, it was a most important element in the development of faculty. Young professors with no more than four years of pastoral experience continued to serve the Church in many ways. They grew in knowledge and competence through study in the great universities of the United States and Europe. Some spent sabbatical leaves in universities in Great Britain and Germany, while others found study in Africa, the Caribbean, and the Appalachian Mountains to be valuable cross-cultural experiences. This contextual education was a significant way of opening windows to a complex and challenging world.

The momentum of support and commitment for Columbia Seminary was slowly but surely increasing in some of the worst financial times for the Church in the twentieth century. The $150,000 campaign in Atlanta Presbytery was pledged and, in spite of the economy, $117,890.61 paid. Again, the end of the year showed a balance of $3.14. It is not too difficult to imagine that the president and others made contributions to avoid any deficit. Even so, there was a call to go much further. The reductions in faculty salary had not been fully restored. The payment of indebtedness was the result of a very stringent operating budget for this entire decade. Sabbaticals were approved for the faculty and initiated in the year 1937–38. The first of these mentions lectures by Professor W. C. Robinson at the Free Church Seminary in Edinburgh, Scotland. The curriculum began to include tentative steps in the use of clinical training in parishes and hospitals.

Though the existence of Columbia Seminary hung in the balance many times, President Richards still added new faculty, such as John S. Foster, who taught homiletics, logic, Christian ethics, and church polity. Charles A. Sheldon, noted organist and choirmaster of First Presbyterian Church in Atlanta, led workshops in music and hymnology. A full time librarian, Harriett Kehre, was appointed. In 1939, Manford George Gutzke came as professor of biblical exposition.

Books by faculty included James B. Green's *Studies in the Holy Spirit*, and W. C. Robinson's *Our Lord, An Affirmation of the Deity of Christ*. Visiting professors included: Fraser Wood, professor of psychology at Davidson College; Egbert T. Smith, field secretary of foreign missions; William Evans of Los Angeles, California, a pastor; Professor W. Taliaferro Thompson of Union Seminary in Richmond, Virginia; and Oscar F. Blackwelder of Washington, D.C. In this small but significant way, the students were confronted with the world of knowledge and ministry.

Moreover, crucial issues dominated the first eight years of the Richards administration and constantly challenged his leadership and the institution. They included:

1. The issue of a merger of Presbyterian seminaries, and especially Union and Columbia.

2. The dire lack of money even for a bare bones operating budget.
3. The state of the Church during the economic depression that was suffocating the area.
4. The exhaustion of the faculty with multiple duties.
5. The need for financial aid for students.

In the constant discussion of mergers in synods and the General Assembly, uncertainty laid a blanket of confusion over people and programs. Debates were quite fierce in the church governing bodies and, what was even more damaging, in local congregations.

President Richards' friend and Columbia's trustee, John McSween, reacted impatiently when he learned the board had, after much deliberation, adopted a "wait and see" position in what was a very real financial crisis. Richards had been president four years, and the Board of Directors had done little to face its challenge. McSween's displeasure centered on an impression that the board wanted the president to be responsible for solving the problems while they appointed another committee to study and report. He wrote:

Frankly I am disappointed in the action of the Board which appears to me indecisive and seems to me to be a typical reaction of so many Boards. It might be expressed crudely: We'll hang on while the President gets out and works himself to death. What I was hoping was either a hearty assent to a merger, or a strong and unequivocal statement to the Church. The word should go out as to the vital nature of the Seminary to our Church, and clearly voice a stand that would revitalize the whole situation. As I see it, we are just where we were before, needing money, with the group designated to plow over ground already well plowed.[28]

A further word of comfort, however, from McSween came to Richards eighteen days later. While it reported a meeting in Greenville, South Carolina, to consider merging Union, Columbia, and Louisville seminaries, he sent a pledge to Columbia for $100. Even better, he wrote:

My heart goes out to you. I realized what you went through last Friday. I hope and pray that you may be successful in this matter and that the Seminary may be saved for this section. With warmest personal regards and grateful appreciation at the noble way in which you are coping with all this,

I am Cordially yours,
John[29]

This challenging period came to a sad conclusion with the sudden death on June 28, 1940, of the man who supported Richards steadfastly and, with him, saved the institution, John Bulow Campbell.

Campbell's official connection with Columbia Theological Seminary began in 1926 as a new member of the Board of Directors. The decision to move to Decatur, Georgia, had been made but the funds to make it possible had not been secured. His initial contribution was small in comparison to what he ultimately would do. Richards wrote: "Before the Campaign was completed, Mr. Campbell had decided to meet the cost of erecting the academic building and to make it a memorial to his beloved mother."[30] Richards often spoke of his quiet and unobtrusive contributions to the life of a struggling institution that was battered by the depression of the 1930s.

On May 27, 1941, the Columbia Theological Seminary community gathered to give thanks to God for the life and influence of John Bulow Campbell. His association with the seminary began in 1926, and he served as a director and chairman of the executive committee until his death on June 28, 1940. Of great importance, also, was his invaluable leadership of the Investment Committee of the Seminary Board. His commitment to the life and work of a struggling institution is reflected in a memorial bulletin dedicated to Campbell:

> His deep concern for it was well illustrated by his quiet statement to the President one day during the depth of the depression. "I lay awake all last night, thinking of your problem." As Chairman of the Investment Committee he gave careful study to the placing of the Seminary's endowment funds and the comparatively high income which these have earned was due to his planning.[31]

There was every reason to offer such praise. Campbell saved the institution. He gave generous gifts and influenced other Presbyterians to give. The ministers who helped bring the seminary to Decatur responded to the appeal. Not only did he solicit gifts but he helped secure loans and at times loaned money from his own resources.

This could have been the end of Columbia, but by the grace of God, due to the sacrificial giving of the Columbia constituency and the improving economy after World War II, the threatening years in the 1930s gave way to a healthier institution in the 1940s and beyond.

The Decade of World War II
1940–1949

The decade of the 1940s began with thanksgiving for the survival of Columbia seminary and, indeed, the nation. The 1930s had sorely tested the whole world economically and, thus, the United States was not alone in a time of trial. The new decade began, also, with encouraging signs that the economy in the

United States was slowly but surely improving. Indeed, with the ominous rearming of a militant Germany, there were examples throughout the world of industrial growth and, thus, less cruel and horrendous unemployment. Though this stimulus was largely produced by the need to prepare militarily for World War II, there were also improving economic conditions for individuals and groups. With few women in jobs that paid wages, and one-fourth of the men unemployed, despair during the 1930s, like poisonous gas, blanketed the nation and much of the world. It is one of the great ironies of the twentieth century that economic recovery came about as nations went to war with each other. By 1940, however, Columbia Theological Seminary had survived the lack of money, the inability of candidates for ministry to have a few dollars to pay even the entry fee, and the hopelessness that suffocated their future hopes and dreams. Pastors of churches, like their parishioners, barely survived. Salaries among small churches were as low as four hundred dollars a year with a supplement of two hundred dollars from the presbytery.

When John Bulow Campbell died suddenly, on June 28, 1940, President Richards suffered a grievous personal loss in the death of his most important partner in the mission of the institution. Atlanta's civic and institutional life also suffered greatly. Adolph Hitler rebuilt Germany during the 1930s, and now began his seemingly unstoppable invasion, capture, and plundering of neighboring states. In passionate but demonic words, he blatantly talked of Germany's domination of Europe and, eventually, the world. He began his heinous attempts to slaughter and eradicate the Jews and anyone else who opposed him. Included in his victims were the ill, the retarded, and the useless in his schemes.

While an economic depression held the nation in its destructive grasp, Decatur, Georgia, was a small town tested like most towns and cities in the 1930s. However, it was relatively untouched in the early 1940s by Hitler's steady expansion in Europe and North Africa. A few young men volunteered for military service in the twelve months leading up to this decade. It was employment and, in addition to clothing, food, and medical care, they were paid a few dollars a month. Most of those dollars were sent home to their families.

At no other time, for various reasons, was there such a close, personal relationship between students and President Richards. In 1942, at a special convocation celebrating his tenth anniversary as president, the student body planned and carried out a personal tribute to him. J. Will Ormond, John H. Leith, and J. Davison Philips spoke of Richards' early life and education, his useful service in the Presbyterian Church (U.S.), and in ecumenical organizations. His leadership of Columbia Seminary was detailed with genuine appreciation. David E. Wilkinson concluded this theme with the presentation of a gift and this personal note: "Dr. Richards, you have been a wonderful inspiration and example for students."

Of course, the institution was still relatively small, the financial support barely adequate, and the faculty few in number, but the president's role was clearly that of a person "in charge," who not only related to every other person on campus, but directed the total life of the institution.

The decade of the 1940s had unique aspects of life on campus. It was a time of surviving during World War II and preparing for the post-war institution. Actually, no one expected the enrollment to double and triple as time went on. The president's role, however, was still that of an administrator in control of events, appointments, finances, and ecclesiastical relationships. The president was an active Presbyter and an ecumenical representative.

Richards supported students from Europe who sought sanctuary in the United States. One such student was from Czechoslovakia. The Committee on Refugee Theological Scholars passionately appealed for admittance, saying it was a life or death decision. Professor Romadka of Princeton Theological Seminary also sought consideration of five refugee students who were safe but still in danger in southern France. They had no hope of paying the tuition, and Richards granted them full scholarships. Haste was imperative. There was no time to get comprehensive application data from them. W. P. Ladd of the American Theological Society detailed the case with both compassion and passion:

> You will at once recognize the steadily deepening gravity of the problem. They have been driven from their positions in totalitarian states whose plight has engaged the concern of the Society. They, if humanly possible, must be enabled to come to this country in most instances completely destitute. Britain could not take any more. In addition to those from Czechoslovakia a considerable number of Protestant theological students from Poland, Holland, and France can look to the United States alone for a safe refuge and completion of their studies.[32]

As the weeks and months moved on with deepening anguish in Europe and frantic efforts in the United States to help, every seminary was asked to take at least one student and one faculty member. Richards agreed and invited Dr. Milio Capek in France to come by the beginning of the term, September 24, 1940.

In addition to survival through the previous decade, the most encouraging thing to President Richards was the slight increase in the number of students. The entering class in September of 1940 was the largest in years, though nothing like the peak years of its early history in South Carolina. I was one of twenty-three members enrolled from Florida to Arkansas and Texas to North Carolina. Nineteen graduated. Before Pearl Harbor, President Richards saw a small but important increase in support from the churches.[33]

During those years of 1940 to 1943, life on campus was somewhat isolated from world events, but by graduation on May 18, 1943, the storms of war and terror had reached across the Atlantic and Pacific Oceans. More and more students were swept up by events as they listened with increasing anxiety to world news each night broadcast by WSB radio. The thundering eloquence of Winston Churchill, and the guttural, manic speeches of Adolph Hitler shattered any sense of isolation. There was much talk on campus of entering the military chaplaincy. The obligation to serve the soldiers, sailors, and airmen grew on seminary campuses throughout the nation. Plans for further graduate study were postponed in order to serve. It did not slow down plans for marriage too much, but world events created quite a different "mind set" in the class of 1943 compared to their attitudes in September, 1940.

Life, however, was quite simple in some ways as the decade began. It slowly but surely became a part of a new political and social culture in the 1940s. President Richards projected a dramatic changing pattern of life in frequent letters to his father. Vegetable gardens were cultivated. Rationing of food, gasoline, and travel were widely accepted. Absorbed in life at Columbia and in the Presbyterian Church during wartime, most members of the class of 1943 were still aware of the changes in the life of the nation and the world. Prayers for peace were offered daily.

Worship in chapel sharpened a focus on prayers also for the survival of democracy as opposed to Nazism. Intercession was made for the victims of Hitler's aggression as Jewish families were sent to camps and death chambers. Pearl Harbor's devastation from a surprise air attack on Sunday morning, December 7, 1941, changed plans and attitudes overnight. In many ways, the turbulent world history dramatically revamped the life and work at Columbia Seminary. It was never the same again. Campus life and work was, inevitably, quite different from that in a small, provincial setting. A world in crisis demanded change, and it happened, both good and bad.

Throughout this decade, President Richards maintained complete supervision and administrative control of the life and work of Columbia Seminary. Even in 1945, he was the final judge and the giver of invitations to visiting scholars. These speakers and lecturers were of national and international influence in their careers. During this period he asked James H. Gailey, an alumnus in graduate study at Princeton Theological Seminary, for an evaluation on scholars there. Gailey's response was immediate and helpful. It was also succinct and to the point: "President Mackay is the most inspiring lecturer by far. Hromadka is a Calvinist, but Homrighausen is a much more popular speaker. Hugh Kerr has an aggravating way of making students think." Gailey also suggested William Albright, a well-known archeologist of Johns Hopkins University.[34]

The war initiated by Germany and Japan ended with a legacy of the horrendous destruction of a fearsome and awesome atomic bomb. By then, much of Europe and the Pacific Islands lay in ruins. Germany and its allies were bankrupt. Sullen hopelessness gripped the defeated countries. Peace treaties dictated by the victors were signed. Franklin Delano Roosevelt's successor, Harry S Truman, had been president only a few months and signed the surrender documents for the United States. Unexpected upheavals in Britain and in the United States resulted from Roosevelt's death on April 14, 1945, and Churchill's defeat at the polls later that same year.[35] Tremendous efforts to rebuild Europe through the Marshall Plan, providing financing and materials, were crucially important. Attention was also given to the Far East, but with less assistance. The rise of communism in China and in other parts of the world seriously influenced relationships with the people and governments in these areas. In all of this worldwide turmoil, President Richards led Columbia to consult with returning chaplains and prospective students before producing curriculum changes and appointing new faculty.

Near the end of World War II, Columbia's professor of church history, William Childs Robinson, preached in the small but worshipful chapel at Warm Springs, Georgia. The date fell on Easter Sunday, April 1, 1945. President Franklin D. Roosevelt attended as he often did while spending time in Warm Springs for physical therapy.[36] The Easter service was held ten days before President Roosevelt's sudden heart attack ended both his life and his career. The *Christian Observer* described the service of worship in vivid terms and concluded its evaluation with the phrase, "The President listened intently."[37]

Robinson immediately dispatched a printed version of the sermon to the president who responded in a letter dated April 11, 1945, and postmarked the day he died. It read in part:

> Thank you very much for your letter of April seventh. I am very glad to have that copy of your sermon, "The Faith of a Soldier," because it gives me in permanent form that very appropriate poem which you embodied in your Easter Day Sermon. That was indeed a grand service and it was wonderful that you could participate. I shall be happy to remember your kind offer to come to Warm Springs again for further ministrations.[38]

The reference to a poem could have been one of the following three included in the sermon.

"The Stirrup Cup"

My short and happy day is done,
The long and lonely night comes on
And at my door the pale horse stands

To bear me forth to unknown lands
But storm and gloom and mystery
Shall only nerve my courage high
To face its close with tranquil heart.
~John Hay

"The Pale Horse"

The Pale horse stands and will not hide
The night has come and I must ride
But not alone to unknown lands
My friend goes with me, holding hands.
~James Powers Smith

More likely, Roosevelt's reference was to the contemporary one written by the mother of an airman who went down in the crash of a B-26 plane near Panama:

God has given me a guiding light
A star called Faith
That substance of things hoped for
That evidence of things not seen
And now within me peace and joy are born
For some day there shall come a resurrection morn
And I shall see again and know my son.

The issue of merging the four seminaries of the Presbyterian Church (U.S.) would not go away quietly after World War II. It started in the late 1930s and did not end until 1950. The reasons advanced were quite familiar. The small numbers of students, the shortage of funds and resources, the appeals to efficiency, and, most of all, the size of the "Southern Church" were reasons for consolidating resources of the seminaries for the education of ministers, educators, and missionaries. The issue seemingly rose from the dead each year from 1939 to 1950.

World War II diverted attention from the issue, but even the post-war surge of enrollments did not extinguish it. Typical of the familiar scenarios was the General Assembly approval of the recommendation of the Works Survey Committee that Louisville, Austin, Union at Richmond, and Columbia be merged. Further, it proposed that an adequate plant be provided in Nashville, Tennessee, near Vanderbilt University. Even the suggestion that merger was an attractive proposal and should be explored created a strong negative response from Columbia's board and constituency.

Though Richards' cautious reaction was one of wanting "to be in subjection to the brethren in the Lord,"[39] the Board of Directors viewed such action as a clear and present danger. The mission of the institution, in the board's view, would be radically changed should the recommendation be approved and acted upon.

A carefully worded statement of position was prepared: "It is the conviction of this board that any removal of this institution from Atlanta would be a mistake." The familiar reasons were once more articulated with conviction and passion:

1. This center offers a strategic center for the service of the South.
2. Moral obligations were laid upon the Seminary to remain here through the large amounts of money contributed to Columbia Theological Seminary by the Presbyterians of Atlanta and Georgia within recent years.[40]

The committee's report recommending this consolidation was written in the years just before World War II, and they did not foresee the tremendous growth of the southeastern United States and Atlanta. Nor did the committee foresee the tremendous growth of the Presbyterian Church (U.S.) in the supporting synods in the area and particularly in Georgia.[41] As the situation changed, consolidation was abandoned as a relevant proposal.

Surprisingly, Britain ousted their great leader, Winston Churchill, in the first election following the armistice in 1945. Even though he had rallied their spirits and efforts in a desperate effort to survive and to win World War II, voters stunned other allied nations by defeating the one leader who had been essential to their survival and victory. Long delayed decisions of equitable pay and social services for the British people were now pressing for implementation and for immediate decisions. The Labour Party won at the polls by promising justice, medical care, and prosperity. Clement Atlee became prime minister. Seismic shocks came in a frightening rush in the domination of Eastern Europe by Russia. In Churchill's vivid analysis, "an iron curtain descended upon Europe."[42] Renewed conflict was ominously threatened.

However, on the seminary campus, life began to quicken with new students, new faculty, and new challenges from the Church in the post-war world. President Richards was also very much in charge of life on campus. The post-war Church, as seen among the Presbyterians of the United States, was committed to welcoming returning war veterans, moving on in the mission of the Church at home and overseas, and seeking to join war relief efforts for surviving nations and churches. Columbia was challenged by the desire of chaplains to have what they called "refresher courses" for brief periods of time. The challenge urged that they be enrolled even though there was a steady and escalating number of students preparing for ministry.

In addition to the strong efforts of various religious bodies, there were some poignant efforts in congregations to bring reconciliation with defeated enemies. Richards often spoke of the work of his lifelong friend, Will Watt, an elder in First Presbyterian Church, Thomasville, Georgia. Mr. Watt initiated a unique effort along this line shortly after the World War II armistice. Watt's two older sons served in World War II. As mayor of the city, he felt some effort should be made by the churches and the citizens of Thomasville to build a peace that would reconcile citizens of the defeated enemy nations with those of the victorious United States.

In a brilliant plan, Watt proposed as a starting point in reconciliation the linking of two relatively small towns of the United States and Germany. Thomasville would initiate this reconciliation through acts of compassion. He recommended that Thomasville, Georgia, form a strong relationship with a town of similar size in the chaos of defeated parts of Europe. Lunenburg, Germany, was selected after careful consultation with the State Department. A proposal was approved that aid would be given to the people of that small town with a population almost identical in size to Thomasville's fifteen thousand people. Over a thousand years old, Lunenburg was now devastated by the battles of World War II. The citizens of that old and historic city were astonished but grateful when two railroad cars of food, clothing, and medicine arrived from Thomasville, Georgia, U.S.A. They were not only recipients of relief packages, but better still, of compassion from their former enemy. It was at least symbolic in obedience to the ancient wisdom of Proverbs: "If your enemies are hungry, give them bread to eat, if they are thirsty, give them water to drink" (Prov. 25:21 NRSV).

An admirable and almost miraculous effort in this attempt at reconciliation came through a Jewish merchant in Thomasville, whose family had come to the United States as refugees. Even though his roots were in Germany, he was approached to give shoes from his store on Main Street for this effort. Thinking that the merchant might angrily decline, Mayor Watt still saw him as the only source in the town for such a gift. In a courageous act, and in fear and anxiety, Watt asked if he could give some shoes that were old and unsold for a number of years. However, in an astonishing and wonderful spirit, the merchant filled up Watt's automobile with the newest and best he had!

The Lunenburg citizens assembled in a town meeting and tried to understand the amazing generosity of their former enemies, these United States citizens, who were sending such desperately needed help. The Marshall Plan, of course, was of utmost importance in the recovery of a defeated Europe. However, this small but direct link with the people of Thomasville, who in the spirit of the Prince of Peace sought reconciliation, produced a bond of such strength that it is still alive and well. The Obermeister of Lunenburg traveled to Thomasville in 1956, to personally express the city's gratitude for aid in a time of great misery. That aid is remembered by citizens of both towns to this day. Indeed, Mayor Watt was made an honorary citizen of Lunenburg, the highest honor the city could bestow. This honor had been granted only three times before in the town's one-thousand-year history. Sweden, Norway, and Germany acted similarly to recognize this compassionate act in a time of great need.

In various sermons and in an address to the Rotary Club of Atlanta, Richards spoke of that compassionate act as one that fulfilled the biblical concept of "the healing of the nations" through the power of simple acts of mercy and concern.

Other important and dramatic changes occurred during this decade. The synods' recommendation that Columbia's Board of Directors revise its membership to strike a balance between ministers and elders was a most important development. This requirement had long been overlooked by many members of the Church in light of focus on the issue of removal. This action brought superb leadership from lay leaders of the Church to the campus and to the whole cause of theological education in the Church.[43]

The evolving role of the president of Columbia Theological Seminary was gathering momentum. The second half of the decade of 1940–50 was a time of enormous transition at Columbia Theological Seminary. World War II was over, and an uneasy and, indeed, fragile peace settled over the world. Europe and Japan were in shambles. Both Britain and Germany suffered in the tremendous destruction of factories, homes, and public buildings. All possible resources were used to fight that war, but at tremendous cost of lives and property. On the post-war campus, President Richards faced new challenges that were changing as the months went by. They brought new pressures to the basic mission of the institution:

Administration. The capacity of Columbia to teach, house, and feed increasing numbers of students was stretched to the breaking point. Only Simons-Law dormitory and Campbell Hall were available. In 1946, twenty students graduated and sought ordination. In 1950, more than one hundred students were admitted to the first year of the three-year bachelor of divinity degree program. The faculty was overwhelmed and courses were taught in duplicate sections. The surrounding housing possibilities in Decatur and Atlanta were quite limited, but returning service men were finishing college and entering theological schools, housing or not. More than half were married. Under a federal government program providing surplus barracks to educational institutions, Columbia installed twelve apartments converted from wartime barracks. They were not sound proof, but they were dry and warm. George William Long Jr., my nephew, was born during this time and spent his first year in one of these apartments. Miss Virginia Harrison, bursar and secretary to the president, said in her Christmas letter: "His birth was the most exciting thing that has happened lately on campus."

If applicants had come immediately after World War II ended, it would have been quite chaotic. However, since some had to finish college first, there was time to plan for space and faculty additions. As they did in many educational institutions, these students brought a maturity and a different emotional frame of reference to the campus.

The role of the president was changing. The Plan of Government was revised somewhat to read, "The President shall be the administrative officer of the seminary. He shall be responsible to the Board of Directors for the discharge of those duties assigned him."[44]

Already, the time when the president managed almost every detail of campus life, including finances, facilities, faculty appointments and duties, ecclesiastical relationships, and admissions, was beginning to change. For example, he had extended conversations and correspondence with Marion Anderson of West Point, Georgia, regarding admission. Anderson was thirty-eight years old with a wife and a small child. He did not have the required college degree. He persisted, however, in his desire to study for the ministry out of a sense of call. Finally, April 3, 1945, Richards mentioned the possibility he might have of ordination under the extraordinary clause provided in the *Book of Order* for those without a college degree.

That change in the president's role escalated as time went on in the postwar period.

Ecclesiastical Relations. There may have been an uneasy peace in Europe, but not even that in the Presbyterian Church, U.S. The critics challenged ecumenical councils for unorthodox positions and for supporting desegregation and racial justice. Richards was the principal target for ecumenical critics. Because of his role in the leadership of the Federal Council of Churches and in various appeals for racial justice, he became the "punching bag" for critics.

The Spillman correspondence circulatated by a layman to every session in the Southeast attacked Professor of Old Testament, E. D. Kerr; Professor of New Testament, Samuel A. Cartledge; and President Richards. Columbia's professors were accused of heretical teaching, and President Richards was harshly condemned for his involvements in ecumenical groups such as the Federal Council of Churches. President Richards' response to all inquires and attacks was almost always a denial that they were true. For example, students' misleading and exaggerated reports on statements by Professor Kerr in Old

Testament classes were sent to the Board of Directors, but later withdrawn by them. The Board of Directors was unanimous in approving Professor Kerr's statement of faith.

More extensive, however, was the critical response to the publication of *A Conservative Introduction to the Old Testament* by Professor Samuel A. Cartledge. Published by Zondervan Publishing Company, it was to be used as a companion volume to a well-received work some years earlier on the New Testament. Although the New Testament volume was frequently used as a text-book by conservative institutions and ministers, the Old Testament one created quite a furor. Accusations of "heretical higher criticism positions" were part of a steady bombardment of charges against Professor Cartledge and his views.

President Richards responded to these vocal critics with a disclaimer. The members of the Board of Directors had not read the book before publication, but he had. While some of his suggestions were not followed, he articulates his position in a carefully worded position:

> I would not stand in the way of Professor Cartledge publishing this book. I should think it a very dangerous practice indeed if the president of a theological seminary were allowed to say what professors of the institution might or might not publish. In reality, such action would involve an infringement upon the right of free speech which is so vital both to democracy and the Church.[45]

Enoree Presbytery investigated the whole matter and filed a critical report. The Board of Directors, however, affirmed Professor Cartledge's status as a valued faculty member.

W. R. Hough of Jackson, Mississippi, circulated the Church with charges of heresy in Cartledge's views. Even after an investigation and rejection of the charges, he still demanded a full public statement of rebuke from President Richards to Cartledge. Richards refused. Other critics included Charles O'Neale Martindale who blamed the Cartledge views on his graduate study at the University of Chicago.[46] In the midst of all this, students and faculty and staff worked to accomplish the mission of Columbia Seminary from a position of intellectual integrity and ecclesiastical commitments.[47]

Financial Health. In an insightful statement to a member of his family, President Richards wrote: "I seem to be doomed to more or less perpetual effort as a fund-raiser. I am at present seeking to secure $100,000 for our Seminary Endowment by January 1, 1946, in order to receive an additional grant of $450,000 which has been promised by a local Foundation if we obtain the objective."[48]

However, the role of the president throughout his entire tenure in that office was officially stated in the Plan of Government. The 1936 Plan of Government said: "The President shall be the presiding officer of the Seminary, and will make the same subscriptions as faculty members."[49]

Furthermore, "The duties of the president relate to securing and maintaining a well-equipped and effectively organized teaching and administrative staff and to the supervision and development of the physical plant and material resources of the seminary. He may delegate the details of the office and he shall have the liberty and authority necessary for the effective performance of this office."

The president was chairman of the faculty and of the executive committee of the faculty. His most important task was to recommend to the board through the Executive Committee the names for faculty and administrative staff to be appointed, and to suggest the appropriate compensation for each. This administrative oversight included the formation of a budget to be approved by the board annually. Perhaps the view of the president's role in days when the numbers were small and later when they were large is found in the words, "the general oversight of the life and work of Columbia Theological Seminary." July 6, 1946, reports to the synods gave thanks for an operating balance of $2,399.04 and an endowment of $859,391.99.

To some, Mission Haven may have been seen as a minor part of the seminary's mission. The use of an apartment in Simons-Law Hall for missionaries on furlough would quickly point a clear way toward Mission Haven, a large cluster of homes and apartments on the northwest corner of the campus. The Women of the Church of the synods in the southeastern United States funded and operated this facility. Many of the missionaries who had a full furlough year every four years also studied at Columbia Seminary. Most attended classes and some earned graduate degrees. From time to time those who required immediate, emergency care would be patients in Atlanta hospitals, and their families had access to apartments at Mission Haven.

The Decade of Growth
1950–1959

The decade of the 1950s not only involved the transformation of nations throughout the world in a significant way, but also the Christian Church on every continent. The new challenges for Columbia Theological Seminary included everyone in some way, and were felt by faculty, students, graduates, and constituency. This, of course, led to a challenging and different chapter in the office of the presidency for J. McDowell Richards. The Church and the culture were changing with population growth, a mobile population, and a world in evolving political ideologies. Inevitably, a new pattern of leadership was required in light of increases in enrollment, and in the numbers and nature of the students. Students from churches in Europe and the Far East contributed much to community life. For Richards, responsibilities were increasingly delegated to faculty, staff, and administrators. The academic program and life on campus needed deans with authority.

In this decade, the enrollments doubled and then tripled. Veterans of World War II and laypersons challenged by the gravity of dangerous world conflict and fragmentation began serious spiritual pilgrimages. This pilgrimage led some to offer their lives for what was called, in a misleading phrase, "full-time Christian service." Ideally, all Christians in the broad sense of the phrase are in full-time service.

The decade of the 1950s for Columbia Theological Seminary was also a time of looking backward and forward. The directors and the campus community looked back on two wars, World War II and the Korean War. World War II was monumental in its impact on Columbia. Four out of twenty graduates in the class of 1943 served as chaplains during the conflict. The enrollment, however, fell by 50 percent. In the years of the 1950s enrollments surged.

The Korean War was also destructive for Columbia Seminary because of its major ties with the Presbyterian missionaries and the Presbyterian Church in Korea. Twenty-two ministers and their families were recent graduates of the institution. That six hundred mile long peninsula was a vassal state of China for two hundred years until occupied by the Japanese from 1910 until 1948. Following the Korean War, it was divided into North Korea with ties to the Soviet Union and South Korea with ties to the United States. China entered the arena of the Korean War when it became apparent that the Communist powers in Korea would be overcome. Under powerful military pressure, the United States and South Korean forces were driven into a small area on the southeast tip of that peninsula. Heavy use of American military power finally brought the area south of Seoul to a relatively free and democratic culture. However, since that time there have been two Koreas, North and South.

South Korea prospered economically, and the Presbyterians of Korea founded colleges, seminaries, and churches. While there are six different bodies in Korea using the word "Presbyterian," there are more Presbyterian Christians in Korea today than in the United States. In North Korea, Christians were under heavy pressure, and preachers were imprisoned and martyred. Only two Protestant churches survived. However the Presbyterian Church in South Korea grew significantly in membership and in candidates for ministry. It steadily developed strong administrative structures. Graduates of Presbyterian seminaries in the United States, including Columbia, had then and still have strong bonds with Korean Presbyterians and their churches.

Three powerful forces made a significant impact on the Richards presidency in this decade. They were:

1. The surging economy in the United States had a dramatic influence on the church and world. Economic inflation also brought great pressures to the nation and to the churches.
2. The scene in Asia and Europe, and particularly its violent political conflicts, was both destructive and helpful in its impact on the United States.
3. The growth in membership and in the numbers of Presbyterian churches and ministers was impressive.

Important insights from a 1954 accreditation program reflected some of these forces. The process underway at the institution included a review of the total life of the school. A long list of areas studied focused on the patterns of administration, physical plant, finances, enrollment, faculty, students, mission, curriculum, fieldwork, clinical training, library, nature of the school as a community, academic standards, and graduate work. It involved significant amounts of time and work by the faculty, administrators, and students. The final report appears to have been

J. McDowell Richards, center, seated, and the faculty of Columbia Seminary in the 1950s.

written by Richards after considerable consultation with the faculty and staff about details. It resulted in accreditation for another four years, but a greater result was observed on campus through the process of research and analysis. Important reports reviewing the academic program of curriculum and faculty were carefully developed. The administration and faculty benefited from the self-study required. Students became more involved in the total life of the seminary. The result was a revealing document of life and relationships on campus. Every group had an opportunity to do serious self-examination and make specific recommendations. What is equally important for President Richards is the suggested scope of the responsibilities of the president and the utilization of faculty and staff. The research and the report were much more than the normal accreditation process usually required. It included several visits to the campus and extended conversations with administration, faculty and students.

The progress made in the decade of the 1950s was extremely important, for it began with a highly unfavorable review of Columbia Theological Seminary from a consulting firm, Cresap and Associates. It was extremely critical, and surely a most discouraging evaluation for Richards. Their "findings" or conclusions, based on the questionnaires, were:

A. From the generally low response level for this type of survey, we can only conclude that either there is a general apathy and indifference to the institution, or its constituents believe that responding would have no effect in generating change and improvement.

B. The public image of the institution needs to be improved, or at least established within the Church constituency, through a vast improvement in public relations and public knowledge of the institution.

C. Improved and enlarged continuing education for the ministry seems in demand, with strong emphasis on continuing lay education through home study materials and retreats.

D. A lack of desired activity in the faculty and advanced students in the Church and within the ministry is evident.

E. Greater assistance in pastoral placement appears to be wanted, including some aid in the complex effort involved in moving to a new pastorate.

F. A request for joint effort by all four seminaries is suggested, as well as greater cooperative effort between local institutions of higher education.

G. Planning for the long-range future of the seminary seems to be of concern, with most groups not aware of any plans or planning effort.

H. Of particular significance, even though represented by a small percentage of returns, is the need for improvement in teaching and teaching programs.

1. The students (15 to 15) believe that the curriculum does not provide them with all the studies they need.
2. The students (16 to 15) believe that the quality of teaching is not satisfactory.
3. More creative teaching is urged.
4. The students report they need better teachers, more counseling and more field education work.[50]

The conclusions reached by this process led the consultants to present a critical report based on quite contradictory data. They concluded:

> The summary of these questionnaire returns indicates that the constituency holds the belief that the institution is drifting rather than forging its own development course, prefers to retire rather than grasp a leadership role, and maintains a faculty and curriculum which is believed to be in no small measure outdated and uninspiring. This, of course, may not be a fair appraisal of the institution, but the important fact is that a good share of the constituency believes this to be the situation.[51]

The response of the Board of Directors and the president was, with a few exceptions, one of negative reaction and disagreement. The small number of responses indicated a negative view of the processes used in this evaluation. They did, however, seek to strengthen the weaknesses and did so before moving on with a major financial campaign. From the viewpoint of the seminary, however, a courageous effort to raise more money in a campaign than in all the history of the institution was a positive step in implementing the report's recommendations. This rather audacious response to the criticisms involved an effort to raise $5 million for basic undergraduate needs. An application to the Woodruff Foundation for a challenge grant over a ten-year period of $2.5 million would stimulate giving by the constituency that would set a new record for a single campaign. An additional $1 million was projected for the initiation of graduate work. The case for the mission of Columbia was succinctly made:

> The future of America and of our western civilization will be determined largely by our attitude toward moral and spiritual values. General Douglas W. MacArthur was right when he declared that the issue before us was "largely theological." President Eisenhower has courageously taken the leadership in declaring the necessity of religious faith if we are to solve our problems, and in emphasizing the importance of the Church in the life of our nation.

> No institutions are so essential to the Church as the schools which train our ministers. Our theological seminaries are the fountain from which the stream of

religious leadership must flow. Without strong seminaries the church cannot itself be strong. This is one form of education which can never be provided out of public funds. Its hope inevitably rests upon church support and individual gifts.

Columbia Theological Seminary is strategically situated to be a major force in the religious life of the Southeast. It has rendered distinguished service for 126 years and is today standing on the threshold of its greatest opportunity. Although thoroughly accredited, its resources are inadequate even for its present student body of approximately 200.

The continued expansion of the Southeast makes it necessary that we provide for further growth as well as for the improvement of our work. In the light of this fact, the Faculty and Directors of the institution have engaged in a careful study of its needs and have charted a ten-year program. It seems reasonable to expect a student body of 300 by 1964. If adequate provision is to be made for that task, the following amounts will be needed:

For basic undergraduate needs:

Buildings and physical equipment	1,500,000
Endowment	500,000
Graduate Program: Endowment	1,000,000

The accompanying statement, "The Crisis of Our Times," is of great importance in understanding the presidency of J. McDowell Richards, his convictions, and his commitments to Columbia Theological Seminary. The major principles reflecting his case for the existence and support of this most important institution are found in selections from that article:

The critical nature of our times and the necessity for keeping the moral and spiritual foundations of our society intact, make self-evident the need of our entire nation for a vigorous and well-prepared religious leadership. It is of our own Southeastern States that we speak in a particular way. The almost phenomenal development of the South from an economic and industrial viewpoint is well known. It is of utmost importance that in our material and scientific progress we should not neglect the things of the spirit. It is essential that the Christian forces of our region keep pace with developments in all other areas of life if we are to become and remain truly strong.[52]

Richards saw a worldwide crisis developing as America faced a philosophy espousing tyranny and materialistic values. The threat of global war and political chaos would ultimately prevail if the Church was weak and ineffective. He passionately describes the need for spiritual nurture and committed service by the Church and her ministers. He speaks of the education of able and devoted ministers:

> In presenting the cause of Theological Education, we believe we are speaking for that which is most vital to the cause of religion. Our theological seminaries are the fountain from which the stream of religious leadership must flow. History shows that the Church has never been stronger than its ministry. We must have able, consecrated, and thoroughly trained men[53] to supply our pulpits, fill our teaching positions, and direct our church boards and agencies if the Christian Faith is to be properly presented in our time. The equipment and techniques of yesterday will not suffice for the needs of education tomorrow in the field of ministerial training any more than in those of engineering and medicine. Not only must the quality of our work be constantly improved, but we must be prepared to train an increasing number of students.[54]

Another revelation of the thinking and the views of Richards is found in an undated description of the qualifications to be sought in a professor of Columbia Seminary. The sixteen items are:

1. A warm evangelical faith and strong Christian character.
2. A first rate intellect and a winsome personality.
3. Competence in his field or proven ability to attain that competence.
4. Loyalty as a Churchman.
5. The ability and desire to teach.
6. A reasonable amount of pastoral experience, if possible, but definitely the possession of a pastor's heart.
7. Convictions deeply held in a framework of charity for all.
8. Concern for the missionary outreach of the Church at home and abroad.
9. Concern for the social problems of our day and for the witness of the Church through action.
10. An inclination to productive scholarship.
11. A youthful spirit with potentialities for continued growth as a scholar, a teacher, and a person. In years, he should not be beyond middle age.
12. Industry, faithfulness and dependability.
13. Soundness of judgment.
14. Humility.
15. Discontent with himself.
16. An ecumenical spirit in the full sense of the term.[55]

While there is no mention of the requirement to be a minister in the Presbyterian Church in order to be granted tenure, this was probably assumed based on the Plan of Government. Later on, with the appointment of faculty who were Anglican in England and Australia, and who were ministers of the Church of Scotland, this requirement prevented tenured appointments of "evangelicals" who met most of these qualifications.

The Atlanta Theological Association, formed as a consortium, included Candler School of Theology, Johnson C. Smith Theological Seminary, Columbia Theological Seminary, and Erskine Theological Seminary. Johnson C. Smith, a Presbyterian institution, was one of the schools of theology in a consortium of primarily African-American theological schools in the Interdenominational Theological Center. This further broadened the life of Columbia through faculty and library resources. Thus, the 1950s further strengthened the educational relationships burgeoning in the Atlanta area.

The image of Columbia Theological Seminary and the work of the president emerging in this decade were most clearly seen in a 1954 report to the Committee on the Study of Theological Education in the United States and Canada. A newly formed Association of Theological Schools requested and received from Richards answers to a fifteen-page list of questions seeking information about the mission of the institution, its governance, and the nature of its faculty and students. The basic data sketched a portrait of a theological seminary with these items:

1. The Seminary was "owned and controlled" by the five synods in the Southeastern United States. The Board of Directors included twelve ministers and nine layman elected by their synods. However, in the practice of this form of government, the chairman of the board, and the Executive Committee had much more active relationships with the president and the seminary. Its functions, moreover, included approval of recommendations from the president regarding faculty, budgets, and the major features of the educational program.[56] What was very important at that time was the effort to be a faithful institution of the Presbyterian Church, U.S. This meant active participation in meetings of presbytery, synods and the General Assembly.

2. A faculty of twelve that included the president, the dean, and the librarian. Only two part time lecturers were teaching and are not included in this number.

3. The enrollment reported in 1955 had risen from 44 in 1935, 66 in 1945, to 209 in 1955. There were five women studying in 1955. 60 bachelor of divinity students graduated. A goal of 300 students was declared, and with the development of other degrees such as the master of theology, the

Th.D., and the doctor of ministry, the totals would be twice that of 1955. Nearly half of the students in the classes of 1950 to 1959 were married. These far exceeded the dormitory rooms and apartments available, and was a very great problem until new facilities were built. All but 31 of the students were from small liberal arts colleges, the majority of whom were affiliated with the Presbyterian Church.

4. The 1954 audit revealed an expenditure of $164,302.86 for the operation of this program. By his retirement, the Richards' budget for operations was nearly $800,000. He always was extremely frugal in such matters. The $52,020.99 from the endowment, $63,549.15 from gifts, and student charges for room, board, scholarship gifts, brought the total to a "balanced budget."[57]

5. The mission of the institution was expressed in the Plan of Government, part II, chapter 1, section 3: "The great purpose of the Seminary shall be to prepare men[58] for the Gospel ministry, to train Christian workers, to protect the standards of the Presbyterian Church in the United States, to contend for the Faith, and to labor for the Kingdom of God." In fulfillment of that provision all full professors were required to subscribe to the *Confession of Faith*, catechisms, and other standards of government, discipline, and worship of the Presbyterian Church (U.S.), but not the students.

6. The curriculum was fairly rigid, with students expected to take 80 percent of their work in the required courses with 20 percent in electives.[59] There were other requirements in supervised ministry placements in churches, counseling centers, and urban ministry practicums.

7. With less than 50,000 volumes in the library, faculty and students made use of the other libraries available to them through the consortium with Emory University, University of Georgia, Georgia Institute of Technology, Gammon Theological Seminary, Candler School of Theology, Agnes Scott College, Atlanta Public Library, and Dekalb County Library. The consortium delivered any request within twenty-four hours by a library truck that traveled to each institution Monday through Friday. Graduate studies beyond the college and seminary basic degrees were at a minimal level for lack of resources in faculty and money in 1954.

This decade claimed much energy and time from J. McDowell Richards. As moderator of the General Assembly of the Presbyterian Church (U.S.) in 1955–56, he traveled throughout the church, preaching and speaking.

Following the year when the denomination declined to reunite with the Presbyterian Church (U.S.), Moderator Richards gave strong leadership to the mission of the church at home and overseas, and continued to serve the major boards and agencies which he had done throughout his ministry. This office gave him a forum and an opportunity to not only serve the church at large, but to bring Columbia Seminary into public view as it had not been seen before.

Near the end of this decade in 1958, the Board of Directors with the support of the constituency throughout the synod constituencies in Georgia, South Carolina, Florida, Mississippi, and Alabama united in honoring Richards for twenty-six years of sacrificial, committed leadership of Columbia Seminary. Actually, the occasion launched a new campaign for resources. Patrick Dwight Miller, Richards' longtime friend and colleague spoke for those present in a succinct, but moving tribute. The essence of his praise follows:

> To no other man in the Church does Columbia Seminary owe so much as to her distinguished President, J. McDowell Richards. Few of the younger graduates of the school know of her precarious condition when Dr. Richards came to be President. He began his work here in 1932 in the midst of the great Depression at a shamefully low salary, and served nine years without a single increase. The Board of Directors was never proud of that fact and we are trying to do better. My point is that Dr. Richards was determined to operate the Seminary on a balanced budget—a thing which he has done for 26 years. It is past time that the supporting synods ceased asking this man and his colleagues on the faculty to make bricks without straw. Dr. Richards himself is one reason why the forthcoming financial campaign for Columbia Seminary should succeed.[60]

The decade was drawing to a close with a faculty of thirteen, a budget of $533,000, and a total enrollment in all degree programs of 273. The new decade of the 1960s would bring tremendous challenges and there would be no rest for President Richards.

The Last Decade
1960–1971

The role of President J. McDowell Richards at Columbia Theological Seminary in the decade of the 1960s was dramatically different from that of the 1930s. In Richards' first decade, 1931 to 1940, economic despair spread like a virus throughout the nation and most of the world. World War II began in Germany and Europe. The diminished resources of the Presbyterian Church (U.S.) affected its mission and ministry everywhere. The existence of this century-old institution, Columbia Theological Seminary, was threatened by lack of money and students. However, by 1941, slow but significant changes were bringing new hope for the unemployed, and for the economy as a whole. In the turbulent years of 1941 to 1950, wars were fought in Europe, Asia, and in the Pacific islands. The nation's economy was spent on the consuming need to rearm and reorganize. Unemployment was replaced by full employment in a truly ironic way—the need for the military production. The post-war decades brought new and demanding responsibilities. For the next twenty years, the pace of life in the nation and in the Church moved from glacier-like speed to that of a swiftly running river.

Richards faced a world changed, a seminary changed, and most importantly, a Church that was changing. No nation, business, or educational institution was an island, remote, untouched, or immoveable. The Presbyterian Church in the United States was never impervious to any powerful influence of change in political and economic power in any era. In the 1960s, however, change was swift and visible. Thus, the seminary was changing with it. Some evidences of a new day at Columbia Seminary were internal, but it was clearly affected by developments in the context of its ministry. Powerful political and cultural changes challenged the Church and the seminary. The internationalization of so much of life in the United States called for the internationalization of the work of ministry and, in many ways, in the new approaches in the preparation of ministers. Life, beyond doubt, was changing as the currents of culture swirled around it at 701 Columbia Drive, Decatur, Georgia.

The decade of the 1960s began when the collegial pattern of life in academia was in its infancy at Columbia Seminary. It rapidly grew. This is not to say that it was easy for anyone—administrators, faculty members, or students. As a first priority, the educational program was strengthened as time went on. Life on campus involved more faculty, more staff, more committees, more meetings, more memos, and more involvement in the changing and divided constituency. The institution moved away from the early decades when the president had sole authority to make faculty appointments, approve expenditures, admit or dismiss students, and speak for the institution in various ecclesiastical bodies.

Moreover, the impact of world events and crises was dramatically apparent in faculty, curriculum, and students. In his President's Report to the Board of Directors near the end of the last decade of his presidency, Richards began with these profound words:

> This is an exciting time in which to be alive. The world in which we live is one of great accomplishments and perhaps of greater failures. Man, in recent months, has many problems, which confront us on earth. Assuredly, these are

days both of danger and of opportunity. Unfortunately, the situation which exists in the world as a whole finds its parallel in the life of the Church today. At a time in which the world has a desperate need "to hear a voice not its own voice" the Church as a whole seems all too uncertain about its mission and its message.

Within our own denomination there is strife and a possibility of future division. While our General Assembly continues negotiation with the other denominations in COCU[61] and initiates negotiations looking to possible union with the UPCUSA Church,[62] large segments within our church are discontent and even threatening to withdraw from the denomination. Should the courts make such withdrawal possible it is almost certain that many ministers and congregations would follow that course of action. In the meanwhile, support is being withheld from the agencies of our church and the missionary activities of our denomination both at home and abroad are being curtailed.[63]

Enrollment throughout this decade ranged between 225 and 265 candidates for degrees. Eighty percent were enrolled in the bachelor of divinity degree. Of great importance to the Church, the first female students seeking that degree were a part of that number. There were also thirteen Christian education students by mid-decade. The master of theology program was popular with overseas missionaries on furlough at Mission Haven, the home built and sustained by the Women of the Church for their use.[64] While not the only significant factor in student enrollment, these programs did provide a broader area of service to the Church, and also benefits for the life and work of Columbia Seminary.

Other reports to the board in the last years of the Richards' presidency carried predictions that ultimately were proven quite accurate. There was a schism in which more than two hundred thousand members and ministers withdrew and formed the Presbyterian Church in America in 1973. In many instances, congregations who left took their church buildings and manses with them under the provisions of the Plan of Reunion. The founding of Reformed Theological Seminary fulfilled the predictions of those who claimed that the theological positions of Presbyterian seminaries were not consistent with the Church's theological standards, and therefore a new conservative institution should and would be formed.

Of even greater significance was the rise of Marxist nations around the world. The result forced the division of both Germany and Korea. The number of graduates seeking mission service overseas declined. When the southern part of the area formerly called Korea became South Korea, many missionaries returned when that country was open to them. Increasing, but still small, numbers of graduates saw the most challenging ministries to be in inner-city poverty pockets or with the Appalachian poor. The most widely known of these, Eduard N. Loring, a 1966 graduate of Columbia Seminary, and his wife, Martha Murphy Davis, a graduate of Columbia Seminary in 1974, founded a residential community in Atlanta called "The Open Door." With a committed group of community members and volunteers, they serve those who are ill, poor, homeless, and hungry. Meals are offered, new residents welcomed, and the cause of the homeless advocated.

Among other graduates who formed new organizations focusing on specific forms of mission, Cody Watson, of the class of 1976, developed a focus on areas around the world where there are great needs, both materially and spirituality. These areas have no specific Christian church or witness, and annual publications provide a list and a careful description of each one. Individuals, who agree to join with others in prayers for a clear witness in these nations, are provided clear information for participants who pray daily for a specific need in a specific place. Other graduates have led congregations to new forms of witness and service in urban areas of great need.

At Columbia Seminary, the effort to craft a curriculum that educated ministers for the realities of varied national and international challenges was reflected in new courses. More importantly, as time went on, year-long internships increased in congregations and ministries in the world beyond the campus. Churches in Jamaica, Asia, and South Africa offered opportunities for learning in those contexts. Years of international continuing education affirmed that nothing educates more effectively than an experience in ministry with people of diverse races and in placements in a wide range of life situations. Richards' reports included data indicating increasing interest among students in a wide variety of such courses on and off of campus.

To Richards' delight, a large proportion of Presbyterian candidates for ministry were enrolled as students at Columbia. With great satisfaction, Richards' last report to the Board of Directors emphasized this evidence of service to the Presbyterian Church, U.S.

> The primary thrust of the training given at Columbia Seminary is toward the work of the pastorate, which we believe to be the very heartbeat of the church. It is interesting to record the fact that although Columbia is not the largest seminary of the Presbyterian Church (U.S.), it graduated last June the largest group of candidates for the ministry of our own denomination of any of these institutions. Indeed, 38.3% of all the candidates for the ministry of the Presbyterian Church (U.S.) graduating from these institutions last year received their degrees from Columbia.[65]

The impact of the world context on the seminary's work led to numerous changes and appointments in the mission of Columbia Seminary. New faculty members from overseas were being called in increasing numbers and, even more importantly, utilized in a revised curriculum. Though significant appointments were made in disciplines such as pastoral counseling, urban ministry, evangelism, and mission, the traditional areas of Bible, theology, and church history continued to dominate the program of study needed for ordination.

With increasing demands in curriculum, a number of professors were added during this period. A most important appointment, too, was that of the Rev. C. Benton Kline Jr. as professor of theology and dean of the faculty. With significant experience as a professor and as dean of the faculty at Agnes Scott College, he brought considerable educational experience and ability to the campus. The office of dean of the faculty at Columbia was much enlarged in scope and responsibility. In 1971, Kline became the fifth president of Columbia Theological Seminary. During this time, the curriculum in various degree programs was enlarged and enriched.

Though still less than that of pastors in strong and generous churches, the salaries of faculty and administrative staff were increased regularly over this decade. Unfortunately, over the thirty-nine years of Richards' presidency, any increase in compensation hardly offset the steady inflationary erosion of the value of the dollar. Through most of the years of his presidency, Richards refused regular salary increases for himself. Inadvertently, this very unselfish attitude resulted in keeping the board from raising faculty and staff compensation. He had good reason for his caution. The giving of the supporting synods rarely kept up with inflation even in the 1960s, let alone with the increased expense of additions in faculty, scholarships, and buildings. Over the years of this decade, contributions from synods' budgets actually declined in amounts and in purchasing power. However, a series of regular campaigns by Presbyterians in these synods provided resources for the construction of much-needed buildings, and in increased endowment. Individuals, churches, and foundations generously supported the mission of Columbia Seminary and continue to do so.

The 1970–71 budget provided for these items for the president's compensation:

1. salary: $17,379
2. the president's home
3. an automobile and all travel expenses

The faculty compensation schedule ranged from seven thousand to twelve thousand dollars in cash salary depending on rank. Either a house or a housing allowance was provided as an additional benefit. Once the Presbyterian pension program was established in 1940, 10 percent of the salary was paid into the

Minister's Annuity Fund. Initially, the minister paid one fourth of this amount. However, within a very few years, the seminary provided the entire cost.

In summary, in this decade, the value of the dollar was seriously diminished. To offset that, the faculty compensation included an increase of six thousand dollars in salary, plus the provision of the relevant payments for major medical insurance, one half of the Social Security dues, and an educational allowance of one hundred dollars per child under the age of twenty-one.

Life on campus continued with Richards' responsibilities involving supervision of everything. In a constantly changing view of faculty housing, he proposed in 1969 to Board of Directors that Columbia Seminary continue to provide housing for faculty in the nineteen faculty homes on campus or in nearby neighborhoods. A grant of one thousand dollars would be budgeted for maintenance of each. As was the usual practice with Richards' recommendations, the plan was unanimously approved. While there was considerable discussion in the faculty about the issue, those who bought and owned homes were pleased that a housing allowance was provided for them.

Columbia Seminary struggled to maintain a compensation level equal to that of other Presbyterian seminaries. In addition, and of great importance to the life and work of the seminary, new buildings were constructed. They included a much-needed multi-use facility at a cost of $1.25 million. Appropriately named the Richards Center, it was then and is now essential to the mission of this theological school. A three-story building, it included the Tull Dining Hall, the Dobbs Room for small gatherings, the student lounges, four classrooms, eight faculty offices, and the book store. It has since been remodeled to provide these plus additional services.

In 1965, the Board of Directors secured the approval of the synods who made up the seminary's governing bodies to seek $5 million to enlarge the library, construct a chapel, a gymnasium, student apartments, and faculty homes. The campaign began with a $1 million challenge gift on condition that $4 million would be raised from the constituency. That effort was a tremendous success and by 1970, the difficult task of raising four dollars to claim one dollar was completed.

The involvement of President Richards in the total life and work of Columbia Seminary led to a continuing focus on the financial health of the institution. Even in the decade of the 1960s, pressures mounted to fund the expanding mission of the campus community. Costs escalated, thus fundraising was always a top priority among the president's tasks.

Two powerful forces were at work in the capacity of the institution to fulfill its mission. The relentless erosion in the purchasing power of the dollar was frightening. The diminished support from the synods of Florida, South Carolina, Georgia, Mississippi, and Alabama in budgeted benevolence gifts was a troubling reality. However, the relationship with these governing bodies began to move from ownership and control to an important resource in the provision of trustees, students, and authorization to campaign for financial support. The synods and presbyteries involved were changing in territory. In this environment, through strenuous and determined effort, campaigns for buildings were effective in providing a much more useful and improved campus. However, the costs of faculty, staff, and supplies were also increasing. Inflation eroded the purchasing power of the dollar in a range between 6 percent and 15 percent per year. In spite of strenuous efforts to keep costs low and to raise more money, the stress on Richards increased. He was, by all the signs, discouraged. The operating budget increased from $350,250 in 1961 to $402,200 in 1963 to $588,596 in 1965. By 1970, it had more than doubled. Further complicating the financial resources was the decline in the value of the endowment. It was small comfort to know that the decline of 29.8 percent was identical with the Dow Jones average decline.

The decade of the 1960s included two study committees whose reports differed in both the analysis of the institution and the recommendations made. One of the most helpful examinations of the life and work of Columbia Seminary in its history was that of the King Committee. The Presbyterian Church followed a much-used tradition throughout the nation of using the name of its chairperson as the designation for the committee. Dr. Charles L. King, pastor of the First Presbyterian Church, Houston, Texas, did much more than lend his name to the analysis of the institution and its detailed recommendations for action. A leader in the Presbyterian Church at every level of its life, Dr. King gathered a group of educators with proven ability in leading institutions both large and small.

After a very careful analysis of the past, present, and future of Columbia Seminary, the committee presented a report with recommendations that would make the institution a strong one with a clearly focused mission. The impressive list of those who were to do this vitally important task for a crucially important time in the institution's life included the following: E. G. Homrighausen, dean of the faculty at Princeton Theological Seminary; Professor Joseph R. Sizoo, George Washington University; President R. T. L. Liston, King College; Dr. O. C. Carmichael, whose former service included terms as chancellor of Vanderbilt University and the University of Alabama; and President Emeritus James Ross McCain of Agnes Scott College.

The report strongly recommended an immediate effort to secure $5 million to enlarge the library, construct a chapel, a gymnasium, student apartments, and faculty homes. Both administrators and trustees felt the goal unreachable. The King Committee, however, was quite persuasive. Over a period of three years, the foundations and churches made an impossible dream a reality.

Richards worked tirelessly to carry the message of Columbia's mission to congregations and governing bodies. Individuals and foundations were persuasively presented with a realistic picture of Columbia Seminary's need and, more importantly, its great potential.

All was not well, however. In 1969 and 1970, the endowment portfolio declined 29.8 percent in market value from $5,217,322 to $4,044,166. Richards' primary concern, however, was the alarming trend of decreasing gifts from the supporting synod's benevolence budgets.[66] In 1946, synods' contributions represented 47.3 percent of the total income; in 1956, 34.1 percent; and in 1966, 20.8 percent. The per capita gifts from the supporting synods continued to decline also. They ranged from twenty-two cents in Florida to sixty cents per member in Georgia. However, the successful campaigns to build new facilities and endow the faculty chairs brought increasing resources from individuals and foundations. The pattern of giving shifted to bequests, special campaigns, and larger current gifts. Of great importance was the offer of substantial grants if they could be matched by gifts from other donors. Whether the match was one dollar for each dollar given, or one dollar for each additional four dollars raised, all greatly strengthened the institution and aided in the fulfillment of its mission.

A very important part of the pressure during this decade came from conservative Presbyterians in congregations that are now in the Presbyterian Church in America. A gift was offered on condition that: "The institution would continue to teach that the Bible is the Word of God, not part of the Word of God, and part of the word of man, or that it becomes the word of God to the individual."[67]

Richards kept in conversation with the donor until she agreed that the condition would be changed to read that "the view of inspiration of Scripture at Columbia be that taught in the *Confession of Faith* of the Presbyterian Church (U.S.) in 1944."

There is no record of a final resolution to the discussion. Indeed, no commitments could have been made permanently unless they were carefully and legally restricted. The Confession of Faith has been rewritten and revised since that time. The incident does show how many different and demanding matters came to Richards for decision and implementation.

As president, Richards related to students, as well as to staff and faculty, with genuine interest and with regular contact. Few details were delegated in any area of the institution's life and relationships. He regularly sought students from the colleges and churches within the constituency. While many came from the churches within the bounds of the supporting synods, others from nearby colleges and universities sometimes went to other seminaries. In spite of his constant personal efforts, the sons of some of his most active members of Board of Directors sometimes went elsewhere. His disappointment was reflected in polite but serious conversations and letters.

Few matters of life at Columbia were more important to him than that of student admission and enrollment. Both received his constant and careful supervision whether the numbers were large or small. Whether Richards' motivation was an urge to build Columbia's enrollment, or even the commitment to serve more adequately the Church in the supporting synods, all motivated the president to search for able candidates for ministry.

Graduates were never far from his attention and interest. While the role of pastor as described in chapter four contains many references to these relationships, none is stronger than those with students from overseas. Poignant evidence of this is the continuing flow of correspondence with students in other cultures and countries. Expressions of interest and appreciation continued at a steady pace to graduates in Europe and Asia. These overseas ministers reciprocated. A young Korean student after studying for a year at Columbia Seminary wrote to inquire about "his" seminary, "I want also to have a catalogue of our sweet and precious Columbia Theological Seminary for 1964."[68]

Richards rarely played favorites with students. Therefore, any student appealing for help would get it. Whether conservative or liberal, gifted or not, nine out of ten times Richards responded with a recommendation when asked for an evaluation of a Columbia graduate. Though he did not appoint to Columbia's faculty conservative students with Ph.D.s such as Knox Chamblin, Wilson Benton, or Norman Harper, he did recommend them when asked to do so by other institutions.

The most unique request came from President Lyndon Baines Johnson. Richards was asked to recommend the Rev. Calvin Coolidge Thielman, the pastor of the Montreat Presbyterian Church, Montreat, North Carolina, to the chief of chaplains, U. S. Navy, for appointment as a chaplain. President Johnson wished to have Thielman assigned as a chaplain at the White House. Ecclesiastical endorsement was needed in the Navy's process, so Richards was asked to assist. As a 1955 graduate of Columbia, Thielman was well-known to him, and Richards promptly did so. However, a problem arose in securing ecclesiastical endorsement from the Presbyterian Church (U.S.) for Thielman. This endorsement was required for all Presbyterian chaplains commissioned by the Navy.

As a high school student, Thielman worked in Johnson's first political campaign in a Texas county. His job was to drive a van through every village and town in this county while playing Johnson campaign announcements on a loud speaker. Johnson won his first political victory by a very narrow margin and went on to be a senator, vice president, and upon the assassination of President Kennedy, president of the United States. Johnson never forgot his young friend's work in the campaign. While visiting the president in the White

House, President Johnson suggested to Thielman that he apply to the U. S. Navy for appointment as a chaplain. Assuming he would be approved, Johnson, as commander in chief, would then assign him to the White House. Some officials in the Presbyterian Church (U.S.), however, opposed the appointment for various reasons. The major problem was the politicizing of the process. They delayed the ecclesiastical endorsement required of the denomination and Thielman withdrew his acceptance of the appointment.

During this whole experience, Richards supported Thielman with letters and phone calls. The final report found in his papers is a letter from Marvin Watson, special assistant to the president, dated October 20, 1965: "We have found Thielman to be a dedicated man of God and one whose single purpose would appear to be to carry out God's will in his life. Nothing more could be expected of this man."[69]

Subsequently, Richards' role was that of a supportive, pastoral counselor to Thielman with encouragement to him to continue his ministry in Montreat, North Carolina. His congregation included students and faculty from Montreat College, as well as residents of Montreat and nearby towns.

From time to time, questions have been raised in the Church about the use of ministers as chaplains in military forces. The practice, however, continues with widespread support. An unusually large number of Presbyterian (U.S.) ministers, seventy in all, served in World War II. Even today, in relatively peaceful times, a small number of graduates from Columbia Seminary choose this place of service.

In another quite different situation, Richards sent warm congratulations to Albert Curry Winn following Winn's election to the presidency of Louisville Presbyterian Theological Seminary. Winn responded:

You know better than most that sympathy is as much in order as congratulations! Misery loves company and it is reassuring to know that other and better men are facing difficulties and frustrations that will soon be mine. One bright spot, however, is that this change will bring us together more frequently.[70]

This characteristic care and concern for individuals continued to the end of Richards' presidency. In the description of Richards as pastor, more extensive analysis will be presented, but in the contemporary view of a president's role, his presidency is unique.

One recommendation of a divorced pastor seeking a call is significant. Earlier in his presidency, Richards would not have done so in view of his conviction that divorce should be granted only on the grounds of adulterous behavior. In this period in his life, Richards strongly commended him to a church, for the minister, in Richards' judgment, had made "heroic efforts to save his marriage."

Richards wrote a lengthy recommendation of a 1953 graduate, Abel McIver Hart, for a pastorate in a presbytery that rather ruthlessly examined him with questions concerning his orthodoxy. He presented a vigorous statement of support for Hart and his theological views. He urged the presbytery to receive him and to accept his theology as a truly authentic reflection of the theology of the Presbyterian Church. Thus, he demonstrated his support of graduates of various viewpoints.

As president, Richards maintained an extensive correspondence with graduates working for the Ph.D. degree in institutions in Scotland, Germany, and the United States. He included in lengthy letters much more than a sincere interest in their progress, but also full reports on campus life. To Thomas J. Reeves, studying with the New Testament scholar, A. M. Hunter in Aberdeen, Scotland, he wrote: "Shirley Guthrie is writing a book on Reformed Theology for the Covenant Life Curriculum. It is to be completed now that he is back from sabbatical leave. Professor Cartledge is also on sabbatical leave in England. . . ."[71] Correspondence with graduates always included one or two brief bits of news. Only in his correspondence with World War II military chaplains and missionaries overseas during four decades are there more or lengthier letters.[72]

The last three full years of the Richards' presidency, 1968 to 1970, should have been days of remembering great accomplishments with one celebrative event after another. Both the seminary and Richards had come through the early years of struggle for survival with little money and few students and much fewer faculty. Vastly improved facilities and finances assured a stable period of Richards' leadership of a very important institution for the Church. It was not to be a joyous and fulfilling time, however.

The difficulties were frequent and varied. Joseph C. Morecraft III, a graduate of the class of 1969, charged the faculty with heretical teaching. A critic from Virginia wrote that candidates from their presbyteries missed a conservative, biblical point of view from most of their teachers. Richards responded cautiously and courteously. He sent a long list of teachers who were biblical in viewpoint, and assured the writer that no faculty member was in any way "a liberal theologian." Indeed, he felt that the points of view of some critics claiming to be "Reformed and Biblical" in theology would not have been approved by conservatives like William Childs Robinson.

Over the course of his presidency, Richards had slowly relinquished his early pattern of total control and supervision of the life and work of Columbia Seminary. That responsibility was gradually delegated to a few key administrators. He had been constantly urged to do this by the Board of Directors and the Alumni Association. Following one meeting of the association, an alumnus, Donald B. Bailey, praised him with these words: "Each time I attend meetings at Columbia Seminary I am amazed at the number of matters which you personally are attending to."[73] Bailey spoke for all who knew the realities of Richards' life and work in his early years as president.

Richards sought scholars from around the world to lecture at Columbia, believing it was vitally important for students to look beyond the church they knew firsthand. International students enrolled in courses and invariably contributed to both the scholarship and the cultural context of the institution. Professor David Cairns of the University of Aberdeen, Scotland, accepted the invitation to give the Smyth Lectures in 1960. The Cairns' children's first question upon meeting President Richards was, "Where are the Indians?" Cairns explained that they watched television programs in their Scotland home that included *The Lone Ranger, Laramie, The Range Rider,* and other "westerns." Richards, with considerable amusement, directed them to the Cherokee Indian reservation in the mountains of northern Georgia and western North Carolina. He firmly assured them that no television program such as those mentioned was remotely like them. Furthermore, he spoke of the injustices Native Americans had suffered over the centuries in the United States.

Richards also sought a close relationship with presidents of other Presbyterian seminaries and colleges. Albert C. Winn, professor of Bible at Stillman College, and later professor of theology and president of Louisville Presbyterian Theological Seminary, discussed with Richards a course he was preparing for the seminary. He surmised that the students in the class were seemingly not interested in traditional medieval piety, but did respond enthusiastically to Howard Thurman's visit and lectures on the need for a utilization of both piety and social ethics. As a result, Winn prepared a course, "The Doctrine of the Inner Life." The catalogue description read:

> How does a human being accept, internalize and make personal to himself what God has done in Jesus Christ? Traditional topics such as faith, repentance, prayer and inward growth are suspect in a secular age. Concentration in this area may be an escape from social responsibility. Yet there is a stream of witness from Augustine to Dag Hammarskjold who maintain that effective work in the world must root in an intensely personal, inward relationship with God.[74]

In every decade of Columbia's work in Decatur, Georgia, Richards affirmed a deep conviction that the spiritual nurture of students was essential. Thus, daily chapel was stressed and lectures on spirituality were given.

Richards' last budget of $849,490 was provided by direct gifts from supporting synods of the Southeast, endowment income, and individual donations. A deficit of $12,090 remained at the end of the year, and a few loyal supporters contributed that amount so that the Richards' presidency would have a balanced budget in his last year.

Two months before Richards received "honorable retirement as a minister of the Presbyterian Church (U.S.)" he made his final report to Columbia Seminary and the governing bodies. Two years before, he had described the world as a challenging time to be alive. In contrast to the reports of 1969 and 1970, the final report was positive and forward-looking.

Though realistic about the enormous challenges faced in the Church and in the world, Richards believed in the concept forged in one of the most threatening periods in history: that during the time of those first followers of Jesus of Nazareth. He believed, as they did, that "The Lord God omnipotent reigned." (Rev. 19:6 NRSV) Through good times and bad, he believed that God had an important, and, indeed, essential, mission entrusted to the institution he served. Thus, he approached retirement with thanksgiving for significant years at Columbia Theological Seminary and great expectations for its' future.

Yet, Richards was gratified that Columbia's service to the Church was significant. At that time, nearly one-half of the Presbyterian ministers in the states of Georgia, South Carolina, Alabama, Florida, and Mississippi were graduates of Columbia Theological Seminary. A similar proportion of ministers and a large number of non-ordained missionaries received their training at Columbia. Over twelve hundred alumni were serving the Presbyterian Church (U.S.) in positions of church vocations in important places. In Richards' view, however, "the harvest is great and the laborers are few" in a very needy world.

In his final year as president, Richards addressed the Board of Directors with a painful analysis of two widely circulated attacks on the theological integrity of the institution he had served for almost thirty-nine years.[75] The charges of "heresy" came from two graduates, Joseph C. Morecraft III and Thomas Dwight Linton. Morecraft was ordained by Abingdon Presbytery in Virginia to serve two small churches and was divested of office without censure by Holston Presbytery on July 20, 1973. He had completed four years of ordained ministry in the Presbyterian Church, U.S.

Richards' immediate reaction was that Morecraft's address to Presbyterian Churchmen United[76] was a serious and damaging one. Although he was within the last year of his presidency, he swiftly fashioned a response that, while strongly defending Columbia's faculty, made extensive inquiries of the faculty asking for specific analysis of each of the examples used. Morecraft claimed that the differences of doctrine and mission among groups in the denomination were not a matter of emphasis but of radically different views of theology. He felt that one view was that of "Neo-orthodoxy" and the other, "Calvinism." While describing each of these, he claimed that the Bible was verbally inspired by the Holy Spirit of God from the beginning of Genesis, chapter one, to the "Amen" of Revelation, chapter twenty-two. It was without error or contradiction in the original manuscripts. Richards' response was that, "We do not have the original manuscripts, and in dealing with those we do have, we believe that the teaching of the Bible as a whole, when fully read and understood under the guidance of the Holy Spirit, is the Word of God to us."

He implemented damage control by sharing the charges of heresy with each faculty member. He was not content until he had received from Morecraft the names of faculty accused, and the exact words of lectures he had cited. He then turned to faculty members for help in responding.

Dr. Ronald A. Wallace of the Church of Scotland wrote from his Edinburgh home with four pages of detailed discussions of Morecraft charges. The accusation quoted Wallace as saying, "the word 'propitiation' should never be in any translation of the Bible anywhere." Wallace's response can be summarized in these excerpts from his four-page document:

> I have always taught that in all instances in which the word "hilasterion" occurs in the New Testament it should be translated "expiation" rather than "propitiation." I look on this as primarily a matter of exegesis. I find that what I believe has better scholarship on its side—though I always point out that Leon Morris disagrees. If I made such a statement, and I honestly don't believe I did, I must be much more stupid and unguarded than I think I am.

> I do not believe that the New Testament teaches that Christ died to propitiate an angry God in the sense that this is taught by pagan religions and believed in by natural man. I teach that nowhere in the New Testament is God spoken of as being reconciled by God. I point out that Paul, in using the word reconciliation deliberately used forms of the Greek verb that are not used in pagan Greek religious circles because he wanted to avoid such interpretation. What I am contending for is that the New Testament and the Old say something quite different from the pagan religions.[77]

Wallace, a conservative scholar in matters of biblical interpretation, went on to speak of his concern for Morecraft and the regret that he was not very regular in attendance at Wallace's classes. He wrote: "Joe was never too good about attending my classes so he always tended to pick up things partially . . . Since I feel Joe has been really unfair to me, I would suspect that he has been no less unfair to my colleagues."[78]

Richards' communication to the Board of Directors also responded to T. Dwight Linton's article, "The Crisis in Missions," which appeared in a conservative magazine, the *Southern Presbyterian Journal.* Unlike Morecraft's criticisms it was, in Richards' view, "rather vague." However, the specific criticism Linton developed was that Columbia Theological Seminary and the Board of World Missions were responsible for the problems in the overseas work of the

Presbyterian Church, U.S. Insufficient resources for overseas mission were a direct result of theological views in neo-orthodoxy.

J. Millen Darnell, a missionary in Brazil and a pastor in the United States replied in a defense of theological positions taught at Columbia Seminary. He specifically questions the concept that neo-orthodoxy was responsible: "It is interesting that Linton states that those who adhere to the theology of Karl Barth do not produce missionaries when Karl Barth's own son was a missionary for years."[79] Furthermore, to imply that either the Board of World Missions or Columbia Seminary teaches and believes in universalism was "not the truth."

Richards ended his lengthy discussion of this issue with positive words. He felt the Wallace response was encouraging and viewed it as exceedingly revealing in showing how his accuser had used an isolated statement to give a completely false impression as to a man's actual beliefs and teachings.

Exhausted by years of leadership at Columbia Seminary and throughout the Church, Richards now seemed weary of the daily stress and responsibility. His retirement was getting closer as the days went by. He welcomed it with some reluctance.

So, four productive decades ended for a hard-working, dedicated president. Richards rescued the institution from an ecclesiastical death and brought it to a strong foundation on which successors have built. The Church recognized his presidency with letters, gifts, resolutions, and best of all, great appreciation. Few institutions have known a president who, like Richards, saved the institution from extinction and developed for it a strong faculty and student enrollment. Through the decades of struggle, schism, wars, growth, and challenge, he survived and, more than that, performed magnificently for Columbia Theological Seminary.

CHAPTER THREE

Preacher

*J*AMES MCDOWELL RICHARDS' SELF IMAGE IS BEST summarized in the words of the *Book of Church Order*, "a minister of the Word and Sacrament." That view was true from July 31, 1929, the day of his ordination as a Presbyterian minister in Clarksville, Georgia, to the day he died on August 10, 1986, in the Presbyterian Home in Summerville, South Carolina.

None of his productive labor as a minister gave him greater satisfaction than preaching. He devoted time and energy to the preparation required in preparing to preach well. The result was a faithful interpretation of a psalm, a proverb, a parable, or the words of Jesus. Similarly, the prophets of the Old Testament and the letters of the New Testament were also the basis for his sermons. Like those prophets and apostles, he felt the deep, driving passion of declaring the whole counsel of God for twentieth-century persons and structures.

His role as a preacher began with occasional student sermons at Columbia Theological Seminary, preceded by a very few in England during graduate studies. His subsequent preaching in a cluster of Presbyterian congregations, Clarksville, Nacoochee, Rabun Gap, and Helen, in the mountains of North Georgia, brought him into the context of a different world than he had known before. The contradictions of the warmth of people, the wonders of a world of mountains and valleys, and the pockets of poverty and illiteracy there shaped a new and challenging context of ministry.

Of course, if the rains came and the roads turned into mud and rocks, his little car would not make it to morning or evening worship in the four churches of the Clarkesville, Georgia, group. From July 1928 until July 1931, he and his people found great satisfaction in opportunities for ministry. Richards' years of education at McCallie School, Davidson College, Princeton University, Christ Church College, Oxford, and Columbia Theological Seminary may have seemed at times worlds away. However, the Church was there in the people of those beautiful mountains and valleys. Richards relished the challenges in the preaching of the Word, the administration of the sacraments, and the pastoral ministry to the people.

Best of all, while there, he met and fell in love with Mary Evelyn Knight, a young schoolteacher at Rabun Gap Nacoochie School. She attended Agnes Scott College and in 1928, after her father's death, she sought employment as a teacher. She often spoke of her delight in teaching.

On December 31, 1929, they married, and it was, indeed, good for both. Together they began the process of forming a home and creating a family. When death came to Richards, they had been married for almost fifty-seven years. In 1931, the call of the First Presbyterian Church of Thomasville, Georgia, took them to a church and a city formed originally by Scottish immigrants. The faith and witness of those Presbyterians significantly influenced that area, as it does to this day. Richards found new fulfillment in ministry in these pastorates, and always remembered the people of those mountain congregations and in the First Presbyterian Church of Thomasville, Georgia, with appreciation and affection. Those years were, without question, a time of great satisfaction for Richards as a person and as a minister of Jesus Christ and a prophet of God.

In all these congregations, Richards proclaimed the gospel, baptized babies, married couples, pastored the sick and dying, and shared the Lord's Supper with the people of God. He was a faithful pastor in these churches and visited in homes and hospitals regularly. The records of his sermons there have not been found, but a significant number of those preached during his presidency are among the Richards Papers. They tell us in detail his concept of worship and, especially, the place of preaching in it. Preaching, to Richards, was a matter of interpreting the Bible, proclaiming the gospel of Jesus, the Christ, and "declaring to you the whole counsel of God."[1]

The form of the Richards' sermons and addresses is that of a carefully crafted written manuscript. Even in the most varied settings and contrasting audiences, his liberal arts education from Davidson, Princeton, and Christ Church College, Oxford, is clearly apparent. Long years of writing papers and a thesis gave him a pattern of language and thought that found their way into his sermons and addresses. Carefully chosen words, clear sentences, and appropriate citations appear. Literary allusions and citations are frequently used. Whether in congregations, governing bodies, academic institutions, class reunions, or in publications, he excelled in the use of vivid words and pictures. However, the dominant themes were drawn from the Bible. Near the end of his life, Richards began to use outlines or abbreviated notes rather than a complete manuscript. These were quite rare, however, in the long years before his retirement.[2] He did recommend to students that they become so familiar with the sermon manuscript that they would not need to take it into the pulpit. He often did that himself. A number of basic elements appear in his preaching.

The exposition of a biblical text was essential, and the chosen text was appropriate for the occasion. At his retirement, the faculty and the Board of Directors published a brief collection of sermons, prayers, and addresses by Richards entitled "Change and the Changeless." They span the years from 1940 to 1972. Even though the settings varied from civic clubs to church groups, from seminary chapel to congregations, the style was thoughtful, appropriate, and relevant. He presented the message in clear language and with practical application.

Sermons were used more than once, even though somewhat revised for each occasion. "The Church and the World Today," delivered on November 4, 1963, to the Alumni Association of Columbia Theological Seminary, appears in revised addresses to church judicatories such as synods and presbyteries. It was printed with minor deletions in the *Presbyterian Survey* under the title "Men Perplexed by a Changing World."[3] Once it was called "The Relevance of the Gospel." After detailing the critical issues of race, covetousness, poverty, sexual and alcohol abuse, he concluded:

> The Gospel of Jesus Christ has much to say about all these matters. It is not its irrelevance, but its everlasting relevance which troubles our souls.

Richards went on to say:

> This Word which teaches men how to live contains the only real answers to how they can die. This is also an aspect of our lives which much of our preaching has neglected. One wonders sometimes whether the church really believes its own message. Certainly we have not declared it with the urgency and the conviction which the issue demands.[4]

Richards was asked to preach to disparate groups in varied settings. They included his fiftieth class reunion at Davidson College, the soldiers at Fort McPherson, Atlanta, the large and small congregations in Atlanta Presbytery, the listeners of the Church-at-large in radio and television broadcasts, and to members of civic clubs. Indeed, some of his most eloquent addresses were found in Christmas and Memorial Day talks to the Rotary Club of Atlanta. It was a time when a message on "The Meaning of Christmas" could be delivered to a group of varying religious backgrounds without strong objections. Today, the situation is quite different. Given the diversity of religious practices by members of Rotary, invocations do not conclude "in the name of our Lord, Jesus Christ." There are no public prayers before football games.

The role of a preacher opened many treasured opportunities for Richards. Sermons were preached and worship was led in an amazing variety of settings. Churches, large and small, invited him for a one-time appearance or a series of services. For the sake of the Church and the seminary, he clearly felt that he must preach in a wide variety of churches, conferences, the governing bodies of the church, and on college campuses. With the growing influence of radio, he valued invitations to preach on the *Presbyterian Hour* and the *Protestant Hour*. He preached because he felt compelled to do so for the sake of his own spirit and mind. Invitations came often to serve as the preacher at Montreat Conference Center, College Religious Emphasis Weeks, Christmas and Easter Services and other preaching missions. The invitations took him to thirty or more places every year. Only rarely was he free to sit with his family in a pew at Central Presbyterian Church to hear his friend and pastor, Stuart Oglesby, preach. Two of Richards' children, Makemie and Charles, are valued leaders in that congregation today.

The themes of these sermons or addresses focused on the importance of the gospel for the world, the challenge of demonic forces threatening the survival of the nation, and the mission of the Church everywhere.

Perhaps the most illuminating way to understand the preacher we find in J. McDowell Richards is to look at specific sections of addresses and sermons. The differences may be found in content, but not in style.

On a number of occasions, Richards was chosen as the preacher for the *Presbyterian Hour* radio program. He could not, as few could, compete with Franklin D. Roosevelt or Edward R. Murrow as an orator. However, he was earnest and sincere, and that, as he said once to a student, "would cover a multitude of sins."

On December 22, 1946, he eloquently described, "The Meaning of Christmas." The *Presbyterian Hour*, recorded on tape, was heard in homes throughout the nation and even on ships at sea for those who agreed to use it. This particular sermon became one of the most requested of that era.

Richards began:

In all the realm of literature there is no story more beautiful than is the record of the first Christmas. So perfect is it, so matchless in thought and in expression, so utterly apart from and about the ordinary experiences of life, that it seems almost as unreal as some well loved fairy tale of childhood.

Richards went on to picture the combinations of wonders it presents, and then focused on "the boy child within the virgin's arms." The climax of his presentation cited an essay by F. W. Boreham, a British preacher. Boreham contrasted "battles and babies" in vivid words picturing the enormous significance of the celebration of Christmas:

Early in the nineteenth century people were following with bated breath the march of Napoleon and waiting with feverish impatience for the latest news of the wars. And, all the time, in their own homes, babies were being born. In one year, 1809, midway between Trafalgar and Waterloo, there stole into the world a host of heroes. In 1809 Mr. Gladstone was born in Liverpool, Alfred Tennyson was born in Somersby Rectory, and Oliver Wendell Holmes made his first appearance in Massachusetts. On the very same day of the self same year, Charles Darwin made his debut at Shrewsbury and Abraham Lincoln drew his first breath in Old Kentucky. Music was enriched by Frederick Chopin at Warsaw and by Felix Mendelssohn at Hamburg. But, nobody thought about babies. The question then is which of the battles of 1809 mattered more than the babies of 1809. When a wrong wants righting, a work wants doing, or a truth wants preaching, or a continent wants opening, God sends a baby into the world to do it. That is why, long ago, a baby was born in Bethlehem.[5]

The Davidson College convocation on November 7, 1948, included graduates and interested supporters of Davidson College, and was the first meeting of persons who were to be key leaders in a major fund-raising campaign. As chairman of the board of trustees, and a very loyal alumnus of Davidson College, Richards gladly participated. In launching such an important effort by the college, and as one who knew it as a student and as chairman of the board, Richards enthusiastically appealed for generous support. The event took place in the context of a world beginning to move beyond World War II to renew and rebuild its structures and values. At that time, worship was a central part of life on that campus, reflecting its relationship with the Presbyterian Church. Faculty and students joined the board of trustees for one of those formal and unique gatherings in academia. There is no title to this copy of the address, but it is essentially an analysis of the context of the world at that moment and the challenge to Davidson College.

The faculty in their regalia, and the students in jackets and ties, gathered for a formal occasion. Those who listened heard a speech that began with a vivid and eloquent description of St. Paul's Cathedral standing in London after everything around it was smashed to bits by German bombs in World War II. Richards imagined Londoners checking in the first hours of daylight to see if St. Paul's still stood, and it did. Such a sight gave them new courage.

The question posed from that moment in history was direct. What would give the post-war world hope? In society, from an economic and political viewpoint, the hope of the world for better days lies in our American system at its best. Most would say that. In the world of 1948, however, that alone was not enough. Richards concluded:

The real hope of the world lies in a new recognition of moral and spiritual values, and in the renewal of true religion. God, not gold, is the key. Davidson College, moreover, is a great institution, because of her contribution to the world through her faculty and her graduates.[6]

That contribution included four areas:

1. Davidson stood for something great—truth.[7]
2. The faculty and administration were faithful and devoted servants. President John Rood Cunningham was an example of this.
3. The students were the finest of young men.
4. Friends financially supported Davidson.

This address concluded with a stirring appeal for gifts of $2.5 million:

Davidson is at the crossroads. Davidson must compete with public institutions which receive vast sums of money from the State. Today is not yesterday. Past achievements cannot be a substitute for true education. High purposes will not take the place of performance. Ideals, fine and essential though they are, cannot be translated into a worthy educational program unless equipment is provided. If we are worthy of our heritage, we shall respond to this challenge that the Davidson of tomorrow may be greater by far, than the Davidson of today.[8]

This eloquent and appropriate address was not the only one of its kind. Richards' presidency went from campaign to campaign for Columbia Seminary for thirty-nine years. After his retirement he sometimes told graduates and friends that he felt like the college president who spent most of his time raising money and, thus, he asked that his tombstone carry the simple sentence from Luke 16:22, "And the beggar died." Needless to say, this inscription does not appear on his tombstone.

During the 1940s and 1950s, Richards often preached for the *Protestant Hour*, a nationwide religious broadcast. He was in a group of well-known pulpiteers such as Peter Marshall of Washington, D.C. One of Richards' brief devotionals presented a unique concept of "Happiness." It is handwritten and a little more than one page in length; however, it reflects his literary style and his conviction that happiness is found only in relationship to God. For, "happy is the man whose help is the God of Jacob, whose hope is in the Lord his God" (Ps. 146: 5).

Richards wrote with clarity and persuasiveness:

I suppose that in reality all men are seeking happiness. It is not for nothing that our Declaration of Independence speaks of the pursuit of happiness as one of the "unalienable rights" with which all men are endowed by their Creator. But what is happiness? We encounter many strange concepts of this term.

Near my home I have often read above the entrance to a certain moving picture theater the enticing words, "Where happiness costs so little." Again and again, we find cocktail bars advertising "The Happiness Hour." Happiness today is being sought by a number of those who practice the use of drugs. On a somewhat higher plane I saw recently a billboard proclaiming that the key to a new home is your key to happiness. Alas, it is not always true.

Happiness is more than being entertained. It does not consist in being enabled for a little while to forget our troubles. It is not long found in what we call security. Assuredly, it does not come through the mad pursuit of pleasure and the promiscuous satisfaction of our bodily appetites. There are few more eloquent or pathetic comments on this latter fact than in the lines written by Lord Byron on the conclusion of the thirty-sixth year of his life:

> My days are in the yellow leaf;
> The flowers and fruits of love are gone;
> The worm, the canker and the grief
> Are mine alone.

The point of this brief message is that happiness is found in a walk with God in true partnership.

Even in the most distressing times in his presidency, Richards' faith in God was clearly displayed. Crises at home and around the world swept across the earth. Even then, his sermons proclaim such themes as "The Lord God Omnipotent Reigneth" and "The Christ of Bethlehem is the Hope of the World."

Richards' extensive study of literature during his time as a Rhodes Scholar in Oxford, England, was reflected again and again in sermons dealing with life in both community and in the world. A striking example of this experience is found in sermons such as those preached at his Davidson fiftieth class reunion, in an armistice address to the Rotary Club of Atlanta, and especially in a sermon, "The Church and the World Today," preached on November 4, 1963.

John Masefield's "The Everlasting Mercy" was frequently used to confirm a point. Among the citations from that poem in sermons or addresses is this:

> And he who gives a child a treat
> Makes joy bells ring in Kingdom come
> And he who gives a child a home

Builds palaces in Kingdom come
And she who gives a baby birth
Brings Saviour Christ again to earth.

"The Seekers" and its theme of the search for the city of God appears three times in the sermon collection:

Friends and loves we have none, nor wealth nor blessed abode
But the hope of the city of God at the other end of the road.
Not for us are content and quiet, and peace of mind
There is no solace on earth for us—for such as we—
Who search for a hidden city that we will never see.
Only the road and the dawn, the sun, the wind, and the rain,
And the watch fire under stars, and sleep, and the road again,
And the hope of the City of God at the other end of the road.

Richards did not dwell on the dark pessimism of those words as much as he did on the concept of the search for God as found in various ways among all people. His appeal was to find Jesus Christ, the "way, the truth, and the life," once that driving desire to search and find hope was focused on Him.

Another poem frequently used in sermons and addresses was "The Crystal" by Sydney Lanier:

But Thee, but Thee, O sovereign Seer of Time,
But Thee, O poet's Poet, Wisdom's tongue,
But Thee, O man's best Man, O love's best Love
O perfect life in perfect labor writ,
O all men's Comrade, Servant, King, or Priest
What if or yet, what mole, what flaw, what lapse,
What least defect or shadow of defect
What rumor tattled by an enemy
Of inference loose, what lack of grace
Even in torture's grasp, or sleep's, or death's
Oh, what amiss may I forgive in Thee,
Jesus, good paragon, thou Crystal Christ.

It would, however, be a serious distortion of the sermonic evidence from Richards' life and ministry if we did not say that first, last, and always he was a biblical preacher. His texts were chosen from all the biblical sources, but often would focus on a simple principle such as: "Unto whom much is given, from them much is required." The responsibility of privilege was like a continuing theme from a Beethoven symphony. There were others, however. The prophet, Jeremiah, was the focus of careful study in Richards' academic efforts, and later, in an occasional course, he taught this powerful book as an elective at Columbia Seminary.

A concise example of the varied themes Richards used as a preacher may be found in a published collection of sermons, addresses, and prophetic statements characteristic of many more. At his retirement, members of the faculty and staff selected fifteen examples of his public papers. They vary in nature and context, but they give clear and important examples of his work. Entitled "Change and the Changeless," the subtitle was "Articles, Essays, and Sermons by James McDowell Richards." Written and delivered over the years from 1940 to 1972, the themes strongly reflect the context in the nation and the world when they were written, and include:

1. Reflections on Armistice Day (1940)
2. Brothers in Black (1940)
3. The Christian Church in a World at War (1942)
4. A Condemnation of Mob Violence (1946)
5. Woodrow Wilson—The Christian and the Churchman (1956)
6. God's Commandment for His People (1956)
7. A Call to Civil Obedience and Racial Good Will (1957)
8. A Prayer of Invocation (football game, 1957)
9. The Strange Story of Our Times (1958)
10. The Relevance of the Gospel (1963)
11. The Holy Spirit and the Church (1964)
12. The Church and Its Ministry (1967)
13. World Missions—A Christian Imperative (1969)
14. The Theological Seminary as a Graduate Professional School (1970)
15. Change and the Changeless (1972)

Reflecting Richards' life and times, these sermons and addresses were analyses of complex situations with theological and sociological responses to them. The great majority of Richards' sermons were clear, well-written, biblical expositions. Even some of these non-sermonic addresses reflect Christian convictions that he held with great clarity and tenacity.

In his most widely publicized and circulated sermon, "Brothers in Black," Richards illumined, like a flash of lightening, the issue of racial justice. That sermon would have been influential at any time, but in the late 1940s it evoked at times vitriolic pronouncements of the defenders of segregation. Those who felt it was the voice of a prophet declaring judgment on racism even in the church applauded. As retiring moderator of Atlanta Presbytery on October 14, 1940, he could have chosen any topic that he might think appropriate. He chose to speak to this issue in view of the scornful remarks about African-Americans spoken by the governor of Georgia, Eugene Talmage. Those hurtful remarks were widely published in local and national newspapers. Beyond any expectation, this clear and courageous sermon to a relatively small group of clergy and laity reverberated in Atlanta, Georgia, and around the world.[9]

> Where is . . . thy brother? The question has no limits in so far as the Christian is concerned. . . . For this little while I want to ask . . . that we face it, not on the basis of self-justification, but as the facts require us to answer it before the throne of God. "Where is thy brother in black?" Genesis 4:9.[10]

When asked to deliver an invocation before gatherings of all types, Richards prepared as carefully as he did for a sermon preached in a worship service. Before a Georgia Tech–Duke football game, he prayed:

> O God, our heavenly Father, we thank thee today for the beauty round about us; for strong young men, for their courageous spirits, and for the love of play. We pray thy blessing now upon the members of these teams and upon the institutions which they represent. Whether in victory or in defeat, teach us all the lessons of fair play, of sportsmanship, and of loyalty to causes greater than ourselves. May thy blessing abide upon our country, that increasingly ours may be a nation exalted by righteousness; that America may be a force for freedom, for justice, for mercy and for peace among all nations. Make us faithful as individuals in the performance of all the duties of free citizens, and use us for the accomplishment of thy purposes, we pray in Christ's name, Amen.

A pastoral prayer could be as long as a two page, double-spaced manuscript. Yet, it was written with care, and reflected the gratitude, the thoughts, and feelings of people in the experiences of daily life.

One of Richards' last appearances at Montreat Conference Center came at a Bible conference. A cluster of able preachers was invited to serve, including Charles L. King, William McCorkle, J. Sherrard Rice, and J. Randolph Taylor. Richards felt he was in good company, to say the least. In the discussion of a common theme which they would all address in some way, the choice was "Renewal of the Spiritual Life of the Church." Richards' suggestion of dealing with the racial crisis had some support, but was not chosen. J. Randolph Taylor proposed that focus of the series be the various roles of a minister as preacher, administrator, teacher, presbyter, citizen, friend, husband, and father. The assumption is that little or no consideration was given to women ministers in that conversation. All that would change very quickly.

At almost the identical time of that discussion, Richards was eloquently continuing the prophetic message of the pressures on ministers who were "suffering for Christ sake." He warned that many ministers were discouraged, lonely, and frustrated in a struggle for racial justice and, especially, in the fierce debates concerning the desegregation of public schools. In addition, the erosion of the life of the Church by the tides of cultural influences threatened morality and decency. That pressure was devastatingly debilitating, to say the least.

His greatest anguish, however, intensified as various pressures brought heavy burdens for ministers who raised the issues and were either silenced or forced to resign. He warned that "we had better stand by our brethren in their struggles whether we agree with them or not."

He had three concerns:

1. The freedom of the pulpit, and the right to declare the Word of God according to conscience.
2. The conviction that there was no area of life exempted from the subjection to the authority of Jesus Christ.
3. In all our efforts to know and do the will of God, the spirit of love must prevail.

It is not just coincidence that his first concern is for the freedom of the pulpit for faithful preachers.

Richards' agenda in preaching included diverse issues such as racial justice, temperance, chastity, family life, the meaning of death, and urgency in the Church's mission in the world as commanded by Jesus. For, he claimed, the world is not "post-Christian, but pre-Christian." He appealed for penitence for failures, and prayers for the future, "We may be disturbed but not dismayed." He concluded with a request for "your prayers that in this, too, our church may be found faithful, and we shall find and take that way which is in accord with the mind of Christ."[11]

Near the end of the Richards' presidency, on November 11, 1968, he addressed the Board of Directors and the faculty on the "State of the Church and the State of the Seminary." Richards' personal pain was evident in his view that the situation in the Church was poor, and that schism was likely soon. That division could take place in three ways:

1. If the courts ruled that a congregation could leave the denomination with its property.
2. If union presbyteries and synods were formed and thus provide an immediate step toward merger of Presbyterian denominations, north and south.

3. If the plan of union with the Reformed Church of America was approved. That action would bring together two groups where opposition to reunion with the United Presbyterian Church (U.S.A.) was strongest.

Richards concluded: "We request your prayers that in this, too, our church may be found faithful, and we shall find and take the way which is in accord with the mind of Christ."

Richards challenged the accusers of heresy to prove their accusations or be guilty of violating the ninth commandment, "Thou shalt not bear false witness." He always affirmed the authority of Scripture as interpreted by the Holy Spirit. Moreover, he never really understood the angry accusations that Columbia Theological Seminary was teaching heresy and, in one instance, did not believe in God.

To his great sadness and in spite of his efforts, the schism took place with the formation of the Presbyterian Church in America in 1973. More than two hundred thousand members and their churches withdrew within six months. Richards' commitment to the unity of the Church was expressed in an address at the centennial of Central Presbyterian Church of Atlanta. He praised Calvinism for its emphasis on education, democracy, and ecumenical relationships. He cited John Calvin's statement, "I would be willing to cross seven seas, if by so doing I could bring Christians closer to one another."

The mood of discouragement in the last few years of the Richards' tenure at Columbia Seminary was like a dark, threatening cloud that would not go away. As the preacher at the commencement events in 1970, he asked the graduates to think of ways to measure life. He began:

Life is the most priceless possession of every individual. How then are we to measure its significance? In what shall we invest it to best advantage? What are the standards or values by which we shall make our decisions and on which we shall base our careers?

With the entire Bible to choose from, the theme of doom and gloom also was found in an undated sermon preached at a gathering of members of the Charleston Bible Society in Charleston, South Carolina. He chose the text, "Is there any word from the Lord?" from Jeremiah 37:17.[12] The sermon begins with a graphic description of disastrous times for the people of Israel. The reluctant prophet hears God's command to go and say to the people of Jerusalem that judgment was imminent. A great army is at the gates, and it is clear that doom is at hand. Then, a frightened King Zedekiak asks the fundamental question, "Is there any word from the Lord?"

Richards answered:

> Word there was, indeed. There was a word of truth, which, if it had been heeded
> sooner would have saved a nation. But, the people and their leaders closed their
> hearts to that light. So it was that Jeremiah, speaking the message God had
> given him, could in the end tell only of impending doom.[13]

A serious mood of anxiety is reflected in an analysis of the state of the world.
Richards was quite right in detailing the problems, even though there were
some positive influences at work in the world that indicated that God was still
at work.

The sermon continued to sound alarm over the world's needs. He declared:

> Men today are perplexed, dismayed, distressed as seldom before in history.
> Confronted as they are by the emptiness of their own lives, by the breakdown of
> civilization, and by the apparent intellectual and moral bankruptcy of our race,
> they are yearning to know with deep intensity where there is any answer to their
> needs, any word from the Lord.[14]

In Richards' view, secular man was like a slot machine with no real power
of choice—drop in the coin of stimulus, and straightway he receives the
particular reaction for which he had bargained.

A further example of this warning is found in the Robinson Lectures at
Erskine Theological Seminary. "Preaching and the Issues of Today" provided
a broad umbrella covering various challenges, but Richards continued to see
the world of the preacher as a world under grave threats. He agreed with
Alvin Toffler's conclusion in his book, *Future Shock*, that Western society for
the past three hundred years has been caught up in a firestorm of change. In
sermons on social issues, Richards supported George Buttrick's position of
avoiding the stereotype of the preacher who "is always pleasant, laughing and
joking when he talks with us, but when he preaches he seems angry and
denounces us." More significantly, he approved Buttrick's conclusion: "In
morals, the upheaval is so vast that it seems at times as if the roads are all
gone, all the bridges are down, and all the floods let loose."[15] He praised
Buttrick's positive approach in preaching on social issues. Richards also
agreed that, "one flashing phrase that cuts like a rapier is better than an orgy
of denunciation."[16]

Furthermore, in dealing with the issue of race, Richards urged ministers to
practice the spirit of love. He believed that this seemingly impotent approach
in a time of great chaos could still create a rapport with the hearers. Using "we"
instead of "I," and "us" instead of "you" was helpful, also. Finally, as was his

custom, he concluded with a call to faith in and obedience to Jesus Christ, the way, the truth, and the life:

> The world has never been Christian. It will never be fully Christian until our Lord returns. But, men are in his hands. The future is as bright as his power and glory. His will shall be done despite the folly of men and of devils. His is an ever-lasting Kingdom. In this assurance, let us dedicate ourselves to the task that is forever relevant and compelling. In his strength, let us faithfully proclaim His word for this life, and for the life of the world to come.[17]

The words of benediction found in 2 Corinthians 13:14, most often used during Richards' years of preaching, formed the basis for an appeal to the Synod of the Southeast:[18]

> The grace of the Lord Jesus Christ, the love of God, and the fellowship of the Holy Spirit be with you all. (RSV)

Richards interpreted them as a call like a battle cry, rallying the forces for the struggle ahead. The sermon began:

> Few words are more familiar to us than these. What meaning do they have for the average person who hears them pronounced by the minister? Perhaps they mean little more than that the service is ended and all are free to go. They are the ecclesiastical equivalent of "have a nice day, or a nice week, or a nice year."

> Are they a form of words spoken by rote, or do they come from the heart as a deeply sincere and moving prayer? Is there any sense of wonder or mystery about them? Are they a soothing formula or a challenge; a benediction or a battle cry, or both?[19]

After examining the meaning of such well-worn words as "grace," "love," and "fellowship," Richards chose to focus on the appeal that he described as a "battle cry." "The benediction is our battle cry. Let us sound the advance. Trumpeter, rally them, rally them, rally them. On to the city of God."

In his prophetic sermon, "Principle or Profit," Richards began with a graphic description of the riot in Ephesus described in Acts 19:23–41. The apostle Paul challenged the worship of Diana in that important city, and a riot ensued. Richards graphically draws a picture of "gods for sale" in Ephesus, and the mushrooming profits for the silversmiths. Then, he asked the Augusta, Georgia, congregation if it had avoided that blasphemy in America. Demetrius blamed this fanatic, Paul, for falling sales and diminishing profits. Said Richards:

Demetrius' speech that day is a classic in how to incite a mob to riot and give them a good reason, if not a true reason, for rioting. He led them through the reason for falling profits and then used religion to authenticate the business. "Diana has blessed us, and this Paul is destroying that. Great is Diana of the Ephesians. . . ."

This story illustrates once again that the quickest way to excite people is to hide behind the flag or motherhood. I pray for my country, and have a genuine love for America. But, I have never subscribed to that rather loose statement, "My country, right or wrong." That is making a god out of patriotism. It is like saying, "My mother, drunk or sober." Granted, she is your mother, but this statement never comes to grips with the problem in her life.[20]

The sermon then made a perceptive application by showing that people have a choice between faith and finances, for the church is not for sale. Also, people have a choice between faith and fear, for they may be afraid to rock the boat or hurt our leaders. The conclusion was that people are, in all things, to choose principle before profit, and above all be faithful to Christ.

Another pattern of Richards' preaching was reflected in a discussion of the potential value of "Discontent." Paul's phrase, "Brethren, I count not myself to have apprehended" (Phil. 3:13 KJV), is the basis for his treatment of this theme. Richards focused his appeal in these sentences:

It is one thing for a man to be happy; it is a very different thing for him to be satisfied. It may be highly desirable that he should be content with his lot in life and with the work God calls him to perform. It is disastrous, however, for him to be content with what he finds in himself and the measure of his service to man and God. Discontent stimulates growth in all things, science, knowledge, artistic arenas, but primarily in the spiritual. Brethren, I count not myself to have apprehended.[21]

As passionate and unique among preachers as Richards was on social issues, he was also committed to concepts slowly passing out of the concerns and lives of Presbyterians. The sermon on "The Christian Sabbath" represented an urgent call to preserve that concept. The use of Sunday as a holy day, not a holiday, was one of the passions of his life. When he spoke earnestly of "The Christian Sabbath in Contemporary Society," he revealed his conviction that it was "a pressing problem," and his alarm at the steady erosion of its observance. Fourteen printed pages affirmed that it was essential to a healthy society as well as a healthy church. It should be a time of rest in body, mind, and spirit, rather than a time for exhausting recreation or dissipation. It, at its best, was a day with and for the family. He said:

It is far and away our greatest opportunity for the cultivation of wholesome family relationships. We need to keep the Sabbath in the home that the Sabbath in turn may keep our homes from decay and disintegration.[22]

He sheepishly admitted that he was away on weekends traveling to speak and preach in various places, and felt guilty that he was torn in two directions. Regretting his absence from his family on many Sundays, however, did not keep Richards from preaching regularly. Worship was a deeply felt part of his calling. Lamenting the growing pagan culture in American society, he feared that the subsequent formation of religious illiterates would ultimately be extremely damaging to the church and the state. In a time when material values had already begun to powerfully influence the culture with a serious erosion of values, the Sabbath was needed to transform that culture.

The Sabbath was, he passionately affirmed, a day that calls us to the public worship of God, for which there is no substitute. He declared:

Nature alone cannot make us good. I began my ministry in the mountains of North Georgia. The region is one of rare beauty. I love those hills and valleys and streams very deeply. Many times I have found inspiration in them. More than once, when I was there, I said to my friends that surely a person could not live in such scenes of beauty without being better for it. However, I soon discovered reality. As sincere as I was in saying that, I was startled later to realize that such words were entirely divorced from reality. Men are neither better nor worse in the mountains than elsewhere. Some of the finest people on earth are there, and some of the worst. You will find poverty and ignorance, degradation and sin abounding in the midst of surroundings which surely should remind men of God and make them better, if there were any power in nature to change the lives of individuals or of the race. There is no substitute for worship in God's house.[23]

There were few themes for preaching ignored by Richards. Special occasions and unique programs created something of a sermonic shape to addresses he delivered. The topic, "Christian Education and Evangelism," was assigned to him at a Montreat conference. Richards introduced the theme, with a focus on the Bible as the basis for both areas of ministry:

The Coat of Arms of Oxford University in England bears a significant device. In its center is an open book. The fact that this volume is not a treatise on philosophy or history, or science, but the Bible, is made abundantly clear by the easily legible words which are spread across its pages: *Dominus Illumination Mea,* "The Lord is my light." Grouped around the book are three golden crowns, representing the three persons of the Trinity. It would be hard to find a more complete representation of Christian truth in condensed symbolic form than that.[24]

Richards reminded his hearers that all the famous universities which kept learning alive in the Western world throughout the Middle Ages were instruments of the Church. In later years in the United States, this was true also of Harvard, Yale, and Princeton Universities, and of institutions founded later on that were established by the Church. On Harvard's gates there is carved a striking reminder of that:

> After God had carried us safe to New England, and we had builded our houses, provided necessaries for our livelihood, reared convenient places for God's worship and settled on civil government, one of the next things we longed for and looked after was to advance learning and perpetuate it to posterity, dreading to leave an illiterate ministry to the Churches when our present ministers shall lie in the dust.[25]

What is more, *Who's Who in America* at that time had a very large number of graduates from small colleges founded by the Church. A large proportion of the graduates of those colleges devoted themselves to occupations that led to the betterment of society rather than to individual distinction or personal gain. Even among institutions founded and sustained for the purpose of educating the Church's ministers, a diversity of purposes exists today. Some are quite secular, and a few are still committed to this original mission. Most are financed through their constant appeals to foundations, individuals, and government agencies. To Richards, these changes were a mixed blessing. Though larger sums of money were obtained, the relationships and their values were lost.

Long-delayed plans for building, stymied by the focus on World War II, were revived and implemented in the years following the war. In 1952, Davidson College erected a Davidson Church sanctuary that would serve a congregation meeting for worship and the college gatherings for convocations and graduations. As chairman of the board of trustees, Richards was invited to be the preacher at commencement and at the dedication services of that church. He delighted in the occasion. The sermon began:

> This is a high day, a historic day for Davidson College and for the Davidson community. This beautiful sanctuary, which we have dedicated, is the fulfillment of many hopes and dreams. It is the answer to an evident need and to a longing in the heart of many a worshiper in the humbler sanctuary which formerly occupied this site. It is the realization of a dream and marks the culmination of much

planning and labor and sacrifice on the part of Christians in this and other communities; of some who hold membership now in the church triumphant[26] as well as those who serve in the church militant. May it also be a place of deeper consecration and of more effective service.

This is also a day of great significance to the graduating class of 1952, and to parents, relatives and friends of its members. A four-year journey has ended and now a larger pilgrimage begins. Today you wait for a little while in the house of prayer which lifts its spire like a pointing finger above the campus we love. . . . This commencement opens a new chapter in the life of Davidson College and the Davidson Church, and it marks the beginning of a new section in the record of your lives.[27]

As usual, in his preaching, Richards used numerous citations from poetry, essays, and historians to support his message. Among these are Francis Thompson's dramatic "The Hound of Heaven" and the lines: "I fled him down the nights and down the days . . . from those strong Feet that followed, followed after." Richards saw that pursuing God as the God of Nature, the God of History, and above all, the God of Scripture and the Father of our Lord Jesus Christ.

The God of Nature was pictured as a deity who is not only in the beautiful part of nature. Rather:

> Tis not in the high stars alone,
> Nor in the cup of budding flowers,
> Nor in the redbreast's mellow tone,
> Nor in the bow which smiles midst showers,
> But in the mud and scum of things
> There always, always, something sings.[28]

The God of History is pictured in citations from authors who by no stretch of the imagination can be called Christian apologists. One of these, Count Volney, in a philosophy of history, *The Ruins*, agrees with the Hebrew prophets that the decline and fall of empires can be traced to the folly and sins of their citizens. James Russell Lowell was correct, said Richards, in claiming that "behind the dim unknown, standeth God keeping watching above his own." What is more, Richards said, Victor Hugo was right in saying: "Was it possible for Napoleon to win the Battle of Waterloo? No. Why? On account of Wellington? No. On account of God."[29]

The God of Scripture is pictured as a God revealed in mighty acts through human history, but focuses ultimately on Jesus Christ. Richards concluded with a deep conviction that it was a great thing to erect that noble edifice, the Davidson College Church, as a witness to the reality of God who was in Christ, reconciling the world unto Himself. It is as though:

> A far more important thing is that the message we proclaim shall become a living force in the lives of those who worship here; that from this church and this school shall go forth those who in all of life will be servants of the living God.[30]

In a reflection of the culture of the Church fifty years ago, the Committee on Women's Work of the Presbyterian Church (U.S.) did not invite a woman for the Conference worship services, as would be the case today. They chose Richards, a well-known male minister, to prepare a service of worship to be used in creating Christian attitudes toward other racial groups. It was, as expected, a carefully structured service. However, it was full of masculine terms such as "men" and "brotherhood." The directions for use, however, included groups of women, couples, and men.

Among the memorial sermons that remain in print, those at services for his good friends follow a pattern of thoughtful expositions of appropriate scripture passages, carefully prepared, and delivered with gratitude for life and witness. The following examples highlight this pastoral style.

Lillian Clinkscales Green

The service of thanksgiving for Lillian Clinkscales Green, the wife of Professor James B. Green, stands out among many of the memorial services. Richards displayed a sensitive insight into her faith and life. He described her influence in the seminary community and at Decatur Presbyterian Church as a positive and valuable contribution to both. She was, he said, an intimate part of the community life of Columbia Seminary. Fiercely loyal to Columbia Theological Seminary and to Decatur Presbyterian Church, she was a caring and helpful friend of students and faculty alike. Although reared in the Associate Reformed Presbyterian Church, Mrs. Green was an invaluable leader in the Presbyterian Church, U.S. She founded the present day Columbia Friendship Circle of Presbyterian Women who support Columbia Seminary with prayer, gifts, and financial aid for students. She asked, in the depths of the 1930s economic depression, that each woman gives one dollar a year for this fund. In his sermon, Richards spoke of her as a devoted wife and mother, and affirmed her highest loyalty, a commitment to Jesus Christ. Then, in conclusion, he felt she still spoke to us as one who could say, "I know whom I have believed, and am persuaded that he is able to keep that which I have committed unto Him against that day" (2 Tim. 1:12 KJV).

Mrs. J. Holmes Smith

Similarly, Mrs. J. Holmes Smith, dietitian and hostess at Columbia Seminary, was described in these words:

> Mrs. Smith was a very great lady, and the thing which made her great was her faith in Christ. She came to the Staff of Columbia Seminary in 1943 with her two younger children after the death of her husband. No service is of greater importance to Church and Country than rearing children for the glory of God. This Mildred Smith did. She was also called to serve the entire church in an unheralded but truly significant capacity, Dietitian and Hostess. She filled this office for twenty-one years, serving with efficiency, as well as with grace and dedication. "Man does not live by bread alone," but we do not live and labor physically and mentally without bread. Scripture says, whoever will be chiefest among you, shall be servant of all. So it is today that a multitude throughout our church and in lands beyond the seas rise up with her children and with us and call her blessed. "The path of the righteous is as the light of dawn, that shineth more and more unto the perfect day." The perfect day has come for Mildred Smith.[31]

Mrs. Smith's daughter, Jane Smith Shields, expressed appreciation for the memorial service and described her mother's response to the call to move with her family to Decatur, Georgia, and begin a new work as dietician and hostess. She wrote: "We agree that Mother was a great lady indeed. When I remember how fearful she was about leaving New Orleans, and taking that step into an unknown situation, we praise her for the courage she showed and continued to show through all the years. She always felt your supportive help which strengthened and sustained her and felt she was a member of a warm and caring faculty family."[32]

Stuart R. Oglesby Jr.

Stuart R. Oglesby Jr., a leader in Atlanta Presbytery, led a congregation through tremendous changes in the center of a great city. That congregation, Central Presbyterian Church, was in the heart of downtown Atlanta, across the street from the Georgia's state capital. Born in Hope, Arkansas, on July 10, 1888, he preceded President William Jefferson Clinton in birth there by many years. Oglesby came to Central Presbyterian Church in 1930, and for the next twenty-eight years was not only the pastor of that scattered congregation, but also a "visiting pastor" in their homes and offices.

Richards quoted Celestine Sibley, the widely read columnist of the Atlanta *Journal-Constitution*, who wrote:

> Hearing he was ill, I wrote my old friend Dr. Stuart Oglesby, longtime pastor of Central Presbyterian Church. Now in his 80s he is very ill and no longer the

vibrant force for good that he has been in Atlanta since 1930. I grieved for Dr. Oglesby when I heard that, but I grieved more for the young people of our town who never knew him, and now cannot call on him for strength and support when a job for the common weal needs doing. Dr. Oglesby was probably the nearest thing to a chaplain the *Constitution* newsroom ever had. We called him "our preacher" for he was so available to us. He brought the weekly ad for Central's Sunday Worship, and sat and talked to us with his hat on the back of his head, reporter style.

Many credit Oglesby for saving the Christian Council of Atlanta, the only association that brings together very diverse Christian bodies in service to the Atlanta community. Further, leading his congregation to engage in ministry of varied kinds to the city's diverse population, he still had time to serve the denomination through its Church and Society Board and programs.

The friendship and esteem Richards and Oglesby felt for each other lasted a lifetime. Richards, in the "Service of Celebration and Praise in Gratitude to God for Stuart R. Oglesby Jr.," spoke of him as pastor and preacher for many. He offered a very special expression of profound gratitude for his ministry to the Richards family. Two of Richards' children are active members and leaders in that church today.

Oglesby was a useful member of the Board of Directors of Columbia Theological Seminary. He was fully supportive of the president and his leadership in Columbia's life and work. He was honest enough, however, to occasionally question the president's recommendations. When the board was once asked to invite the Rev. Dr. James S. Stewart of Edinburgh to become professor of worship and preaching in the hope that this unsought and unexpected invitation would persuade him to accept, Oglesby responded with abrupt honesty. "What is Stewart's response?" Richards sheepishly confessed that he had not yet been approached, but he felt a firm invitation might open the door to consideration. Oglesby was right, for there turned out to be no chance Stewart would leave his beloved New College professorship.

Richards spoke of the uncommon pattern of Oglesby's pastoral ministry as one who visited members constantly. Oglesby averaged one hundred calls a month in offices and homes of the people. Even more significant, though, is the great role Oglesby assumed in leading the Presbyterian Church in support of the efforts for justice and righteousness in the church and in the city. Richards concluded his meditation by using a long passage from *Pilgrim's Progress* when Valiant for Truth passed over, and all the trumpets sounded on the other side. He was confident that all the trumpets sounded when Oglesby passed over.

Patrick Dwight Miller

Using words from the story in 2 Samuel 3:31 of David mourning for Abner, Richards began by citing those ancient words from that account: "Know ye not that there is a prince and a great man fallen this day in Israel. A prince in Israel is gone from our midst."

Richards then spoke of Miller:

> A greater man than Abner has fallen. His life, and his death bear a different and a higher witness upon which I invite you to reflect with me a little while . . . If Dr. Miller were here in person, he would accept no praise, but would say with the Apostle Paul, "by the grace of God, I am what I am. All is of grace." His grace, which was upon Dr. Miller, was not in vain. Like Paul he was not disobedient to the heavenly vision.[33]

Richards reflected on causes for gratitude for Patrick Dwight Miller. They include Miller's personal character and conduct, his life as a sermon on the importance of the Christian family, his service as a faithful and effective minister, his commitment to Christian stewardship, and his leadership as an executive of great ability and rare business acumen. During his tenure as executive secretary of the Board of Church Extension from 1955 to 1965, the Presbyterian Church (U.S.) had its most rapid growth. Though the reference to Columbia Seminary was brief in this sermon, Miller served as chairman of the Board of Directors and was a visiting professor at the seminary.

Richards concluded his memorial message with a statement of hope:

> For all these things, we remember Patrick Dwight Miller with love and gratitude today, and lift up our hearts in praise and thanksgiving to the God who ordained and used this man as His servant on earth, and who now has called him home.

> Years ago, when we were both young ministers, Dr. Miller and I used to discuss many matters and often talked about our preaching. I remember still how he called my attention to a significant passage which is found in the opening verses of the book of Joshua, and which he had used as the theme for a commencement sermon: "Now it came to pass after the death of Moses, the servant of the lord, that the Lord spoke to Joshua, the son of Nun, Moses' servant, saying: 'Moses my servant is dead now, therefore, arise, cross over this Jordan.'"

> Humanly speaking, the death of Moses might well have been an occasion for discouragement and despair. He had been the leader in the liberation of Israel and the prophet through whom the Law of God had been given. Who could

replace him? What hope was there now for Israel as it faced strong enemies and unknown dangers in a hostile country? Yet, God's call is to advance.

God never leaves himself without an instrument. He buries his leaders but carries on His work. That which has been accomplished in the past is but preparation for the future. Patrick Dwight Miller has served God faithfully and well in his generation. It remains for us to continue his work, to enlarge the undertakings to which he gave his strength, to build higher and stronger the edifice of the church upon which he labored, to claim new lives and to possess new territories for Christ.[34]

Eugene T. Wilson, pastor of Peachtree Presbyterian Church, Atlanta, Georgia

The memorial service for this faithful, hardworking, and forward-looking minister included a prayer of thanksgiving by Richards. The prayer, as typical of his practice, begins with praise to God, for our times are in God's hands. It moves to praise for God's servant, Gene Wilson, and for the relationships formed with him. The list of causes for gratitude includes the godly home from which he came and in which he came to know the Lord Jesus Christ. There follows a long list of significant reasons for gratitude. They included the home he established with his wife, Martha, his children and grandchildren, the abilities he had which were dedicated to the service of Christ, the institutions which educated him, Presbyterian College, Columbia Theological Seminary, and every worthy influence which shaped his character. He continued:

> We are grateful tonight for his steadfast faith, for his loyalty to Christ and to the Church; for his faithfulness in preaching "the old, old story, of Jesus and his love." We thank thee for giving him a pastor's heart, for his ministry, for his humor, for his ready smile and his warm friendship; for the sympathy which enabled him to share in the joys and sorrows of his people and hence to minister to their varied needs. We thank thee for the courage with which he faced and overcame physical ailments, and for the vision which led him to undertake great tasks for his Master. And now, our father, we thank thee for this church, an outward testimony to his faith and labors, a symbol of that which through him became a reality in the lives of many, a gift laid at the feet of his Lord and Saviour.[35]

The second half of this memorial prayer was full of praise for a God who is "not the God of the dead but of the living." On that basis, Richards offered prayers of intercession for Wilson's wife, his children and his grandchildren, and his friends. The list is extensive and included the work of Peachtree Presbyterian Church, the pastors and people alike, the preaching of the gospel, the teaching of the Word, and the work for righteousness and justice it provides. The whole church around the world is included in intercession. The closing petition was for wisdom and strength to live and work in such a way that God would be glorified, love shed abroad, and purposes fulfilled. The Lord's Prayer in unison concluded this prayer of praise and intercession.

It is important to see Richards as one who carefully prepared and wrote out thoughtful prayers in memorial services. Moreover, these prayers were never even close to chatty talk with the Deity, but were always a serious, reverent, insightful communication with God.

What impact did Richards' preaching have in the minds and lives of listeners? No doubt, the ultimate response was that of a new understanding of what authentic biblical faith is and could be. Those who heard these sermons, of course, experienced various reactions to this new understanding. They often responded with new faith and obedience. Many would find forgiveness and renewal, thanksgiving and rejoicing, repentance and commitment, and wisdom and courage for various human experiences. They heard a clear word from the Lord to experience new life, and to see the Church as worldwide in worship and life.

One layperson, Kate Willis, wrote to describe her deeply felt appreciation for Richards' sermon on the cross. As a delegate to the Synod of Florida's Conference for Women, she listened to his interpretation of the cross of Jesus and its meaning for the faithful today. She responded specifically to the relevance of the message with words and feelings written in the context of one of the greatest tests of faith for any parent, the loss of a child:

> The Cross has a personal meaning for our family, too. Last summer we went to Clearwater, Florida, so I could take training in the Area Laboratory School at Peace Memorial Presbyterian Church. Our beautiful and beloved little five-year-old son drowned in the Gulf. After it happened I wanted to die, but that was physically impossible. It was impossible because of Jesus. In perfect love He had borne his cross so that my son could have eternal life and I knew that for Him, I had to bear mine. It was a small exchange on my part, but it took mighty effort. After my decision was made, I was made aware that it must go farther than just bearing my pain. I must bear it in a manner that would glorify Him, and that is with cheerfulness and hope and faith. For some the gift of acceptance comes easily, but though I do not have this gift, He has been by my side through every day. I know that His love will sustain me until my final victory is won.[36]

Richards warmly affirmed and supported Kate Willis as she expressed her faith and the meaning of the sermon at that moment.

The Richards Papers include grateful letters from ministers and lay persons for his sermons. However, the response was mixed when the sermon appealed for justice in the efforts to eliminate the worst forms of segregation and the impact on African-Americans and the very poor. On occasion, worshipers may have heard or read a sermon and responded by thinking it is an excellent one, but irrelevant to them. However, more often than not, they heard an assurance of God's mighty acts in history and God's work in them and in the church and the world. Laypersons more readily listened for a word from the Lord concerning their daily lives in all its dimensions. Family, work, and the realities of the seasons of life itself, were often seen with new insight and new commitment.

In the first half of Richards' presidency, he had more time to preach at weeklong series of services. However, he continued to do so along with all of his active ministry but with far less frequency. Designed to inspire the faithful, and nourish the life of the Church, he also had an opportunity to counsel with pastors and usually left them with new hope and inspiration.

After a weeklong session in Augusta, Georgia, Hubert G. Wardlaw, pastor of Covenant Presbyterian Church, wrote:

> Your coming to our Church was a God-send. I feel your spirit and presentation of the Word of God for our Church today met a real need here and that our people will begin to work together again for the main purpose of the Church. All of us are so grateful for your coming to us. The Sunday morning services were best attended but I feel the Monday night message went home to key leaders in both sides of the church's factions today.[37]

Wardlaw also spoke with much appreciation for the inspiration to "those of us in the Manse." The fact that in 1969, near the end of the Richards' presidency, his preaching brought such a response is significant. The issues of controversies, divisions, and suspicions were weakening the mission of the Church as it always does.

Whether the church was large or small seemed irrelevant to Richards. In 1945, he shared a week with the First Presbyterian Church of Andalusia, Alabama. William H. Boyd, a 1943 Columbia Seminary graduate, was serving that church until the pastor could be released from the military chaplaincy. Boyd wrote:

> There is no doubt as to the blessing that we received from your visit. I personally and we as a congregation wish to express to you our genuine appreciation for your kindness in coming to be with us for the week of our services. We are all gratified by the outward manifestations of God's blessings upon us as the result of your ministry here. The Spirit of God moved in our midst to stir us in a spiritual way. Three families will unite with our church and another is probable.[38]

After a series of services in Red Springs, North Carolina, in which Richards used the overall theme of the nature and mission of the Church, the pastor, Thomas A. Fry Jr. wrote:

> I want to thank you again for coming to Red Springs and bringing such helpful messages on the Church. One of our ladies told me yesterday that it was the finest thing that had happened in Red Springs in many a year. It was a great blessing to our people to have the opportunity to know personally one who is associated with the Church in all its world wide work.[39]

Richards, in the first twenty-five years of his presidency, led Holy Week services throughout the Southeast. Even though he missed being with his family at Easter, he relished such opportunities. An example of such special services was a preaching mission in Daytona Beach, Florida, with Dr. Paul Edris and the Daytona Beach Presbyterian Church. He preached on Palm Sunday and at daily noonday and evening services. The grueling schedule included a three-hour Good Friday service. He was, without doubt, weary when he returned to campus.[40]

In wartime, Richards was much interested in chaplain's retreats and in the invitations that came to speak at military bases. The post chaplain at nearby Fort McPherson, D. H. Funk, was one of many who invited him to preach in chapel. Since attendance was often required, Richards had large congregations. Chaplain Funk wrote on April 17, 1944:

> I want to express to you the thanks of the Commanding Officer, the Chaplains and the entire personnel of this post for your kindness in bringing us such an inspiring Easter message. Your message contributed greatly to the success of our post-wide Easter Service and we are in hopes that you will be with us again.[41]

The response to Richards' messages broadcast through radio was positive. In the days before television and even for a decade later, the *Presbyterian Hour* invited him to preach frequently. In addition, churches such as the First Presbyterian Church of Atlanta embraced the communication age and began using radio in the 1920s to reach more people.[42] The response Richards received was encouraging to him.

Richards regularly received invitations from stations that were motivated by the license requirement to schedule a wide variety of programs. Indeed, for years free time was given in substantial amounts for such broadcasts. Today, they have been diminished in number by the expense for television and radio time. Rarely, if at all, are they without cost to the church.

One sample of Richards' preaching in this media is a list of topics for a radio devotions program. Based on the epistle to the Romans, they make up an interesting assortment of theological topics:

1. The Life of Faith (1:11–17)
2. The Sinfulness of Man (3:9–20)
3. The Humility of Faith (3:27)[43]
4. The Faith of Abraham (4:13–18)
5. The Peace of the Believer (5:1–4)
6. Faith and the Law (7:14–28)
7. The Triumphant Assurance of Faith (8:28–39)
8. Confessing Our Faith (10:4–10)
9. Faith and Missions (10:11–17)
10. The Consequences of Unbelief (11:17–24)
11. The Proof of Faith (12:1–11)
12. The Obedience of Faith (16:17–27)

Obviously, those topics would probably not evoke curiosity or interest from a non-religious person moving over the dial in search of a program that would entertain. But, the irony is that the content of Richards' message might be far more relevant to their lives and to the world around them. Those who responded in writing were no doubt only a small percentage of radio listeners. However, it is significant that some persons, both lay and clergy, did respond with a letter of thanks.

Dr. W. H. Hudson, whose ministry was largely overseas as a missionary, wrote an appreciative letter to Richards in January 1944, after hearing Richards' sermon, "The Meaning of Christmas." Richards responded in typical fashion:

> It was most thoughtful of you to write to me after hearing my message on radio last Sunday, and your letter has been a source of real approval of my sermon on that date, and I am glad to know that you feel it would be profitable for it to be in print.[44]

Mr. and Mrs. George F. Nixon, from Rome, Georgia, responded in these words:

> It was such a delightful surprise to hear your message over radio from First Presbyterian Church, Atlanta. The weather and neuralgia kept me home from service today. We appreciate so much your Christmas message which has now been sent to us. We hope we have many opportunities of hearing from you. We are hoping to have our boys home again before springtime, and have "goodwill toward all nations" before another year.[45]

One more, from Dr. and Mrs. D. P. McGeachy Sr., also affirmed the message:

> Mrs. McGeachy and I had time this morning to hear your radio sermon and we are glad. You preached a good sermon, and your voice came over as naturally as though we were sitting in plain sight and listening to you face to face. We thank God for you and the story you have to tell. This radio business is a wonderful thing.[46]

Richards never thought he had a good voice, and even took lessons from Huburt V. Taylor, professor of speech at Columbia Seminary, seeking improvement. The message itself was uniformly of high quality.

After attending the first meeting of the World Council of Churches in Amsterdam Holland (1948), Richards returned home inspired by this new ecumenical gathering. He found there, as he often said, a common loyalty and common purpose. The experience helped Christians understand one another better, he confidently claimed, to find new ways of cooperative service, and to manifest to the world the essential unity of all who believe in Jesus Christ as God and Saviour. Two weeks of meetings were not marked by complete agreement, but, as Karl Barth put it, "the disagreements were within the agreements." Inspired in this way, Richards delivered a radio address on World Communion Sunday, October 3, 1948, which included, he felt, a stunning declaration of faith. He used these words to describe it:

> The world is in the hands of the Living God. It is in hands of Jesus Christ, who lived and died and rose from the dead. God has broken the power of evil once and for all, and opened for every one the gate into freedom and joy in the Holy Spirit. The final judgment on all human history and on every human deed is the judgment of the merciful Christ, and the end of history will be the triumph of His kingdom where alone we shall understand how much God loved the world. . . .
>
> In all earnestness, we would invite you to enter His church, to accept Him as your Lord and Saviour, and to unite with us as we seek in the greatest fellowship on earth to know Him and make Him known.[47]

In summary, Richards had a lifelong love for preaching. Throughout the Church and indeed in many parts of the world where the Presbyterian Church had partnership with Christian churches and institutions, Richards gladly responded to invitations to preach. In retirement, he served as interim pastor for the one-thousand-member Bethesda Presbyterian Church, in Camden, South Carolina. He relished the opportunity.

Richards was truly "a man for all seasons" as a preacher. He fashioned appropriate sermons for varying occasions and settings. He carefully crafted biblical themes and applied them to contemporary settings. In the depression years, the wars, the times of controversy in nation and in Church, he steadfastly focused "The Word of the Lord" for persons, structures, society, congregations, academic institutions, and national life. He made the most of his opportunities using his gifts of mind and voice. As always, as in all human endeavors, the final judgment is God's. Many who listened to him during the decades of his ministry would say, "Well done, good and faithful servant."

CHAPTER FOUR

Pastor

*I*N THE RICHARDS PAPERS, WE CATCH THE CHARACTER and spirit of his pastoral care in his genuine concern for missionaries, chaplains, pastors, presbytery executives, and for a surprisingly large number of laypersons. Much of the material available reflects a sensitive and supportive concern for each individual.

Richards' correspondence with graduates through the years often came during a time of trouble or a time of great celebration. Always, in both, he was sensitive and compassionate. Pastors could be failing, or depressed, or quite unwise in actions and attitudes, but the flow of concerned and compassionate correspondence never stopped. It continued even in the age of the telephone and travel. They could need wisdom and advice as a presbytery executive, a minister in graduate study, a missionary, or a chaplain in the military and in hospitals, and for all he was an available listener. What was also positive and supportive were the letters of congratulations for a marriage, a new call, the birth of a baby, or the recognition of a governing body. They kept going out from his first floor office in Campbell Hall on the seminary campus to persons scattered across the world.

Richards' role of the pastor was reflected in various ways to persons in disparate situations. Prospective students, missionaries, chaplains in World War II, and pastors were recipients of Richards' prayerful concern. Indeed, lay leaders of the Presbyterian Church were among those who welcomed his words of encouragement, commendation on service, and counseling. This pastoral concern appears particularly in stressful times of racial conflict, economic stress, and drastic changes in the Church. Whether a single occasion, or a continuing correspondence, the Richards' letters were often two and three pages, warm and considerate, reconciling and yet bearing an authentic pastoral witness. Richards' approach as a pastor, both written and verbal, was considerate and humble, but absolutely clear. No fuzzy equivocation, no talking out of both sides of the mouth, and no backing down under attack found a place in his correspondence or in his pastoral care of many persons. Moreover, Richards offered hope in a variety of ways and patterns.

Arch L. MacNair, class of 1939, spoke of his experience with J. McDowell Richards as a trusted, helpful pastor in these words:

> When I entered Columbia Theological Seminary in the fall of 1936, I had $10 for the first year, and no further aid came from home. Dr. Richards welcomed me and helped me through three years of Seminary. I thank God that I came under the influence of this gentle, Christ like man.[1]

Following a year of graduate study in 1946–47 at Scotland's University of Edinburgh, MacNair was actively seeking a pastorate in the southeastern United States. He appealed to President Richards for help in securing a pastorate: "This is a report from the unemployed. I have had some inquiries from churches but nothing definite has resulted. I need to find a call soon and hope that you can help me."[2] Shortly, through Richards' efforts, a number of churches became interested in MacNair, and he accepted a call to a new pastorate in Deland, Florida.

A pastor arrived on campus without an appointment in the midst of a Board of Directors meeting. Richards, rather than send word to him that he was busy and could not see him, came out into the hallway for a fifteen-minute conversation. Later, Richards wrote: "I regret very much that I was under such pressure at the time of your unexpected visit and consequently, may have seemed less sympathetic and interested than was actually the case."[3]

Richards was much pleased to receive a letter of profuse thanks for the conference. A grateful graduate replied:

> I do want you to know that I am sincerely grateful for all that the Seminary has meant to me. These years have been rich in God's blessings and I am aware of the efforts which you and the other faculty have made to make them so. Your interest in the details of the students' lives has been of real blessing to us.[4]

Words of appreciation such as these reflect the pastoral spirit of J. McDowell Richards. For more than thirty-nine challenging years, Richards provided personal, honest, and prayerful counsel for thousands of ministers and lay persons. In good times and bad, in simple and complex situations, and, above all, in the spirit of Jesus of Nazareth, he exemplified the title—pastor.

Even in retirement, he was a useful staff member in various churches as interim pastor or as a pastoral visitor. He found an important place of service on the staff of the ten-thousand-member Peachtree Presbyterian Church of Atlanta. He visited members in hospitals almost daily and, in the traditional and some would say old-fashioned way, he prayed at the end of each visit. One of Atlanta's outstanding businessmen, J. Erskine Love Jr., spoke to me with a sense of awe as he marveled at Richards' gifts for such pastoral visits and, particularly, Richards' prayers for him.

Whether professor, administrator, staff member, or maintenance employee, Richards was personally concerned for each individual at Columbia. An example was Joe Dixon, an amazing man who served as janitor and groundskeeper. Dixon worked long and hard for the seminary in Decatur. Dixon had lost an arm in his youth, but was able to use wheelbarrows, lawn mowers, and other equipment by inventing straps and slings to compensate.

One of the angriest letters in Richards' collection is addressed to a loan company in Atlanta. Dixon's daughter missed payments on a small personal loan, so her father, a cosigner, was threatened with garnishment of his salary and of other assets such as his small home. In distress, he presented Richards with the facts, believing that the world was crashing in on him and he would soon be penniless, homeless, and jobless. Richards' strategy was to send a special delivery letter to the company detailing his outrage at the threats against an honest, hardworking man like Joe Dixon. Furthermore, in time, Joe Dixon would pay the loan for his daughter, but it would take many months.

The company backed down and the loan was paid. Richards' pastoral support was immensely helpful to Dixon and his daughter. Though Richards' action might seem paternalistic to some, the entire seminary community was gratified that the problem was solved and the debt ultimately paid.

Most institutional leaders will agree that food service is often the most difficult part of campus life to be administered satisfactorily. Further, the budget resources available in three of the four decades of the Richards era were minimal at best. Richards called Mrs. J. Holmes Smith of New Orleans, Louisiana, to the position of director of food service. She had four children, three in college and seminary during her period of service at Columbia. Her husband, a surgeon, died. She was persuaded in 1943 in the midst of World War II to take this position at a very low salary, and to live in an apartment in the dormitory made up of four former student rooms and one bath. It was minimally equipped with kitchen facilities.

She would not have come if she had not seen in this position a great opportunity to serve the Church, the seminary, and the students. She did so with distinction and effectiveness in one of the most difficult positions on any campus. In a service of worship and thanksgiving for Mrs. Smith, Richards spoke of her as a devoted Christian, a great and gifted lady, a worthy mother, and an example to all in matters of faith and witness.

Plato Henderson, chef for forty-one years, faithfully served the institution and especially students and staff members. Beginning on February 14, 1919, in Columbia, South Carolina, Henderson became a friend of faculty and students. The number of meals and the statistics on students served set a record that is unmatched today. In a report full of gratitude on May 8, 1962, Richards offered high praise: "Plato Henderson holds a large place in the hearts of generations of Seminary students. Now old and infirm, I am recommending that he be retired at the end of May, that the Board of Directors send him a message of appreciation, and that a modest pension be provided for him."[5]

For thirty-six years, Miss C. Virginia Harrison was an invaluable part of the total life of the institution. Truly, a "woman for all seasons," she was a hard-working and able colleague in the treasurer's office. She functioned as seminary bursar and as personal secretary to Richards.

Richards regarded her as indispensable in the life and work of Columbia Seminary and was protective of her in the light of her tremendous workload. Richards was asked to participate in a depression-era program by the federal government agency, the Works Progress Act (WPA). A researcher paid by WPA would index all of the graduates of Columbia Seminary. Richards' reply was quite cautious:

> If the project could be carried through next summer and if the worker assigned the project at Columbia Theological Seminary could come here during the summer months when our office work is comparatively light, we should be glad to cooperate. The primary source material for the survey in connection with Columbia Seminary could only be furnished by my personal secretary. The latter is already carrying a double load of responsibility by reason of the fact that she is also our Seminary Bursar.[6]

The most important profile we find in Richards' role as pastor was his deep and abiding interest in graduates from the first day to the last day of his life. Four decades came and went with the incredible changes in the culture and challenge of a lifetime of ministry. Immediately after assuming the presidency, Richards faced the devastating impact of the economic depression of the 1930s. In all four decades of his presidency, the pressure to secure much-needed financial support remained. Like a kind and generous parent, he was there to help and to make every possible attempt to meet the needs.

To William H. Boyd of the class of 1943, he wrote:

> It is indeed hard for me to believe that you and the members of your class have been out of the Seminary for five years, as I note that the years go by with a

rapidity which is in direct proportion to my increasing age. I continue to follow all members of your class with very real friendship, but feel an especial interest in you and in your family. I trust all is going well in your work and you are happy in the field of service to which you are called.[7]

Richards practiced a pattern of attention to individuals in pastoral care. In a lecture, he presented the importance of pastoral care of individuals. To support that position, he cited with approval a conversation with Stuart R. Oglesby[8] of Central Presbyterian Church of Atlanta. Oglesby was one of the most useful and beloved ministers in the Presbyterian Church (U.S.). For twenty-eight years, he served Central Presbyterian Church, a strong congregation in the center of the city. Richards inquired of Oglesby the secret of his longevity and, particularly, his relationship with difficult persons in that congregation. Oglesby said with characteristic directness, "Just stay so close to them that they can't kick you."[9]

Again and again, kindness was shown to students with problems and needs. In varied situations involving pastoral care, Richards spent significant amounts of time in dealing with individuals. Whether in student divisions and debates in the last decade of his presidency, or in advising graduates on graduate school, it was most often a "one on one" pattern. In extensive correspondence with John H. Leith concerning plans for graduate school in 1944, every response was supportive, direct, and specific. In the last few years of his presidency, Richards met again and again with student leaders, one by one, and occasionally as a group representing the "conservatives" and the "liberals" on the Community Life Committee dealing with extensive student unrest. That unrest was a combination of many factors, but included dissatisfaction with courses and professors.

Richards was compassionate even in his directness with students. Once he relayed to a senior the evaluation by a church of the student's summer internship. Evaluation was, and is, a most important part of theological education. Among other comments, good and bad, the church recommended much-needed voice training. The student, astonished and defensive, nonetheless responded to Richards' firmness and took the lessons. He was, he declared, "determined to make this weakness a strength."

Through the early years of the Richards' presidency, he was *the* pastor to graduates. The numbers were small, the relationships close, and the possibilities for other counseling few. Whether by mail or in person, he was usually available to them. They would arrive at his office without an appointment, but with serious conflicts and concerns. Graduates would be shocked to find that he was in New York, New York, or Jacksonville, Florida, at meetings. They thought that he was always in his Campbell Hall office and available to them.

Surprisingly, 70 percent of the time he was. But by 1950, and throughout the last two decades of his presidency, appointments were needed. The number of meetings escalated rapidly. Still, the letters went out to clergy and laity troubled with various emotions and circumstances from one they regarded as their only pastor—respected, trusted, and available. The numbers were small, and the correspondence was cost effective compared to the telephone and travel norm.

Invariably, the letters reflected the financial pressures on all Presbyterians during the great economic depression of the 1930s. Ministers were called with no firm commitment to receive a specific salary. Bonneau H. Dickson, a graduate in 1936, said that not one member of his class received a call with anything but a promise to pay what the congregation could, share the vegetables and meat which they raised on the farms, and provide a manse. His first salary was four hundred dollars a year plus two hundred dollars from presbytery. He received the four hundred dollars, but not always the two hundred dollars. At that time, there was no pension program. Graduates rarely had five dollars for a diploma and, thus, received a blank piece of paper at graduation. A few manses had no running water, but provided a well from which to draw needed supplies. Richards' role was to support them and their churches with fervent prayer and numerous letters of encouragement. He understood their situation, for there were also desperate needs for money at Columbia Seminary.

This succinct overview of the amazing scope of Richards' service as a pastor to many persons in many circumstances is evidence that he actually spent the majority of his time and effort in counseling other pastors. He compiled extensive records of consultation with those who served as pastors of churches, chaplains in the military and in hospitals, and those in colleges and seminaries. The use of his time and energy in the role of a pastor to pastors may be found most often in four specific areas: pastors in difficult situations, pastors seeking a change of location, missionaries, and military chaplains.

The difficult situations for pastors had a common basis. Usually, they involved graduates under painful stress in complicated pressures from congregations and communities. Their communications vividly described painful problems with angry people, including members of the Session. Unhappiness on the part of a spouse was also distressing to the marriage and the ministry. In those days, the spouse was usually a wife, but inevitably, the entire family was swept up in crises and buffeted by merciless pressures. Financial problems for ministers and their families were serious and detrimental. Minimal compensation in the depression of the 1930s and inflation in the decades after the war exacerbated the spirits of many. They ranged in extremes from a manse with no running water in it, to persons who seem cruelly demanding. One poorly paid director of a community center in Birmingham, Alabama, was understandably discouraged because he was expected to raise the entire amount needed for operations including his own salary each month. The distraught minister received a strong letter of encouragement from Richards with assurances of God's grace in those circumstances. Richards enclosed a check for five dollars as a symbol of his personal support.

Some wounded ministers pled for help in securing a call to a new pastorate. One such minister, disappointed in the places where Richards had recommended him, angrily accused him of "letting him down." He found fault with every church that went through the process of visiting, conferring, and indicating interest in calling him. This was too much for Richards, and a firm letter of rebuke was on its way like lightning and thunder in summer storm. On the other hand, most graduates of the institution during Richards' years were appreciative of his support and actions in their behalf.

One "suffering servant" is a relatively extreme case, but was not alone in the anguish of ministers who faced seemingly insoluble problems. He described the situation in graphic terms:

> The Session has finally agreed to grant me permission to teach the course at the Seminary for two days a week during one month. The action is based on the condition that Columbia Theological Seminary sends acceptable supplies at Seminary expense. Two of our elders are brothers, but they do not speak to each other and always argue about every matter coming to the Session. We have four out of sixteen elders who have been for 25 years a malignant minority that eventually will have to be operated on and cut out. Our official life needs new, progressive, Christ-like blood. Well, is it worth the struggle? Why should I, one man, stay here and bleed my heart out, and after these years of trials one day have a real good Church? . . . Why do I write you all this? Well for a long time I have wanted to go to a father-confessor and, to earnestly request that, if convenient, you recommend me to another field immediately. . . . I am sick and weary of lying awake nights worrying about fundamental ecclesiastical and spiritual problems. I have done my share toward rehabilitation. Now, let some other Presbyterian minister come and have his chance, too. . . . What is your wisdom and counsel? There is a great deal more, if we were talking face to face, but I fear I have already bored you with these gory details.[10]

In his usual way, Richards was more than a "father-confessor." He offered sympathy and support. However, he strongly urged this troubled pastor not to give up. While he would help secure a call for him, he also suggested that he draw support from those members who serve with him and support him. Above all, Richards reminded him that God had not forsaken him nor the church, and with patience and prayer, the difficulties could be resolved. In time, the result was that this troubled minister was given leave by the session to teach the course in public speaking. What is more, a church much nearer Columbia Seminary called him.

Such pastoral care was given in every decade of Richards' presidency. It was offered to a wide range of persons with disappointments, pain, and suffering, and to those with great rewards in ministry. He rejoiced with those who rejoiced, and grieved with those who grieved, and gave each personal advice and counsel. Richards offered support to all who sought it.

An important part of Richards' pastoral ministry is found in numerous expressions of concern and comfort to lay persons. Richards expressed his sensitivity for the feelings of Oscar Dugger of Andalusia, Alabama, during a major career change.[11] Richards began a two-page letter with personal thanks for the gift of a plate and cup to their baby son, Charles. He quickly moved the focus of his response to the news that Dugger had sold the newspaper that he had worked long and hard to develop. It was a typical rational view of all the issues involved in the impact upon Dugger's life, and especially the inevitable and powerful emotions he must have felt in such a move:

I know this step must have been a hard one for you to take, and probably it has left you with a rather lonely and lost feeling on these recent days. Nevertheless, I believe that you were wise in the action, and I hope that your release from this duty is going to bring you an increasing sense of peace and a deep joy in being released for other service. I trust that by being freed from the responsibility of editing the paper your life will be prolonged many years, and that you will thereby be enabled to increase your usefulness in the church and community.

I do not know whether you realize how deeply you are loved by the congregation of our church in Andalusia and how they look to you for leadership. Your life and influence are a benediction in that community, and I am sure that only eternity will reveal the real extent of the influence that you and Mrs. Dugger have exerted for good. I trust that our heavenly Father's blessing may abide upon you both in the fullest measure as you come to the evening time of life and that he will bless and use you both abundantly in His service through many years to come.

Sincerely, your friend,
J. McDowell Richards[12]

While more evidence is available in correspondence in the 1930s and 1940s, there are numerous instances in all four decades of Richards' presidency of appeals from ministers for counsel, assistance, and wisdom in a wide variety of situations. As the telephone and face-to-face conferences grew in number and in effectiveness in pastoral care, the loss of written material is a

definite handicap in evaluating Richards' pastoral care in the last twenty years
of his presidency. Those who know Richards' ministry patterns best would
agree, however, that his pattern of counseling remained the same. He was
usually direct, but supportive.

It was not unusual to receive a phone call, a letter, or a request for an
appointment that was more a cry of pain and anguish than a specific appeal:

> The conditions here are about to get the best of me. I have tried to do every-
> thing in my power to be happy and contented here, but have been dissatisfied
> for the whole two years and four months. We do not have any real close friends,
> and I don't think that it is altogether our fault, for never before have either of us
> found it to be difficult to have at least a few close friends.[13]

How did Richards deal with such a situation? Probably much more was
needed than could be given by mail. However, he responded at length with
consoling words, suggestions that the minister be patient and prayerful, and an
offer to help him find another call in due time.

Sometimes this worked, and sometimes it did not. A pastor's wife argued
quite defensively in confronting criticism from the congregation. She admitted
she had a temper, but was trying to control it. Furthermore, she was staying
home with the children more and was not going to the movies. These seemed
to be serious issues with the members of the church. She, moreover, appealed
for help and especially with calls to North Carolina churches. Investigation
revealed the other side of the situation. The minister did not pay his debts and
he, too, had a rather explosive temper. Evidently, nothing resolved the problems and her husband "divested the office of ministry without censure" using
the provisions of the *Book of Church Order* of that time.

A very promising young minister was called to two small rural churches
fairly near a large university where he hoped to do graduate work. After an
exhaustive and insightful three-page analysis of both the town and country
around it, he expressed a feeling of being overwhelmed by the Baptists. The
heart of his evaluation of the problem was found in these words:

> The Baptists work the area intensely, and the First Baptist Church is like a large
> city Presbyterian Church. I am sorry I have written so much, but I am now far
> away from the Seminary and don't get to see you and ask your advice and
> discuss problems. This letter takes the place of a conversation. I really did enjoy
> getting to see you at Montreat and hope I will get to see you there again.[14]

The response was one of compassion for "God's suffering servant," but
diverted attention from the situation with suggestions that he pursue graduate

work part time at the nearby university in the Ph.D. program. The minister did this with success, and went on to happier and more fruitful days as a pastor in strong churches.

It was not unusual for Richards to revise his appraisal of a developing crisis after receiving new information about it. Initially, he sternly challenged a minister who accepted a call after serving three small churches for only a year. During that time the minister spent significant amounts of time using a fellowship to do graduate work at Columbia Seminary. At the first mention of the minister's accepting another call, the Commission on the Minister and His Work in the Presbytery charged him with dishonesty.

After reviewing all of the facts, however, Richards reconsidered his position after thoroughly analyzing the details of the situation. He ultimately supported the minister's position, and urged the commission to reconsider the problems there. There was no manse available. The congregations only wanted preaching on three out of four Sundays. One of them had a disturbed member who was a major problem. A woman in one of the churches felt that she should have weekly visits from the pastor, and wept when she heard anyone else had been visited.

The problems of pastors and congregations were neither few nor simple. Even in the best of circumstances, there was sometimes at least one church member who was an implacable adversary of the minister. John Haddon Leith, class of 1943, had a distinguished and productive period of ministry throughout his life. As a pastor in Auburn, Alabama, and as professor of theology at Union Theological Seminary in Richmond, Virginia, he was a gifted preacher, pastor, scholar, teacher, and administrator.

While pursuing graduate work in Nashville, Tennessee, Leith served a church near the Vanderbilt University campus. After completing a master's degree, he earned a Ph.D. at Yale University. In one of the first exchange of letters with Richards, August 2, 1943, he wrote of receiving a "splendid library" from an older minister. He was almost ecstatic about the gift:

This relieves one of my fears. I have always been afraid that I might not be able to accumulate an adequate library to preach during the first years of my work. I think I have a better library than the average preacher now. I have been given a typewriter which is practically new and a number of other valuable things. I have also done better financially than I ever hoped. Providence has been so good to me during the past year or so that I am almost afraid of the future. Everything has been ideal for me here except "your friend." However, even the fact that he is here is good experience. I feel certain that I shall never have to deal with an elder more skillful in the art of being "a pain in the neck" than he is. I don't think such incantations occur very often.[15]

Frequent consultations by mail and in person continued until a most unfortunate rupture of their friendship occurred when Richards postponed a recommendation to the Board of Directors that Leith be appointed professor of theology. The conservative leaders in the Southeast opposed this appointment because he was too liberal. The evidence showed, however, that Leith was then and is now strongly committed to Reformed Theology. Apparently, Richards' strong appeals for racial justice in the Church had disturbed his critics. At a time when the synods in the southeastern United States controlled Columbia Seminary as members of the Board of Directors, Richards was bombarded with letters and phone calls opposing the appointment. He wrote Leith that he would postpone the recommendation to the board for a year or two, in order to deal with these criticisms. Leith was almost immediately offered a position at Union Theological Seminary in Richmond, Virginia, and went on there to have a distinguished career as teacher, author, and church leader. Leith was especially gifted in preparing students for the Church's ministry.[16] Ultimately, a healthy degree of reconciliation was developed between Richards and Leith.

Another pastor, facing a serious problem with the Church's session, sent a frantic plea for support and guidance in these anguished words:

> One elder is largely the source of the trouble, for he has influence over certain officers and church members. He attempted to do an underhanded thing, and has lost most all the confidence that was placed in him . . . So God's deliverance has come. It was at the cost of suffering to me and the rest of the Church family, but I rejoice as I understand more fully the meaning of that passage of scripture, "I beheld Satan as lightning fall from heaven."

He goes on to cite another verse, "I had fainted, unless I had believed to see the goodness of the Lord in the land of the living."[17]

Richards responded immediately with positive and celebrative words:

> I can understand what real joy and hope this must bring you. It is often difficult for us to understand these things at the time, but it is good that we can always rely on a higher wisdom than our own and that we can so often see in time the way in which that wisdom has directed our lives.[18]

In keeping with all kinds of letters in all kinds of situations, this one ends with a word about a "good opening of the seminary on Thursday with a fine new class enrolled, and I am hoping that one of the finest years in the seminary's history lies before us."

Richards' approach to ministers seeking a change of pastorates varied only in small details. Whether seeking a first call, or a move after many years in a single church, pastors received affirmation and encouragement from Richards. For instance, a minister who served only three years in a pastorate contacted Richards for help. The urgency to find a new pastorate was both apparent and frantic. The pastor wrote:

> In this particular community, I feel like I'm wasting my time. . . . It is not wise here to try to become too progressive. It is not welcomed, and it's miserable to have to choke and crucify one's ideals and hopes. Frankly, I can't recall being in such a state of mind. Willing, and, I believe, equipped to do some things, but not permitted to do so is my situation. Respectable sinners are very difficult to help and that is my situation here.[19]

Richards' response was immediate. He offered both "interest and sympathy" and agreed that it would be helpful to move. He promised to assist in opening doors for him.

In later years of the 1960s, Richards recognized that sometimes the problems moved with the pastor. Richards' approach in the last decade of his presidency became more realistic but still helpful. Understanding a continuing difficulty, he would arrange for graduate study at Columbia or another institution. This type of "sabbatical" was a renewing, clarifying and healing experience for many.

The emphasis on continuing education as a means of renewal has grown steadily during the last three decades. Unfortunately, funds for advanced study were not available until that decade. When they were, wounded ministers experienced a renewal of both mind and body. For example, one pastor was given an additional $250 per month by his presbytery to experience the seminary and its life and work for several months. Richards wrote: "Because of the tension in his church and community over the racial situation, he is really here to recuperate rather than study for an advanced degree." Richards helped him find a new pastorate after his educational program was completed.

At times, Richards' pastoral care was like throwing a life preserver to a drowning man. Frank Alfred Mathes was pastor of a number of strong churches throughout the Southeast. He wrote often to Richards, in poignant and painful expressions of discouragement and disappointment. Letters arrived from him in the spring of 1969, while he served as the pastor of the Independent Presbyterian Church of Savannah, Georgia. "Independent" and "Presbyterian" are words that contradict each other in the categories of Church identity and government. Originally started by the Church of Scotland missionaries, its ministers for a number of years were members of Savannah Presbytery and contributions were sent to it. The congregation, however, felt independent.

Mathes became quite depressed and frustrated over the growing atmosphere of either benign neglect or actual hostility in the attitude of the congregation toward the Presbytery of Savannah. It was even more indifferent toward the Synod of Georgia and the General Assembly boards and agencies of the Presbyterian Church, U.S.

He wrote:

> There are great problems here. Independent Presbyterian Church maintains an attitude of total indifference toward the Presbyterian Church, US. The core of the officers is a hotbed of fundamentalism and is very unpresbyterian.

> The situation does not improve with time, and after five years of hard work, agonizing prayer, and much patient and painstaking pastoral care, I am convinced that I am not the leader for this church. There are some good Christian people here and they have been good to me personally. So, you see what we have been up against. Thanks to you from the bottom of my heart for your concern and counsel.[20]

Even when Richards was within two years of retirement, his pattern of conscientious care of graduates continued. He did not retire from a pastoral concern for graduates. For example, a graduate was deeply frustrated and indeed wallowed in despair after seeking medical aid for an inner ear problem. Surgery at Duke Medical Center was of no help. Richards approved and encouraged a plan for him to take courses in pastoral care and supervision with Professor Thomas H. McDill, and to consider working as a hospital chaplain. Unfortunately, the graduate did not have the necessary grade average required for graduate school. Richards remained concerned and interested, but there was no evidence that he could do more than offer prayer and sympathy.

The continuing stream of letters from Richards to graduates was most effective during the time when there were few alternatives. Counseling centers for ministers were rare. The pastoral counselor, Ruell Howe, developed two-week seminars in Michigan. In response to the appeals from all sides, presbyteries formed counseling centers for ministers and other church leaders and provided resources in staff and money to help troubled participants. It was the only counsel some ministers received. For example, in a small mining town in Virginia, a pastor wrote in response to a letter: "Your recent letter was much consolation. I get disheartened sometimes. I need someone like you to talk with about the situation. I am not bad with people. Further, most of them would want me to stay. I just feel I could do more in another field using what I learned here."[21]

Another minister went through the call process in a small presbytery to serve as pastor of a strong town church. The presbytery's committee approved him for that position. Before the congregation could meet to ratify the call, conservative members of the presbytery called a number of key leaders in that congregation and labeled the candidate "a liberal." They charged him with voting to retain the denominational membership in the National Council of Churches. Indeed, they researched every vote he had made and reported a number of them to these critics. He wrote Richards a letter full of anger and pain: "I feel stabbed in the back. I am a man without a country. What am I to do? I must be a failure in the ministry."[22]

With compassion and eloquence, Richards urged him to remain in the ministry because he had real promise in that calling. He reached out to him as a brother in the faith, and assured him that he would do all in his power to help him find another call. Most importantly, he suggested several places where a recommendation would be sent immediately with a full explanation of the injustices the minister had suffered.

However, there was growing evidence that some ministers needed extensive therapy for various forms of mental illness. Symptoms included severe depression, paranoia, and an inability to relate to people. However, conclusions about these types of illnesses can only be matters of conjecture when the only data we have are letters. It was a field which was new and different to a person with a classical college and theological education. The fact that Richards' influence was the determining factor in the appointment of Thomas H. McDill as professor of pastoral care and counseling is significant evidence, however, that he was increasingly concerned. He concluded that students and pastors should have some understanding of the human condition—mind, body, and spirit.

For example, a brilliant student with a university degree from a prestigious institution functioned well at Columbia Seminary as a student. He received a fellowship grant for further graduate study. As he deteriorated emotionally, with frequent outbursts of anger and occasional withdrawal from basic responsibilities, his parishioners became greatly alarmed. Richards expressed his own feeling of frustration. He commiserated with a pastor with whom this student served in an assistant pastor's position. All involved were troubled that the problem did not go away, but grew slowly and surely to a critical point. Richards wrote:

Frankly, I am baffled by this situation. Mr. ——— was a better preacher and more promising minister as a first year student than when he graduated. Now he has failed . . . Try to be an understanding friend, and find out why he lost confidence and has withdrawn into a shell, so that it is now very hard for him to mix with people and to preach effectively. If you can help him regain his confidence and his effectiveness you will have done a great thing for him and for our church as well. Please keep me advised.[23]

He, tragically, never found his way to health and did not continue in the ordained ministry.

It did not come easily, but based on his experience over many years, Richards came to agree with the psychologist, William E. Crane, that psychological testing and counseling should be given to every student entering the ministry of the Church. Crane wrote: "No student is adequately prepared to deal with the problems of men and women as a pastor until he gains understanding of himself."[24]

One pastor, while serving a small town church in the South communicated frequently with Richards, as did many graduates in their first pastorates. While describing in rather vivid ways the problems of a small church, he complained, with good cause, of the way one or two persons could make life miserable for a pastor:

> With the exception of four united sisters, two married, and two desiring to be, we have no serious obstacles in the church. These individuals I refer to as the BIG FOUR are constantly on my neck about certain programs of the church. For example, they oppose enlarging the Sunday School as it will be harder to win a Presbytery banner for per capita offerings. Such matters look small to an outsider, but in a small town where everyone has some relationship, it is a big problem. Especially when the preacher is trying to reach a group of cotton mill people they care to have nothing to do with. O well, we all have our problems and these stumbling blocks make us keenly aware that we cannot fulfill our calling in our own strength.[25]

Difficult and complex pastoral needs were occasionally found in faculty and administrators. Richards faced various forms of mental and emotional illness in a half dozen troubled persons during his tenure. The treatment for these serious problems was not very well developed in the first two decades of Richards' presidency.

A colleague wrote about a friend who was:

> ... going through a spiritual crisis. He has been battered for several months and is no doubt having quite a struggle. From all I am able to learn he has had a Christian experience and enjoys a living relationship to Christ. I should not deny that his experiences have been somewhat narrow as related to some people here, but not so in his surroundings elsewhere. The frame of his religious life according to some of his associates has been that of conforming to a set of standards quite negative, approaching social asceticism. On the other hand, through

his family (paternally) there has appeared the other extreme from time to time. Then through the church, summer conferences and college he has had a sane and wholesome Christian environment. This is the background as I see it.[26]

Richards responded with assurances that he was in touch with him. He felt that, "he is too fine and promising a young fellow for us to lose and I certainly hope that he will be able to find inner peace and assurance in the early future."[27]

The records do not detail any direct approach from Richards, however, but evidently there was help, for the "young fellow" went on to serve as a Presbyterian minister with effectiveness and distinction as pastor of several very strong churches. Whenever depression returned, the treatment for such problems was steadily improving.

In another graduate's illness, Richards felt helpless to offer any constructive counsel. The minister was in and out of hospitals and ultimately demitted the ministry. Nonetheless, Richards was sincerely grieved over such a situation. He wrote: "I trust you will continue to gain strength steadily, and that you will soon be restored to health and strength. I am sure you will have a real opportunity to witness to Christ while you are in the sanitarium. I shall join with you in the prayer that you may have the strength to exert a strong Christian influence while you are there."[28]

Encouragement was a part of the Richards' approach. H. G. Wardlaw of Conway, South Carolina, responded quickly to such an approach. He wrote:

> I want to express my deep appreciation to you for sending Mr ———'s letter on to me and also say that I am grateful for the things you had to say about our work. As much as I appreciate these things, I am humbled by them. I am beginning to learn that the grace of encouragement is one of the greatest forces for good within the grasp of mortal men. As I think back over Seminary days I realize that you have known and practiced this fine Christian art often when it was needed most in someone's life.[29]

In the experience of ministers, some felt great frustration when there was no forward movement by the congregation in difficult situations. For example, a restless minister felt that, after a year, he had exhausted the potential in the neighborhood, and thus in the church. The building was hidden away on a side street where few people ever passed. The minister's restlessness increased when he was unable to persuade them to move from "the back street to the crossroads." Richards was sympathetic, especially since it came in 1945, when the post-war period was moving ahead with great promise for growth. However, he counseled patience, for it was just too early to give up yet.[30]

Richards was not always supportive in the ways he dealt with ministers. He never abandoned anyone who sought his help, but in situations where the minister was divorced, he would recommend that minister only if there were "biblical grounds for the divorce." That, to him, meant unfaithfulness on the part of the spouse from whom he was divorced. A minister, a chaplain in World War II, asked for recommendations to churches. Richards' response was consistent with his views:

> In the light of the unfortunate history of your marriage, my personal opinion is that you would be advised to stay permanently in education work. Divorce unfortunately stands in the way of usefulness in the pastorate except in rare instances.[31]

This advice was given in spite of the fact that the spouse absconded with the considerable amount of money that the chaplain sent her while overseas. He intended to use the funds for their needs in the post-war world.

At times, Richards listened, but apparently was unable to offer any simple solution to a minister's problems. Letters, however, continued to appear in the president's office from around the world, and especially from the supporting synods. A member of a presbytery staff, Rose B. Smith, had studied at Columbia in courses preparing to be a "church worker." In an eight-page letter, she described her work and her feeling of loneliness. Thus, when she asked for current information about Columbia's curriculum possibilities, the information went out immediately. Richards was kind and responsive to her and to her situation. This exchange took place in the winter of 1949, a time when the climate where she worked in the Appalachian Mountains was cruelly harsh. However, there is no record that she returned for further study.

At times, all Richards could offer was an assurance of support in the situation and a warm welcome when pastors visited the campus. A pastor wrote with grief and anguish of his efforts to reconcile with his estranged wife. He went to the city hundreds of miles away where she and their children lived. She not only rejected any program leading to reconciliation, but also refused to see him: "Save your money, I have no interest whatever in you. I am living a new life. Your children hate you as much as I do." Richards evidently helped the minister in a significant way with wise counsel and pastoral support. One of Richards' letters was three pages long.[32]

As could be expected, there were ministers who simply refused any semblance of appropriate counseling. It was considered either a stigma to do so, or a lack of faith, or even a mental illness which would "destroy my ministry." Such a point of view also resulted in living a charade under the delusion that the fault was with others. An alumnus reported to Richards that he must get another call as soon as possible. He described a luncheon with three ministers who helped him see his mistakes in his overzealous attacks on members of his congregation. "Should I stay or seek another call?" he asked. Richards was in the second decade of his presidency, and followed his practice of encouraging a minister to find another place of ministry. He was cautious and wise enough, however, to say, "Don't repeat your mistakes."

As often was the case, more than a change of location was needed in this instance. The minister soon moved to a new work and, quickly dissatisfied, applied for overseas mission service. He was dismissed to the Methodist Church not long after that in a failed effort to solve the problems. A move that carries the problems along like baggage is doomed to a repetition of them.

While Richards responded in some way to every appeal for counsel or advice, some graduates developed a very close relationship with him that was almost like a father-son experience. W. Frank Harrington was one of those who regularly sought advice and wisdom for the experiences of the pastorate. Whether at First Presbyterian Church in Hinesville, Georgia, North Augusta Presbyterian Church in North Augusta, South Carolina, or the Peachtree Presbyterian Church in Atlanta, Harrington sought and received counsel and pastoral care throughout his ministerial career. These three churches differed in settings, size, and culture. In Hinesville, Harrington faced the pressures of the 1950s and 1960s, when racial problems and vigorous political pressure from the local John Birch Society formed a formidable context for ministry. An example from this period was the accusation from members of that group that the Presbyterian Church (U.S.) was high on their list of Communist sympathizers. Harrington was sustained by correspondence and conversation with Richards in a time of great turmoil. On March 17, 1964, Harrington wrote:

> Our Communist battlers are rather stirred up again, and are convinced that our Church (i.e. Presbyterian Church, US) is tolerant if not downright "pink." I covet your prayers for patience and understanding as I seek to minister to their spiritual needs.[33]

Frequently, ministers in those critical days remembered Richards' sermon, "Brothers in Black." Preached in 1940, it courageously called for Christian treatment for African-Americans. Based on the biblical text in Genesis 3:9, Richards asked, "Where is thy brother, the Negro?" He was one of the first ministers in the nation who, in 1940, showed concern and compassion for African-Americans. They believed that Richards understood their problems and would help to resolve them. Also important, he strengthened the courage and the witness of other pastors of that period by affirming their witness. Better still, these pressured persons believed he would come to their rescue, as he did on numerous occasions. Even more importantly, whites and blacks knew they had someone to talk with who would support them with concern and counsel.

Harrington spoke for numerous Presbyterian ministers, most, but not all, of whom were graduates of Columbia Seminary when he wrote: "For about two years I was under intense pressure, and you and Dr. P. D. Miller walked beside me and you served as a tower of strength during that time."[34]

All too often, the only answer was to help move ministers who were under fire for conscience's sake in the Southeast. Richards made that a priority for his immediate assistance. Moving was not the final solution, but it saved the ministry of some very useful pastors. Some presbyteries financed graduate study at Columbia for a quarter or for a year.[35] It was usually a healing time and a renewing of perspective and commitment.

A different challenge pastors faced was in the community at large. An unusual example was that of the position of Prince Edward County, Virginia, and the Farmville Presbyterian Church. J. Hoge Smith Jr. described the situation he faced as the pastor there in crystal clear images:

> The public schools are closed. Only a white Academy remains. In Brazil, I worked with and worshipped with a racially mixed community of Christians. I was happy to do so. But now, here, what am I to do? Would my resignation from a comfortable, good life, at the cost of income, be a good protest producing action? I remember your "Brothers in Black" Sermon in 1940.[36]

In response, Richards offered genuine sympathy and concern. He wished he had a "clearer word from the Lord" to speak in reply:

> I do not think you are selling your integrity for a comfortable life as a minister of the Gospel. Everywhere, we find Christians with blind spots on issues such as this. However, much can be done in pastoral relationships. You cannot be silent. If another call comes, perhaps you can accept it. Perhaps, a prophetic but loving word of farewell would be appropriate. I am not sure a gesture of resignation now would have any real effect, though I would admire you for it.[37]

The issue of racial justice had many twists and turns. The simple act of seeking to relate to black groups in Nashville, Tennessee, drew "fire." George D. Carter reported that the area nearby was steadily becoming black. Among other things, he began a coffee house sponsored by the church and, although it drew primarily white high school students, it came under great criticism. The local newspaper reported that drugs had been found there. Though never substantiated, the report produced a withholding of eight thousand dollars in pledges at the time of the annual stewardship effort. Carter said: "I have taken some knocks from trying to be innovative in reaching people. The methods we have used are strongly criticized. I need to move."[38]

Richards was cautiously approving, but wondered about some of the aspects of the activities at the coffee house. Was the program there fully controlled? He, as usual, was willing to help Carter find a new church.

One other variation in this area of pastoral care of troubled ministers was a report from Savannah, Georgia. J. Walton Stewart was pastor of the only church in Savannah Presbytery in May 1965, that voted to accept the action of the General Assembly of the Presbyterian Church (U.S.) to seat anyone who came to worship. African-American visitors were specifically included in this action. Stewart reported, however, being somewhat irritated by the way groups came twenty minutes late when the service was well under way. They always sat in the front seats. He referred to this as a "grand entrance," and thought they were missing a great opportunity to be a part of that worshiping congregation.

Richards suggested that he ask the leaders not only to come on time, but to remain and visit with the congregation. Most of all, Richards commended Stewart and First Presbyterian Church, Savannah. Furthermore, he urged them to continue their policy patiently.

There is no doubt, however, that much of Richards' pastoral care was for those with difficult congregations. He never ignored the problems of the pastors involved, and he freely gave his wisdom and support to those who lived in constant tension and discouragement. One desperate appeal began:

> Frankly, it is time for me to move. The counsel I received that I stay away from this church was a bit late in arriving, but I think it is well said. One minister told me, "there are no big issues in that church, just little people." They seem terribly immature and naïve to me as Christians, Presbyterians, and even people. . . . Meanwhile my tendency to want to tell people off wells up stronger and my impatience both to do what is to be done, and also with those who will not do, tries its best to boil over from time to time. . . . It is hard for a man to know his own heart, but I think it is time for me to move.[39]

With only an exchange of letters, it is impossible to tell if a move to another responsibility was the solution. It, however, is the kind of situation—all too common—that led Richards to support the courses in pastoral care and counseling. They began at Columbia Seminary in 1951, taught by certified pastoral counselors with extensive training.

This is not to imply that his pastoral care and counseling was given only to those in great difficulty. There were important moments of care when a minister sought advice on career decisions, and also when there were marriages, births, and other causes for celebration. Ph.D. degree awards were noted and applauded. The birth of a baby was an occasion for prayerful good wishes.

Richards also supported with encouragement and praise those pastors who thrived in difficult situations. One such minister was Laurence Beaver Robinson, pastor of Central Presbyterian Church in the inner city of Newark, New Jersey. Robinson's report on his life and work there left Richards tremendously encouraged and almost ecstatic as he read over his report. Robinson went to Central Presbyterian Church when it was declining in membership, the buildings and neighborhood were in disrepair, and the racial makeup of the area was becoming Hispanic and African-American.

> In spite of the challenges, much has been accomplished. 80% of my congregation are African American, 10% Puerto Ricans, and the others a variety of backgrounds. However, attendance is up 50%, repairs have been made to the manse and the church.

Robinson went on to compare his previous pastorate in Honea Path, South Carolina, with the one in New Jersey as going from hell to heaven. His explanation no doubt induced Richards' chuckle. Robinson played with words because the Shell Station next door to the church in Honea Path had lost the "S," and became the "hell station." A famous African-American minister, Father Divine, was located nearby in New Jersey. Father Divine called his church a heaven. So, Robinson did go from hell to heaven![40]

The situation at Central Presbyterian clearly turned around in the years of Robinson's pastorate, 1956–65. Richards warmly commended Robinson and quickly spread the news to faculty and students.

As the international dimension of seminary life grew, so did Richards' relationship with students from overseas. Nam Chin Cha, a professor in a theological seminary related to one of the Presbyterian churches in Korea, spoke for many when he wrote:

> I cannot forget my sweet hours in our dear school, Columbia Theological Seminary. Often I have you and my Columbia Theological Seminary, our dear school, in prayer.

> There are in Korea today painful divisions among Presbyterians in Korea. . . . Personally, I want to heal these groups, for it is too bad to have gaps in Christ's body.[41]

Richards' response was full of affirmation and gratitude. Richards commended Nam Chin Cha's work as a student at Columbia Seminary, rejoiceed in his service as a seminary professor, and encouraged his efforts to heal the divisions:

Today, it is distressing that there should be so much division and strife among the servants of Christ. I am glad that your own influence is on the side of unity and good will, and I hope very much that your efforts in this respect will meet with good success.[42]

Distressingly, there were signs that many ministers felt the loneliness of pastorates in the cities and in the towns where they served. Indeed, it was at times, though certainly not always, a smothering blanket of hopelessness and frustration. They expressed these feelings to Richards, who like a trusted friend and mentor, would be that "someone to talk to."

Alton Glasure, a minister in a large congregation, expressed this sense of the value of such pastoral care in these words: "I appreciate, more than I can tell you, your willingness to counsel with me at lunch, yesterday. The preacher, who counsels so often with others, also needs a counselor. You have always been most helpful."[43]

On occasion, as we have seen, he could be frank and direct in his analysis of individuals and situations. A minister seeking to move to a new pastorate was visited by several committees from churches seeking a pastor. None of them responded positively to the sermon. He wrote quite frankly to the minister to encourage him to improve in the content and delivery of these sermons. A very defensive response came back after several weeks delay. The minister wrote:

I have seen no more committees nor have I heard anything since your letter . . .

That sermon must have been worse than the committee suggested to you. Really, I still think it was pretty good. Probably, one big trouble with it is that it did have only two points rather than the orthodox three. In spite of my satisfaction with my past productions I suspect that my congregation has seen somewhat more of the skeletons of the beasts, or assembled dinosaur bones covered with transparent flesh or perhaps the better word is mouse. At any rate, the committee does not know how much it has missed in the way of obvious sermon outlines in the last four or five weeks.

I appreciate your good words about me and your confidential information to me. When there is a nibble by some committee, I am for a while fairly plagued with unrest, not so much I think from a desire to move as from curiosity. Of course, there are times when I do want to move but, then, there are actually times when I do not. But I am always filled with anxiety.[44]

In the middle years of Richards' presidency from 1945 to 1965, the Presbyterian Church (U.S.) sent men and women in large numbers to overseas mission work in Korea, Japan, Taiwan, Mexico, Brazil, and the Congo. Because of the presentations in the World Missions, courses at Columbia, and the expansion of personnel overseas in the Presbyterian Church (U.S.), Columbia provided a substantial number of missionaries. During the fifteen years of post–World War II history, approximately half of all the evangelistic missionaries appointed by the Presbyterian Church (U.S.) were graduates of this institution.

What is more, the lay missionaries provided a superb variety of gifts. They included indispensable persons such as physicians, educators, and administrators. Most received a year's valuable training at Columbia Seminary. The Board of World Missions gave their strong endorsement to this part of the required preparation before they went abroad. Mission Haven, the facility and program begun on the Columbia Seminary campus, grew to seventeen apartments and homes for those on furlough. Mission Haven continues today in its service to a wide range of missionaries and ministers. Its comprehensive group of services program is provided by a splendid staff of volunteers. Mrs. Joseph E. Patrick of Decatur, Georgia, has led the program for many years.

As a member of the Board of World Missions of the denomination, and as chair of the Candidates Committee, Richards made a significant contribution to this period of overseas ministries. He was especially grateful for Columbia graduates serving overseas. His opportunities in the leadership of the Church in the United States and the world, further inspired him to urge assistance to developing nations, and the churches in them. These Christians, moreover, showed a magnificent devotion to their own churches. With rare exceptions, they welcomed assistance from overseas in creating educational institutions, hospitals, and much needed facilities for local congregations.

Equally important was the thoughtful and continuing correspondence with overseas personnel throughout the year. Beyond special events such as the birth of a baby or a return to "the Field," Richards wrote just to be sure they knew they were remembered with prayers and commendation. To Dr. and Mrs. James R. Boyce, in Frac, Ixta, Mexico, he sent assurances of interest, prayerful support, and his pride in them. In addition to much news from Columbia, he concluded:

> Trusting that you will be divinely led and blessed in all of your service for Christ in Mexico, and with warm regards and every good wish for each member of your household, I am

Sincerely, your friend,
J. McDowell Richards[45]

Similarly, to Mr. and Mrs. Ira Moore, Richards sent news of the seminary's life. He expressed his delight in the addition of J. Holmes Smith, class of 1943, to the large Columbia contingency in the Congo mission staff. He added with great appreciation that Smith's mother, Mrs. J. Holmes Smith Sr., would assume duties at Columbia Seminary as matron of the refectory. A steady stream of reports and personal newsletters from them matched the Richards' letters to those overseas. James R. Boyce wrote: "On a recent vacation, we enjoyed being with another missionary family. They have a little boy just two months younger than our Jimmy. One or the other of us has to continually untangle them from their many fights every day. The saving element is that children don't hold grudges."[46] Dr. Boyce also reported on the significant plans for a seminary in Mexico that would draw from all of Latin America as the medical school there did.

Twenty years later, Richards sent a long and thoughtful letter of condolence to Robert N. Montgomery in Kualien, Taiwan, on the death of his father. You can imagine the warm response from Montgomery as he read:

> Your father was a great and good man, and I count it one of the real privileges of my life to have known him. Only eternity will reveal the real significance of his labors as a minister, and as a missionary of the Gospel. Our Church will always be indebted to him and to your mother for the work which they have done. We are also deeply grateful for their unfailing loyalty to Columbia Theological Seminary, and it was a joy to have contact with him as with your mother on many occasions in recent years. We cannot mourn for your father since we know that he has entered into a greater fullness of life and joy in the presence of the Lord whom he loved and served so well. . . . At the same time the experience of separation from those whom we love can never be easy and I know that there has been much sadness for each member of your family in your father's death.[47]

After eight years of pastorates, in three small churches in South Carolina and Georgia, Malcolm and Sally Bullock began a ministry overseas in Taipei, Taiwan. In their second year of service, a letter from Richards brought this significant response: "It is such an encouragement, to hear that our ministry here is being supported by your prayers and loving concern."[48]

The Board of World Missions, in view of the emphasis at Columbia Seminary on service overseas, strongly recommended its program to candidates for missionary service. In addition to the program leading to ordination, a one-year course for laypersons was also suggested to educational and medical personnel. The curriculum for that year contained work in Bible, mission, and church history.

Richards taught regularly in these courses and formed a pastoral relationship with the appointees. Thus, he could serve pastorally from the basis of a personal relationship with many of them. The facilities at Mission Haven, the furlough apartments and homes on campus, and the seminary educational program were an important part of the entire relationship from the beginning to the present day. Often they wrote as soon as they arrived to serve a new overseas term, asking for a reservation for one of the apartments or homes at Mission Haven four years hence.

While the Montreat Conference Center was a most important part of missionary life in the summer school attended by appointees, the educational program at Columbia provided opportunities for serious study leading to a master of theology degree in some useful biblical or mission area. The furlough year in the United States after a full term overseas made this possible. Actually, the furlough year was so fully utilized in both continuing education and in preaching and teaching throughout the Church, that it was a most demanding time for missionaries. Thus, the churches and educational institutions of the Atlanta area were also important elements in the total picture.

Even today, when many "short term" overseas assignments are made rather than a lifetime appointment, the seminary and Mission Haven have much to offer the residents there and are constantly utilized.

Perhaps this section of a Christmas letter of December 1, 1955, will represent best the pastoral concern and care of Richards for missionaries:

> I am writing this note in the hope that it will reach you before Christmas Day to bring a message of remembrance and good wishes from the Columbia Seminary family. We are deeply interested in your life and work and are grateful for the fact that Columbia Seminary can claim some small share at least in the work which you are doing. Hence, at this season particularly we want you to know that you are not forgotten by us and we take this opportunity to wish for you not only a truly joyous Christmas season but a new year filled under the blessing of God with all that is good. Each member of the staff would wish to be remembered to you. . . . Also, we are glad to report that the missionary interest continues to be high on the campus and that we are increasingly going to be well represented on the foreign mission fields. Three seniors are volunteers.[49]

While many letters in return spoke of much satisfaction in overseas service, it was not unusual for a missionary family to decide to end that chapter in their lives. In reply to a 1948 Christmas letter, Walter Swetnam wrote that he was coming home. He explained his decision in these words:

I have resolved to seek work in the United States at this time partly on account of the education of my children and partly because I feel that I am getting into a rut and need a change. I am 48 years old, and if I should return for another term, I would be too old to get any other work at all. Perhaps I am now, but I hope not. . . . I am uncertain whether to go back into pastoral work, or go on teaching. We will need a call providing $3000 per year, plus a manse. Perhaps, a church near a college where our oldest daughter could commute would be ideal. I daresay that by this time your senior class has grabbed off everything desirable but there might be something that would appear about the time of the spring meeting of Presbyteries.[50]

Dr. Swetnam served churches in Amite, Louisiana, and Citronelle, Alabama, from 1949 to retirement.

Richards' era launched the beginning of the service of pastoral counselors and chaplains in hospitals and institutions. However, a concern for authentic pastoral care by ministers may well have begun, though in a rudimentary way, with the military chaplains in World War II and, to some extent, the Korean and Vietnam Wars. Though the largest number of chaplains were appointed in World War II, each of these conflicts saw significant service on the part of Columbia graduates.

Seventy ministers from the Presbyterian Church (U.S.) were called to duty as chaplains in World War II. A few may have been called up from the Reserve Officer Corps, but all were transferred to the Chaplains Corps. One of the best known and most highly decorated was Eugene L. Daniel, chaplain with the United States Army in the North Africa campaigns. During a fierce attack by a German armored division, Chaplain Daniel was captured with four wounded American and German soldiers. In a letter to Mrs. Eugene L. Daniel, the commanding officer, Lt. Col. Robert R. Moore, wrote from North Africa, April 6, 1943:

Chaplain Daniel's capture happened this way. We had four wounded men with us, all stretcher cases, three Germans and one American. We had carried them five miles when we started to receive machine gun fire. Gene told the Stretcher Bearers and the attending Medics to go ahead to safety and he would remain with the wounded. The Medics were to tell me that he would see me. It was the greatest thing a man could do. I only wish I were half the man Gene was. His advice to myself and men was most timely and the comfort he gave to the men was far beyond words. His loss to this Battalion is one of the hardest things we have had to overcome. He taught us all to pray and our prayers that night, or rather mine, were to get all the boys out and for strength and guidance. I have no fear for Gene for I feel he is safe and may God bless him and comfort you folks. Sincerely, Robert R. Moore, Lt. Col. 168th Infantry, (North Africa).

(Mailed, April 10, 1943 after passing the Censor, and received by Mrs. Daniel, April 24, 1943)[51]

Chaplain Daniel's experience as a prisoner of war is described in his book, *In the Presence of Mine Enemies.* In correspondence and in face-to-face conversations, a detailed account from Daniel provides a significant record of his thoughts and feelings during this time. With heartfelt admiration, Richards added his own record of that time in the foreword to Daniel's vivid account of that part of the war. Daniel's book is a unique and valuable record of events and experiences following his capture in North Africa and his subsequent ministries in two prisoner of war camps in Germany. He might have made it to his unit safely, but the medical corpsman refused to stay with the wounded German prisoners, saying he had joined the U.S. Army to serve sick and wounded American soldiers. Daniel felt, as a matter of conscience, however, that if at all possible, someone should remain. Thus, he waited with the wounded Germans until daylight and managed to surrender to the German panzer unit that had broken through and captured a large part of the area. He wrote from his stalag: "My main concern was to find a way to deliver them to the German Panzer Unit without getting killed."

In a splendid, realistic account of his experience, *In the Presence of Mine Enemies*, Daniel described the moment of capture:

I took a white towel and waved it in the direction of some German troops I saw in the distance. Then, the wounded German soldier put his arm around my shoulder and I put my arm around his waist and we proceeded to walk slowly over the desert toward the highway and the German troops. After we had walked about a mile we were seen by a German motorcycle patrolman who came speeding toward us. The motorcycle was equipped with a sidecar and had a small machine gun mounted on the handlebars. When the rider came within about a hundred yards of us he dismounted, drew his automatic pistol and walked toward us. The wounded German with me called to him and evidently told him I was unarmed, so he put his pistol back in its holster and came on toward us. As he was coming, the wounded man spoke to me in broken English, "I want to say something." So I said, "All right." He repeated this sentence several times, and I said, "all right." Finally, he said very deliberatively and clearly, "Americans are very gentlemanly." Later, the wounded soldier left behind was also rescued by the Germans.[52]

Daniel's ministry in two prison camps was as significant as that of any chaplain in World War II. Those imprisoned with him lavishly praised his dedicated and insightful concern for them. On March 9, 1945, Richards' letter to Daniel showed his respect for Daniel's devoted service. He wrote:

> Your fine letter of January 18, 1945, from prison camp reached me yesterday and I cannot tell you how much it was appreciated. I was glad to know that my two letters had reached you on January 8, and was delighted to have the news you gave of yourself. I am glad indeed to know that you are well and hope that you continue to have large opportunities for work among the men with whom you are associated.[53]

Richards went on to express appreciation also for suggestions concerning the life and work at Columbia in the post-war period. Letters from chaplains and other persons in military service were read at chapel to faculty and students. They created extensive discussions in faculty meetings and led to significant curriculum revisions. Among the most strongly supported additions were pastoral courses in preaching, counseling, and administration. Chaplain Daniel's suggestions for the post-war curriculum at Columbia Seminary were in the dual realms of Reformed Theology and social action.

As was his pattern in pastoral care for all chaplains, Richards focused on those overseas. Personally, twenty-four letters from him came to me while serving on the island of Guam in the Pacific for nineteen months. Again and again, he wrote of the seminary's prayerful support of graduates scattered across all the war zones. As usual, he included news of the institution and of the church at home. Since my wife, Katherine Wright Philips, studied at Columbia for a nine-month term,[54] he included a word or two about talking with her. I value to this day the lengthy reports and the assurances of prayerful concern from Richards during those unique and challenging times. Particularly, his simple message of congratulations and prayerful good wishes when we were married in the midst of World War II on September 15, 1943, meant much to us.

All World War II chaplains received advice and counsel on post-war plans for continuing education and recommendations of them to churches seeking pastors. All were asked for suggestions concerning the curriculum and faculty at Columbia Seminary. Some six-page responses were received in response to the request. As a result, the post-war curriculum was developed at Columbia on the basis of specific pleas from chaplains for courses in counseling, preaching, and administrative work to supplement the traditional areas of theology and Bible.

To supplement this picture of pastoral care, it should be noted that Richards kept up a friendship by correspondence with friends around the world. Particularly, he exchanged long letters with friends he met as fellow students during his Rhodes Scholar days in Oxford University. To Charles B. Arbuthnot Jr. of the staff of the World Council of Churches in Geneva, a tongue-in-cheek style emerged in a letter reporting on a mutual friend:

> You may be surprised to know that our mutual friend, P. D. Miller, has accepted the call of the Druid Hills Presbyterian Church in Atlanta, and he will move from San Antonio, Texas to this city about Jan. 2. After all his boasts about the wonders of Texas and his Church in San Antonio, one would never suppose that so humble a state as Georgia would be able to attract him. Doubtless he would say, however, that it was purely a sense of duty and that he feels called to missionary work in this area.[55]

Throughout his presidency, Richards was an effective counselor and pastor with a personal interest in every person related to Columbia Theological Seminary.

CHAPTER FIVE

Presbyter

O F ALL OF THE VARIED ROLES IN THE LIFE AND WORK OF J. McDowell Richards, perhaps the most distinctive was that of presbyter. A vast amount of responsibility and activity in the Church and in the world utilized his gifts of ability and wisdom. Few Presbyterian ministers throughout our history as a Church have given such long and effective periods of consistent leadership over four decades. He regarded these duties in the governing bodies and agencies of the Church as a blending of obligation and privilege. The attendance at meetings all over the world, both routine and historic, and especially in the Presbyterian Church (U.S.), was an exhausting reflection of a Calvinistic sense of duty and privilege. Three pages of single-spaced type list Richards' memberships in the boards, agencies, and committees of the General Assembly, synods, and presbyteries. This is an impressive group of ecclesiastical agencies, both local and international, reflecting significant causes to which he devoted travel, time, and vision. As the four decades of his presidency picture it, the pace escalated like that of a speeding train leaving the station.

"Presbyter," in the usage of the word over twenty centuries, means more than a literal concept of an "elder" as a person in an older age bracket. Beyond that, a presbyter is a person who leads, teaches, guides, and governs in the life of the Presbyterian Church. For Richards, as a Presbyterian minister, "presbyter" became a many-splendored word. It included participation in the Presbytery of Atlanta, the Synod of the Southeast, the General Assembly of the Presbyterian Church (U.S.), and the reunited Church in the PCUSA. It also involved a large variety of national, international, and regional ecumenical groups. Among them were the Federal Council of Churches and its successor, the National Council of Churches, the World Council of Churches, the Presbyterian World Alliance, and the Christian Council of Atlanta. Other local committees included those seeking greater justice for minorities, particularly African-Americans. A few causes were quite different, such as one that sought strict observance of Sunday as the Sabbath Day.

For thirty-nine years of service as president of Columbia Seminary and even in the first few years of retirement, Richards maintained a frenetic pace of travel, meetings, lectures, and preaching. He saw all of them as a part of a cluster of obligations as a presbyter. While the word literally means "elder," it was used in the Presbyterian Church to designate a minister or a layperson who attended meetings of the governing bodies of the denomination. Even during the first decade of his presidency and the struggle for the continuing existence of Columbia Theological Seminary, Richards was a faithful participant in the Presbytery of Atlanta and the Synod of Georgia. He was twice moderator of Atlanta Presbytery and the moderator of the first meeting of the Synod of the Southeast that included Georgia, Florida, and South Carolina. In 1955, in the aftermath of many conflicts in the post–World War II Church, Richards was chosen as moderator of the General Assembly of the Presbyterian Church (U.S.), the highest office in the denomination. All the time, however, he provided devoted supervision and productive leadership for Columbia Seminary. The result was a surge of growth in student enrollment and important additions to the faculty. At the same time, he led an impressive program of expansion of the campus and its facilities. He was faithful to his ordination vows which included a strong commitment of time, vision, and leadership to the total life and work of the denomination. All the roles of his ministry—preacher, pastor, president, and prophet—came together in Richards' brilliant leadership in the Church and the world as a presbyter. We shall look at this role in some detail in both basic ecclesiastical leadership and in relationships with leaders of the Church.

In Richards' final report to the Synod of Georgia, Presbyterian Church (U.S.), on March 12, 1971, his stance as president of Columbia Theological Seminary reflects a mutually dependent relationship with the Church. It was quite clear that Columbia Seminary's status was one of "ownership and control" by the synods, as the Plan of Government at that time expressed it. It was quite clear, also, that the ecclesiastical frame of reference for Columbia's life and work was found in the churches, presbyteries, synods, and General Assembly of the Presbyterian Church, U.S. From the beginning of this institution in Lexington, Georgia, in 1828, with Thomas Goulding instructing five young students in the manse of the Presbyterian Church, to this day, the mission of educating ministers is the basic reason for Columbia's being. Though the synods no longer make direct contributions to Columbia Theological Seminary from their mission budgets, they do schedule important special campaigns in order to raise endowment, scholarships, and building funds from Presbyterians in these synods. The members of the seminary board, once called directors, are now trustees. The number of ruling elders on the board has increased significantly, and ministers are chosen from other synods. Throughout Richards' presidency, only the supporting synods with ownership and control elected trustees. Columbia Seminary's president was inevitably, as a Presbyterian minister, a presbyter with responsibilities, activities, and commitments. If neglected and avoided, an enormous cost to integrity and faithfulness resulted. Thus, boards and agencies, institutions and their leaders looked to Richards for wisdom, direction, and support. Among the groups he served as trustee or member were Davidson College, Board of World Missions, Board of Church Extension, General Assembly Council, and the Federal Council of Churches.

Beyond surface appearances, the astonishing fact of the matter was that Richards went far beyond expected attendance and observance of Presbyterian polity and theology. He not only faithfully attended meetings of presbytery, synod, and the General Assembly, he responded to an astonishing array of requests to lead and guide committees and boards. He was elected to the highest offices of the denomination, presiding with fairness and effectiveness. Whether moderator or committee member, he was faithful to the tasks, and diligent in the responsibilities assigned him. Elected president and professor of practical theology at Columbia Theological Seminary in 1932, he did not withdraw to the confines of the campus, but served the whole Church. He gave years of service to General Assembly committees, institutions, and ecumenical groups. Among these were:

1. General Assembly's Committee on Social and Moral Welfare (1935–49).[1]
2. Delegate to the World Alliance of Reformed Churches, Toronto, Canada (1937).
3. One of the founders of the University Center in Georgia, a consortium including Agnes Scott College, Emory University, the Atlanta Art Association, and Columbia Theological Seminary (1939).
4. Moderator, Atlanta Presbytery, Presbyterian Church, U.S. (1940). He chose the topic, "Brothers in Black," an eloquent appeal calling for racial justice, as the moderator's sermon. The sermon was circulated around the world.
5. Member, the Editorial Council which instituted the publication of *Theology Today* (1944).
6. Represented the Presbyterian Church (U.S.) on the Executive Committee Federal Council of Churches of Christ in America; vice president, (1942–44).

7. Elected to Board of Cooperators, Presbyterian Ministers Fund, Philadelphia; president, Presbyterian Education Educational Association of the South (1947).
8. Chairman, Executive Committee on Negro Work, Presbyterian Church (U.S.) (1947–49).
9. Delegate to the World Alliance of Reformed Churches, Geneva, Switzerland; moderator, Synod of Georgia, Presbyterian Church, U.S.
10. A participant in the establishment of the Protestant Radio Center and a trustee (1949).
11. President, Atlanta Christian Council (1950–51).
12. Member, Constituting Convention of the National Council of Churches (1950).
13. Representative of the Presbyterian Church (U.S.) on the General Board of the National Council of Churches (1950–51).
14. Member, Board of Church Extension, Presbyterian Church (U.S.) (1950–56); chairman, (1953–56).
15. Moderator, General Assembly, Presbyterian Church (U.S.) (1955–56).
16. Member, Board of World Missions, Presbyterian Church, U.S.; chairman, Committee on Candidates (1960–66).
17. President, Georgia Council on Human Relations (1959–60).
18. Leader in planning and organizing the Atlanta Theological Association, a cluster including Candler School of Theology, the Interdenominational Theological Center, Erskine Theological Seminary, and Columbia Theological Seminary (1966–71).[2]

It is quite clear that Richards took the responsibilities of a presbyter very seriously in representing the church in denominational and ecumenical agencies.

What is even more significant, however, is Richards' response to the policies and recommendations of presbytery, synod, and the General Assembly. He was an active participant in those meetings, and felt a serious responsibility to implement the basic positions of these groups in matters of mission, program, and social policy.

In what way could Richards be called conservative and in what way could he be called liberal? Labels, like misspelled words, are really as meaningless at times as the word Democrat. He was both. He reflected the theology of the Church as found in the *Westminster Confession of Faith* and its polity and government in the *Book of Order*. These important documents were revised somewhat in his lifetime, but he was correctly identified and rightly known as a Presbyterian and a presbyter of the Presbyterian Church, U.S.A. In both theology and ethics, he faithfully practiced these standards. In addition, he was Presbyterian in worship and in practice. Thus, he was a rather unusual

Presbyterian, conservative in theology but "liberal" as the word was used at that time, in views on race, justice, and ecumenism.

Richards' sermons and addresses offer insight into the ways in which he participated as a presbyter. They do not follow a cookie-cutter pattern, but rather range from brief statements to complete sermons and articles. Selections from a few of Richards' important addresses to presbyteries and synods provide a consistent pattern of carefully prepared, well-written efforts.

Sermons

As early as the late 1930s, Richards led the governing bodies of the Presbyterian Church to heed the call for racial justice. A flow of correspondence on this theme often challenged his positions, but some did support him with tremendous appreciation for his witness. Thus, whether by phone or by mail, a variety of views and convictions were expressed. Outrage at worst, and calm rebuke at best, came from those who disagreed that segregation must end and justice must begin.

"Brothers in Black" is Richards' best-known sermon on any topic. As moderator of Atlanta Presbytery, Richards chose this title for his final moderator's sermon on October 14, 1940. More than fifty thousand copies were distributed around the world. It deserves special recognition as an example of his leadership as moderator. A fuller discussion of this sermon is found in chapter six, "Prophet."

It is from consistency, not coincidence, that Richards' sermon, "Brothers in Black" and its eloquent appeal for justice for African-Americans, was based on the persuasive teaching of Scripture. The Bible was used to support the total mission of the Church and to invite response to Richards' preaching and writing. The context of Christian responsibility was apparent. As a Presbyterian, he served major Presbyterian causes including world mission, church extension, education in the churches and institutions, and the governing bodies of the whole Church. As a presbyter, however, his leadership was on the front lines of the efforts to effect growth and change. For a number of reasons, we turn first to his unique role in racial justice as a unique part of service as a presbyter.

In other sermons delivered to the Church's governing bodies, Richards spoke and wrote with compelling eloquence of Scripture passages which he believed pointed a way out of the crisis in society. One, the letter of Paul to Philemon, was brief but relevant. Onesimus, a slave, fled with money stolen from Philemon. Through the ministry of Paul, Onesimus became a Christian and was ready to return to Philemon, confess his guilt, and plead for forgiveness. "I appeal to you," wrote Paul, "on the basis of love for my child, Onesimus." Paul comes to the point with a passionate urgency, "Receive him no longer as a slave, but more than a slave, a beloved brother!"

This influential sermon was circulated throughout the South and beyond. Many a graduate and preacher were sustained by Richards' strength and commitment in a very tough time for the Church. African-American Christians rejoiced in his preaching and writing on these themes.

Thus, Richards reflected his role as a presbyter in his support and implementation of positions of the Presbyterian Church, U.S. It was not enough to attend governing body meetings, serve on demanding boards and committees, and participate in decisions. He took the role of a prophet with courage and conviction. It was as essential to that of a presbyter as breathing is to life.

The Christian Church in a World at War

The Presbyterian Church in the United States in 1934 took what was then a highly controversial step in establishing a committee on social and moral problems. As the United States prepared for World War II, this committee asked Richards to prepare a paper on this theme, "The Christian Church in a World at War." It was adopted by the General Assembly at its meeting in 1942. The essential appeal in the paper was to remember that there were Christians on all sides of the conflict, that all humans were made in the image of God, and God in Christ loves all. One of the more important projects in a long list of duties was The Commission to Study the Basis of a Just and Durable Peace. Under the leadership of the great statesman, John Foster Dulles, the Federal Council of the Churches of Christ in America asked five members of the council to prepare a plan for the Church's witness in a post-war world. Walter W. Van Kirk described the effort in a letter to Richards:

> Mr. Dulles and I feel that the time has come to mobilize public opinion in support of the Guiding Principles approved at Cleveland. Could you meet with Mr. Dulles at the National Arts Club, Friday, January 22, 1943 to discuss this matter with him? I am asking you and five other members of the Executive Committee to meet with us. Mr. Dulles and I feel that before proceeding with this matter it would be advisable to counsel with a few of the members of the Executive Committee.[3]

The attachment included a proposed position of the Federal Council on the problem of the future world order in the post–World War II period. The statement listed political principles that must be implemented by any just and durable peace. They were:

1. The peace must reflect justice, not vengeance, toward our defeated enemies.

2. The peace must provide the political framework for a continuing collaboration of the United Nations, and, in due course, of neutral and enemy nations.

3. The peace must make provision for bringing under international supervision and regulation those economic and financial acts of nations that have widespread international repercussions.

4. The peace must make provision for an organization empowered to adapt the treaty structure of the world to changing underlying conditions.

5. The peace must consecrate the goal of autonomy for all subject people who desire it, and it must establish an international body to assure and to supervise a realization of that goal.

6. The terms of peace must establish procedure for mobilizing preponderant moral, economic and military power against any individual or group that would defy the lawful decisions of the new organizations contemplated hereby.

7. The peace must incorporate a universal bill of rights to religious and intellectual liberty by the individual.[4]

The application of these very general principles resulted in detailed ideals and plans for a United Nations organization. Richards joined in the general concept and sought much more detailed programs in implementing them. Of course, there have been enormous tensions and wars since World War II in many parts of the world, but at least a voice calling for peace among the nations was heard.

Ecumenics

As the years moved on, responsibilities and tasks as a Presbyterian minister increased for Richards through membership on boards and committees and, most significantly, in ecumenical agencies. He was a trusted and respected leader in groups as diverse as the National Council of Churches and the Committee on Sabbath Observance. A pattern of full participation in Presbyterian committees and boards began early in his presidency.

As a presbyter, Richards accepted numerous assignments in the ecumenical relationships of the PCUS. He defended participation in these activities and programs by detailing their work in programs of evangelism, religious liberty, war and post-war service, and the spiritual bases of peace. These activities dealt with the mission and ministry of Protestant churches. They included a witness in cities, on college campuses, and with military forces. Christian education through the churches was a significant part of the witness of congregations and presbyteries. Overseas, a crucial issue was religious liberty for Protestants in countries dominated by the Roman Catholic Church. Peace issues in the post–World War II culture, and their spiritual basis, resulted in overseas aid for churches. The two most influential Presbyterian ecumenical leaders from the South were John M. Alexander and J. McDowell Richards.

A point of tension for Richards and Alexander was the tendency of Federal Council staff members to appear at congressional hearings of pending legislation and speak without authority or action by the Council Executive Committee. They urged representatives of the council staff to use officially approved documents in their testimony before Congress.

Of all the activity as a presbyter, Richards' membership in ecumenical councils created more criticism and tension than any other. Through articles and editorials in publications such as Carl McIntire's *Christian Beacon* and the *Southern Presbyterian Journal*, many Presbyterians came to believe that the Federal Council of Churches was anti-business and was extremely liberal in its programs and proclamations. Presbyterian laymen who were officers of various companies and law firms began to send strong letters of criticism to Richards objecting to positions taken. L. E. Faulkner, general manager of the Mississippi Central Railroad, was one of the most widely read critics. Faulkner circulated material to Presbyterian business and professional laymen regularly. In reply to good friends among Presbyterian elders who sent him critical materials, Richards responded as a loyal presbyter and yet with sensitivity and understanding.

One of his close friends and loyal supporters, Lamar Westcott of Dalton, Georgia, reported to him that materials were coming to him and all the elders of his church concerning the Presbyterian Church and its involvement in the Federal Council of Churches. Mr. Westcott's plea was outlined in a hope that "Christians could get a better understanding of each other's positions." On January 14, 1947, Richards responded in a carefully worded two-page document. He wrote:

> Your letter of January 7 with enclosures has been received and I wish to thank you sincerely for it. I am greatly interested in the matters about which you have written, and I appreciate the spirit in which you have set them forth. I agree with you most heartily in your statement that you wish there could be a better understanding and a more sympathetic attitude between our church people and that we should endeavor to work in harmony instead of at cross purposes. I do not know anything more tragic than for Christian people to spend their time and energy in fighting one another when the forces of evil in this world are so strong and we are continually challenged to stand together for righteousness in the name of Christ.[5]

Richards presented the case for support of the Federal Council of Churches in a rationale that is reflected in several comments such as these: The largest item in its budget was for evangelism. It was the only organization calling Christians to unite in facing the needs of the world. The Catholic Church was strong through its unity, and Protestants could be also. What was significant, Richards believed, was that John Foster Dulles, a leading Republican, was a committed board member of the Federal Council of Churches and brought leaders together to work for peace in the post–World War II world.

A part of Richards' response focused on the values of the free enterprise economic system in the United States. Though imperfect, he still felt it was better than any other system throughout the world. An elder commissioner, Ewing S. Humphrey, contracting engineer of the Virginia Bridge Company attended the General Assembly meeting in May, 1948. He was so impressed by Richards' report to that governing body detailing the work of the Federal Council of Churches that he wrote:

> It is hard for me to find words to adequately express my congratulations to you for your wonderful talk to the General Assembly[6] Monday afternoon. It assured me that the truth you gave them had a lot to do with the final vote on our church's continuing membership in it. . . .
>
> I am truly grateful for you and your leadership, not only on the Federal Council but at Columbia Seminary and in all the activities of our Church. The debates I heard at this Assembly made me more conscious of how much we need you, and men like you, in keeping our church from going off at a tangent. I want you to know that I am most grateful. I truly thank our Heavenly Father for you and I am so proud to call you my friend.
>
> Very Sincerely,
> Ewing Humphries[7]

Two important educational consortia were the University Center in Georgia and the Atlanta Theological Association. The University Center in Georgia began with Agnes Scott College, Emory University, Georgia Institute of Technology, the University of Georgia, the Atlanta Art Association, and Columbia Theological Seminary. The Atlanta Theological Association was formed with the Candler School of Theology, the Interdenominational Theological Center, Erskine Theological Seminary, and Columbia Theological Seminary.

It is quite clear that Richards' membership in important boards and councils was never casual or perfunctory. Attendance at these meetings was a matter of great importance to him and to the other members of boards and agencies. In a family letter, September 23, 1955, Richards described a fairly typical schedule at that period of his presidency:

> I believe that when I last wrote home, I was on the eve of going to New Orleans, Louisiana, for the Services in the Carrollton Presbyterian Church of that city on September 11. Following my return from New Orleans, I spent two days in the mountains of North Georgia with the members of our faculty on our annual faculty retreat. We had a very pleasant and also helpful and stimulating time talking about the work of our school year. On Saturday evening, I went to Laurinburg, North Carolina, where I preached on Sunday morning in connection with the twenty-fifth anniversary of Dr. S. H. Fulton as Pastor of that congregation. I got home again on Monday morning and left that night for Orlando, Florida where I attended the meeting of the Synod of Florida on Tuesday and until early afternoon yesterday. I then flew home in time to be present for the reception in honor of our entering class, and I am to deliver the address at the opening exercises in our Chapel this evening. I am to preach next Sunday at the morning service of the Presbyterian Church at St. Simons Island, Georgia.[8]

A clear witness in times of controversy and even in schism was Richards' first priority. In such times, letters, phone calls, conferences, and meetings were opportunities for developing thoughtful analyses and wise positions. Above all, he stressed the centrality of teaching of Jesus of Nazareth for the mission of the Church in every age.

The history of all four decades of Richards' presidency and the years of retirement included records of high-level consultations and carefully worded recommendations. One example is a resolution Richards wrote for a group of representative leaders in 1947. As soon as World War II ended, debates and arguments began. As a presbyter, he was genuinely distressed by the divisiveness being formed in various groups. Eighteen ministers and elders representing various points of view signed this appeal for consideration of others in church debates, and active support of the Presbyterian Church (U.S.) in a campaign for the agencies and institutions during that post-war period. In that effort, called the "Program of Progress," the Church was urged to do a positive thing and renew mission for the denomination. The resolution was as follows:

> We, the undersigned, representative ministers and laymen of the Southern Presbyterian Church,[9] having been called together by the Moderator of the General Assembly to consider the serious crisis which confronts the church because of sharp differences which have arisen in connection with the discussion of the questions of church union and the relation of the church to the

Federal Council, after full and prayerful consideration, have reached the following conclusions:

1. We are profoundly concerned that the wide differences of viewpoint which exist among us shall not lead to ill will and bitterness, or to disruption of our church's work in the vitally important fields of Evangelism, Christian Education, and Missions.

2. We pledge ourselves, so far as in us lies, to conduct our debate on these issues in a spirit of fairness, of mutual esteem, and of brotherly love, recognizing our own lack of wisdom and realizing that in spite of our differences we are united by our common love for our Lord Jesus Christ and a common loyalty to His Church. We would earnestly call upon all church courts and other groups which debate these matters to see that their discussions are pitched upon the highest possible plane and are kept free from personalities and from bitterness.

3. We urge that the full support of our Church be given to the Presbyterian Program of Progress and that the controversies in which we are presently engaged be not allowed to divert our attention from a movement which holds such tremendous possibilities for good in the advancement of our Lord's work.

4. We covenant with one another to pray for each other and for our beloved church, asking that the matters before us may be settled in the spirit of Christ and in accordance with the will of our Heavenly Father. We call upon all others of like mind to join with us in this prayer.

Signed: R. W. Cousar, J. R. McCain, G. T. Gillespie, John Alexander, Daniel Iverson, J. McDowell Richards, R. A. Lapsley Jr., T. K. Young, J. P. McCallie, William V. Gardner, Charles G. McClure, E. T. Thompson, John R. Richardson, Charles E. Kraemer, Aubrey N. Brown, Henry B. Dendy, W. T. McElroy, and John R. Cunningham.

Richards also led the Board of World Missions in an intense analysis of its role:

The primary purpose of the Board of World Missions is that of being an instrument of the Church in the fulfillment of its Christ-given mission to proclaim the Gospel of the Lord Jesus Christ to the ends of the earth through preaching, teaching, healing, and every means of God's appointments.[10]

Richards continued with extensive analyses of the Church's achievements in mission overseas, the relationships established with other churches abroad, and the effective work of other church agencies such as church extension, women's work, and Christian education. He felt very strongly that the need for interpreting the responsibilities of the Board of World Missions to the entire Church should have renewed emphasis. Richards' focus on the congregations' obligation for intercession, service, and stewardship was evidence that no board representing the entire Church could provide all that was needed.

Unique among these recommendations was an emphasis on evangelism by the Church in the United States using the resources of the world church. This effort, also, would provide a way for Christian lay persons from the United States who are living and working overseas to share their abundance for the physical needs of the people around the world.

The most impressive quality of Richards' service as a presbyter was his sense of responsibility. When his nine-year term of service on the Board of World Missions of the Presbyterian Church (U.S.) ended, the Administrative Council of that board praised Richards in an unusually specific way:

> As your nine years of service on the Board of World Missions draws to a close, the Administrative Council desires to express its appreciation for the leadership you have provided. Your faithfulness is shown in the record of attendance. What the record does not show is the deep commitment, wisdom and understanding your attendance has always provided. Your preparation and study before each Board Meeting has given testimony to your commitment as a member and as chairman of the Candidates Committee. Your wisdom has passed a strenuous test. Your participation in the discussions of the Board has given ample evidence of your understanding. We are grateful for the way you have shared your life and leadership with us.[11]

Schism

The life of a presbyter as Richards knew it was lived in a continuing context of varied pressures and controversies. In the thirty-nine years at Columbia Theological Seminary, and years of service in the Church before and after that period, as the saying goes, "If it wasn't one thing, it was another." The most painful of all for Richards was the continuing threat of schism in the denomination. *A Pastoral Communication on the Issues before the Church* expressed his conviction that schism was contrary to the will of God and detrimental to the health and mission of the Church. As the first moderator of the newly formed Synod of the Southeast, he wrote to the churches of Georgia, South Carolina, and Florida, enclosing this pastoral communication. He began with an analysis of the state of the Church:

These are difficult days in the Presbyterian Church, US. Charge and counter-charges are being made. Suspicion, distrust, and sometimes bitterness have been aroused. A goodly number of congregations have voted to withdraw from the denomination and plans are being made for the organization of a new Church. Other congregations are being urged to withdraw. Are such steps wise, necessary and justified? In the belief that they are not, the writer of this paper, without criticizing those who hold a different view, seeks to discuss some of the issues which led to the present situation, and to plead for understanding, love, and unity among brethren.[12] We may differ on many points, but the things on which we are agreed in the face of an unbelieving and often hostile world are immeasurably more important. Above all we are united by a common faith in and loyalty to Jesus Christ as Lord and Savior. This is the central fact which we must never forget.

The act of separating from a parent denomination is of an exceedingly serious nature and not lightly to be undertaken. Such action should come only as a last resort and if a church has clearly and irrevocably departed from the Christian Faith. The Presbyterian Church, US, imperfect though it be, has not so departed.[13]

In 1964, Richards developed a call to the Church to turn away from divisiveness and move on in mission. It was widely circulated. As moderator of the Presbyterian Church (U.S.), he asked a small group of leaders to develop an appeal to the whole Church to end conflict and create a new unity of faith and mission. In essence, it appealed on the basis of "two fundamental facts:"

1. First, our Church is, by the grace of God, a part of the Body of Christ. . . . We belong to Him. Because we belong to Him, we belong to each other. Because we belong to Him, we also belong to other members and other parts of the Body.
2. The second fundamental fact is that we are a Presbyterian Church. Our congregations and church courts form one organic whole. Every member, every congregation, every presbytery shares in our representative government and participates in decisions reached through the Presbyterian system. Such official positions are not binding on the individual conscience. They allow for dissent, which is under girded by love for the unity and program and order of our whole Church and by trust in each other and the Presbyterian system.[14]

The appeal to the Church to move beyond divisiveness was passionate and persuasive. Tragically, it was not enough to avoid the separation of two groups in the denomination.

In the life of the Presbyterian Church (U.S.) during the remainder of Richards' life, there was a mixture of growth and decline in membership and in mission. Since the reunion of the two major bodies of the Presbyterian Church, the US and the UPUSA, there has been a small decrease annually in the number of members. That factor has caused endless analysis and discussion. The irony in the situation is that polls indicate there are twice as many persons listing Presbyterian as their religion as can be found in any Presbyterian church of any kind in the United States. Now, well into the twenty-first century, the threat of further schism and separation continues, but even more serious is the number of Presbyterians who are inactive in the categories of attendance and membership. While there was an increase in interest in worship following the catastrophe at the World Trade Center in 2001, it has since declined.

Theological issues also remained with constant pressure for resolution in a divided Church. At the height of theological tension during the last years of his presidency, Richards sought to deal helpfully with critical questions raised by the constituency. Paramount among these was the doctrine of the inspiration of Scripture. In a very important address to the Board of Directors and the faculty on November 11, 1968, he presented an eleven-page lecture entitled "Columbia Theological Seminary—Its Present and Future."

The fear of schism in the Church was fully justified in Richards' analysis. In a relatively brief summation of the crisis in the Presbyterian Church (U.S.) as he saw it at that time, he said, with sadness:

> Conditions existing in our church are not good. In fact, it would appear that there is real danger of the disintegration of our denomination if present tendencies continue. This is not my opinion alone, but seemed also to be that of the Presidents of our other Seminaries.[15]

Thus, Richards began by describing the possibility of a damaging breakup of the Church in which he was nurtured and in which he had served with devotion and hope. The first possibility for that to occur was dependent upon the issue of church property. Did the local congregation have total ownership or control, or did the denomination have a vested interest in it? The interpretation in the official documents of the denomination provided ownership and control for the local congregation, but the church could not be moved to a new location or into another denomination without the approval of the presbytery.

A prospective ruling by the Supreme Court on the issue of ownership was of great significance. Two churches in Savannah, Georgia, won an appeal to the Supreme Court of Georgia that they had a right to withdraw from the denomination and take their property with them. In Richards' view, this would encourage a significant number of churches to leave. He was relieved when the United States Supreme Court overruled that action. It is possible to withdraw with property only if a presbytery allows and approves that procedure. Few presbyteries appeared to be willing to do so.

Another possibility included in this scenario was the proposal for union synods and presbyteries. Should that take place, those opposing a new ecumenical status for the denomination would also resort to schism. Even a plan proposed for union with the Reformed Church of America, which allowed congregations the right to take title to their property, seemed unacceptable. Those who favored reunion with the UPUSA were fearful that union with the Reformed Church of America would threaten this effort to unite the two major Presbyterian bodies. While seeking to be positive and hopeful about it all, Richards said: "Insofar as the future of the church as a whole is concerned, I am an optimist because I am a Calvinist."[16]

Nevertheless, he sought to be realistic, and to face things as they were. Should a schism occur in the Church, Richards felt that Columbia Seminary would be affected more than any other in the denomination. It was located in the area of the Presbyterian Church (U.S.) that would be affected most. In the southeastern United States, the issue was most fervently debated, and the danger of division leading to schism was most likely. He wrote:

> If there is division in our church, it will most certainly affect our synods more than any others. That section of the denomination, which would be recognized as the legally continuing church, would presumably own Columbia Seminary. It is likely, however, that its constituency would be much smaller and that its financial support would be correspondingly decreased . . . In the years ahead, however there is a real possibility that we shall face a decline in the size of our student body, and a decrease in the financial resources available for its support.[17]

Kenneth Keyes, president of Concerned Presbyterians, published accusations against Columbia Seminary that fueled the schism. The first issue questioned the interpretation of Scripture. Richards' affirmation of Scripture was as follows:

> What do we mean by saying that the Bible is our only infallible rule of faith and practice? It simply means that, while we recognize the human element in Scripture, and are not afraid to subject these writings to the most searching examination, we believe that the Scriptures are God-inspired and that in all matters pertaining to what we are to believe and how we are to live they constitute our divinely given and authoritative guide. In other words, taken as a whole,

they are doctrinally infallible. We do not understand them as being given to teach us particulars of science or of history, but rather the way of eternal life. In the words of the Shorter Catechism they principally teach us "what man is to believe concerning God and what duty God requires of man."[18]

Richards said again and again:

There is not a member of the faculty of Columbia Theological Seminary who does not accept the full authority of Scripture. Each one of us in his ordination vow has declared that he believes the Scriptures of the Old and New Testaments to be the Word of God, the only infallible rule of faith and practice. Several years ago, when our faculty received an inquiry from Central Mississippi Presbytery, it replied unanimously by declaring afresh the faith to which we had given assent at the time of our ordination. These are not light words and they were not lightly used by any one of us.[19]

Richards conceded in such discussions that there is a difference in views between those who think the manuscripts are verbally inerrant and without a mistake or contradiction of any kind and those who do not. However, he acknowledged that there are errors in the Greek in some of the manuscripts. An example from the Book of Revelation is cited. In addition, the four Gospels have differing titles for Jesus on the Cross. Richards strongly argues that these slight differences do not change the truth implicit in them even though they are not identical.

Furthermore, Richards agreed that the original manuscripts may have been without error, but we do not have these documents. However, he believed the message of the Scripture presenting Jesus the Christ is, as a whole, clear and persuasive.

A second issue raised by Keyes claimed that students were taught to preach something called "ecclesiastical sociology." Richards replied that the definition of that term was not provided to him in correspondence, and thus he found it hard to respond to the accusation. He did believe, however, that the gospel had to do with all of life. Moreover, if that gospel was applied only to Christian concern for justice, righteousness, and mercy in social and political matters, and not in individual lives, then the charge was half right. He wrote:

There is but one message for the Christian minister. It is the message contained in Scripture that Jesus Christ is our Lord and Savior. There is no one on our faculty who is not committed to this truth and who does not teach it to our students.[20]

The third accusation was an amazing statement that Columbia Theological Seminary's faculty did not believe in God. Richards responded:

> This report is so absurd that I have taken a certain amount of satisfaction in it. No person who knows anything about the life of this institution could believe the statement to be true, and the very fact that it can be solemnly uttered is indication of the somewhat hysterical state of society and of our church at the present time. Even so, it is disturbing to reflect that there are individuals in our church who know very little about this institution on any first hand basis and who may be misled by just such wild reports as this one.[21]

Richards communicated with the supporting synods by forcefully challenging the accusation. He also wrote the author of the accusation, Kenneth Keyes, to share with him what Richards had said to the synods and would continue to say unless Keyes had valid evidence to support his charge. Many weeks went by before a reply came, and it was unsatisfactory to Richards since it neither retracted the charges nor offered evidence to support them. Richards concluded: "I am sure you will be able to judge for yourselves the reason no evidence has been produced. No valid evidence can be produced because the statement simply is not true."[22]

Richards also informed the board that the chairman, J. Davison Philips, had received a report from one of his elders of charges being made against Philips by a representative of Concerned Presbyterians: "When Dr. Philips leaves your Church you will not be allowed to call a pastor of your own choice."[23] This conclusion seems to contradict another made to this elder, that "Dr. Philips is one of the swingingest members of the Fellowship of Concern."[24]

The Fellowship of Concern was made up of hundreds of ministers of the Presbyterian Church (U.S.) committed to give financial and spiritual support to ministers driven from their pastorates by militant segregationist groups. After a few years it was expanded to serve a more comprehensive mission.

First known as "A Fellowship of Concern," its purpose was carefully worded and its membership formed by laypeople and ministers of the Presbyterian Church, U.S. It invited those who shared a desire to see the Presbyterian Church in the United States more relevantly related in program and service to the critical issues of the twentieth century to unite around a statement of purpose. The covenant was formed with five commitments:

1. To interpret the Reformed doctrine of the sovereignty of God in its authentic application to all of life.
2. To seek for our Church a more vital role in the struggle for social justice and the search for Christian unity.

3. To take appropriate action in local congregations and beyond to bear our witness in the face of contemporary issues.
4. To help the Church assert moral leadership in the changing patterns of racial and cultural revolution.
5. To support those who have been under extreme pressure because of their faithfulness to the Church's social witness.[25]

Richards was committed to these general goals, but wanted more. In addition to supporting those ministers in difficulty because of the Church's social witness, he urged a broader plan of action.

A most important effort toward the reunion of presbyteries in the PCUS and PCUSA arose when union synods and presbyteries were proposed. In geographical areas with significant numbers of churches in both denominations could be found, they merged as presbyteries and synods. Richards was skeptical about the implications of such a plan:

The possibility of suspicion, ill will, and open strife between Christians in local congregations as well as synods and Presbyteries should any of these eventualities some to pass is painfully real. I am not a pessimist, however, but a realistic optimist.

Columbia Theological Seminary is in the heart of that section of our church where the present agitation is at its maximum. There will always be a Columbia Theological Seminary in Atlanta, but its constituency would be smaller, and its support correspondingly decreased.[26]

That prediction has been partially fulfilled. The reunion of the two major Presbyterian denominations in the United States has lessened the sense of "ownership" of Columbia Theological Seminary by the Church in the southeastern United States. It has, however, enlarged the geographical areas from which it draws students.

In the tumult of argument, division, and factionalism growing in the Church in the 1960s, pastors and elders seeking information and wisdom often consulted Richards. The major tensions were related to issues of the reunion of the Presbyterian denominations, racial justice, ecumenical bodies such as the National Council of Churches, and the orthodoxy of the faculties of theological seminaries.

As the decades of Richards' presidency moved on through troubled waters, the pain of schism and separation grew day by day like the dripping of a leaky faucet. Paul Coblenz, a Presbyterian missionary in Brazil, wrote to the Covenant Fellowship of Presbyterians formed in the late 1960s, expressing his feeling of hopelessness about the Presbyterian Church (U.S.):

> I am driven to the conclusion, upon examining the state of our church, that the
> positions taken by the leaders of certain boards, the men of dedication in our
> church, the debasing of our primary goal as servants of Christ, and the blind-
> ness to some of the havoc which their strong opinions are causing, that your
> organization has arrived much too late to bring about any substantial change in
> the direction of this sad cleavage There is no middle of the road left. The polariza-
> tion has gone too far. Your engineering to build bridges within the denomination
> is great, but the chasm has become a grand canyon.[27]

Richards, in contrast, never gave up on the Church as it existed in every
decade of his adult life. He kept preaching, teaching, praying, and serving. As
difficult as it was, major issues were faced and decisions made.

Some of them were minor "housekeeping" matters, but were still very
important. Presbyteries and synods were reorganized and often had other
priorities than seminaries and colleges. All causes suffered to some degree
with the exception of children's homes and retirement facilities. The choice
was a slowly weakening relationship with governing bodies or independent
fund-raising. The decade of the 1960s was, in every way, the most challenging
and discouraging period of Richards' administration. He had always had a very
high view of the responsibility of Columbia Theological Seminary to these
governing bodies, and to the very end clung to the relationship as indispensable. The defection of churches that joined the Presbyterian Church in
America, and their constant criticism of the theological position of the seminary kept Richards on the defensive.

A close friend, G. H. Achenbach, advocated withholding funds for the
budgets of the governing bodies of the church. Richards countered that idea
by demonstrating that the innocent would be penalized, and worthwhile causes
such as overseas mission, food, medical care and clothing for the poor, homes
for children without a home, and the church's institutions would be damaged.
Ironically, this view was supported by all sides in the conflict within the
Church, but some wanted to choose and support only a few causes. During this
decade, it was very difficult to schedule a capital funds campaign for endowment and new buildings at Columbia Seminary. Governing bodies had their
own interests and priorities. Directors on the seminary board were dismissed
and replacements chosen with no consultation with the trustees nor with
Richards. Again and again, however, Richards presented the case for unity
rather than schism. He said, "I am deeply concerned for the welfare of our
Church and that there shall not be a real cleavage between the ministry and
laity of our denomination."

That sad cleavage in the region of Columbia Theological Seminary was often a cleavage in families. Richards' family was no exception. Reunions took on a new atmosphere of debate and disagreement by a few. One member of this generation commented, "that we must be of all people the most butt headed."

As early as 1955, Richards grew increasingly weary of carrying the main responsibility for defending the ecumenical movement and its organizations. To him, it was like swimming against a powerful tide. He declined an invitation from *Life* magazine to participate in a national symposium on racial issues. He was feeling the pressure of the seminary's constituency who disagreed in a significant way with him. He felt that others should take up the cause of racial justice. He did, however, take a public and forceful stance when the residential areas around Agnes Scott College and Columbia Theological Seminary began a transition in the mid-1960s from all white owners to an increasing number of blacks. Representatives of the two institutions helped greatly during those days of rapid change to unite the town and strengthen the public schools. He felt the public schools should be supported whole-heartedly. A major study of the entire area by the community planning consultant and landscape architect, Clyde D. Robbins, recommended that the two campuses ultimately be joined.

This has not been done and is highly unlikely to occur in the future. Actually, the city of Decatur has experienced a great influx of young families drawn by neighborhoods and the public schools. The public schools are approximately 50 percent white and 50 percent African-American and Asian. The area south of the seminary campus in DeKalb County is predominantly African-American. Richards affirmed the right of freedom of housing for citizens to buy property and to live in the community of their choosing. He concluded his report to the board by saying:

> Up to the present a few Negro families have purchased homes in close proximity to the seminary. It is our hope that these, and others who will follow them, will be welcomed by their white neighbors. If we can solve the challenge of integration here upon a Christian basis, we shall make a real contribution to the life of the nation and of the church, both south and north.[28]

Perhaps the most important aspect of Richards' experience as presbyter is that he was faithful to the end of his presidency, and indeed throughout his retirement. In his last year as president, he wrote J. G. S. S. Thomson of Edinburgh, Scotland,[29] a Christmas letter which included a description of seminary life in 1970:

> This has been a good year at Columbia Seminary. Our student enrollment is approximately 200 and the spirit of the group this year has been particularly

good. Conditions in our church as in the world are troubled and these young men are facing a much more complex situation than seminary students did even at the time you were here. It takes courage for a young person to enter the ministry in these days and we rejoice in the fact that there continue to be those who are ready to dedicate their lives to the service of Christ in the Parish ministry as well as in the mission field.[30]

Faithful in attendance at meetings, useful in serving on any committee or board when asked, devoted to Columbia Theological Seminary and to the Church around the world, Richards was an exceptional presbyter.

CHAPTER SIX

Prophet

*J*AMES MCDOWELL RICHARDS WAS A USEFUL PRESBYTERIAN
minister, a Rhodes Scholar, and, for most of his adult life, a theological
educator. A trusted and able leader in the committees and agencies of the
governing bodies of the Presbyterian Church (U.S.A.), Richards was one of a
small group of Presbyterian ministers elected as moderator of the General
Assembly of the Presbyterian Church, U.S. What is even more significant is
that although thoroughly committed to the Presbyterian system of doctrine
and polity, Richards was deeply involved in ecumenical groups and social
action issues. Ordinarily, this would appear to both conservative and liberal
observers, at best, unique, and at worst, inconsistent. This, however, is the way
he applied theology and polity to racial justice and ecumenical commitments.
All four relate to each other and were formative influences that reflected
President Richards' attitudes and actions as a Christian and as a Presbyterian.

Richards was a unique combination of Presbyterian statesman and world
Christian. An examination of his ministry as pastor, educator, and presbyter
has revealed a consistent and comprehensive practice of leadership in the
Church and in the world. We shall also look at examples of his prophetic
ministry in race relations and ecumenism, based on Presbyterian theology and
polity.

Racial Justice

As early as the late 1930s, Richards preached and wrote concerning relevant
issues of racial justice. The impetus for this conviction can be traced to the time
Richards spent at Oxford University. Europe and the Near East were in great
flux, and the changing world had a profound effect on Richards. The wave of
political change created ecclesiastical change as well. In this context, the

prophetic activity in both word and deed in Richards' life and work grew into a lifetime of commitment:

> His years at Oxford (1923–26) covered Hitler's "Beer Hall Putsch" in Munich, the death of Lenin and the rise of Stalin to power, and in the Near East the movement of hundreds of thousands of refugees across national orders, the first of those "displaced persons" in modern times.[1]

Indeed, while studying in Oxford, England, entries in Richards' diary in 1923 reflected an uneasy conscience. Had he chosen to be defensive, Richards could have responded to criticism of the United States in racial matters by pointing out British practices in the history of its colonial expansion in India and other countries. However, he wrote:

> Can our treatment of the Negro be in any way reconciled with Christianity? Perhaps so, but it is hard for me to see just how.[2]

A few days later, October 22, 1923, he responded to another student from England who asked about "Jim Crow" practices in the United States. When told that in some areas African-Americans were segregated by white authorities in separate railroad cars, his friend replied, "What horrid people!" The next morning the student apologized. Richards wrote: "But, after all, was he not right? What would Christ's attitude be toward the Negro?"[3]

Fifteen years later, on October 14, 1940, in his most widely publicized and circulated sermon, "Brothers in Black," Richards illumined, like a flash of lightening, the issue of racial justice. That sermon would have been influential at any time, but in 1940, it evoked vitriolic pronouncements by angry defenders of segregation. However, some in the Church felt that they heard the voice of a prophet in Richards' sermon declaring judgment on racism. As retiring moderator of Atlanta Presbytery,[4] October 14, 1940, he could have chosen any topic for his final sermon that he might think appropriate. He chose to address this issue in view of the scornful remarks concerning African-Americans spoken by the governor of Georgia, Eugene Talmage. Those hurtful words were widely published in local and national newspapers. Richards described those moments in a brief review of his days at Columbia Seminary:

> Race was one of the dominant questions facing the church during this period. No question has had more influence over the South or over the Church in the South. As a son of the Old South, I confess that my conscience in racial matters was slow in developing. Members of my family and I simply accepted segregation in the early years. Granted, we were opposed to injustice within it. But it did

not occur to us that we could get away from segregation. At one time, I thought that trying to abolish segregation would likely result in bloodshed, and in certain parts of the South it did. Yet we began to change and to see, step by step, the injustice of segregation itself.

One step came in the early 1940s when Gene Talmage, then Governor of Georgia, stated that the poorest white man was better than the best black. That stirred me up considerably and as retiring Moderator of Atlanta Presbytery, I preached a sermon on "Brothers in Black." Today, it seems a rather straightforward appeal for simple justice and the recognition of black men as our brothers, but at the time it aroused much excitement. The sermon was printed and distributed in a number of churches. In at least

J. McDowell Richards at age twenty-four while attending Oxford University in England.

one congregation an irate member gathered all the copies and burned them. Others reacted differently. An incident that happened to me as a result of this sermon told much about the times.[5]

This incident involved a most moving response from a black porter on a train Richards frequently used:

It was my custom to take the Pullman overnight on various trips for the Seminary. Shortly after I had preached this sermon, the black porter on the Pullman I was riding said to me, "I believe you are the gentleman who made that nice speech recently, aren't you?" I was at first perplexed but then realized that the *Atlanta Constitution* had given perhaps three paragraphs on a back page to an account of my remarks. Hence I said, "Yes, I suppose I am. How did you know that?" Well, he said, "I heard the people who brought you to the Pullman say, 'Goodbye, Dr. Richards.' When I went home, my mother had this article cut out of the paper and I said, 'I believe I know that gentleman. I think he rides on my car, sometime.'" Then he added, "Everything you said was true, but it seems like nobody will take our part," but he seemed to find tremendous encouragement in the fact that someone had at least spoken on the subject. My attitude would never be the same after that.[6]

As timely and relevant as anything said and done in that crisis, the response to Richards' appeal to hear the Word of God for this time and this issue was both immediate and public. Even the most racist spokesmen fumbled their opportunity to respond, as if to ignore it would silence it. They were mistaken. "Brothers in Black" and its powerful text, Genesis 3:8–16, was read, and its message heard around the world. Within weeks fifty thousand copies were distributed. Homileticians would say, with some reason, that the text, "Where is . . . thy brother," was lifted out of context, but that did not diminish its power. "Brothers in Black," unlike most sermons, was debated and discussed in newspapers, radio broadcasts, magazines, and pulpits.

"Where is thy brother who is black?" became the penetrating question in this sermon addressed to a meeting of ministers and elders of Atlanta Presbytery. Richards carefully reviewed the role of public officials as a "very special reason for us to ask that question here today." While acknowledging that he was limiting the application of the text to the racial issue, it seemed appropriate because of insulting and humiliating statements concerning African-Americans made in various public places and even in the Senate of the United States. For, said Richards:

> We cannot overestimate how much has been done to aggravate prejudices and to increase evils which were already sore enough. I am not undertaking to discuss politics here. I speak today because Christian principles and spiritual interests are at stake. These actions of political leaders are but the natural outcome of a racial philosophy, which, though contrary to all Christian principles, is all too commonly held by the man in the street and too little opposed by the man in the pew. The Church of Jesus Christ has not given the leadership which her Faith demands of her in making this kind of philosophy impossible.[7]

The relevant point, however, was eloquently stated in prophetic sermons and articles. African-Americans must be treated justly, respectfully, and fairly.

His most frequently cited Scriptural passages were the questions in Genesis: "Where art thou?" (3:9) and "Where is thy brother?" (4:9). The passages deal with the unjust treatment of Joseph by jealous brothers, but, in an imaginative way, are applied by Richards as a principle for all human relationships. The clear teachings of Jesus of the "servant" pattern for Christian life in the gospels, and later reflected in the epistles, were foundational in his views.

Again, drawing from Scripture, the sermon began with a profound question:

> "Where is thy brother?" (Gen. 4:9): This query comes to us out of one of the oldest and most familiar stories of Scripture. It is the second question recorded in the Bible as being asked by God. In the third chapter of Genesis we find that

when man had first made the choice between good and evil and had fallen into sin, God called to him in his place of hiding in the Garden saying, "Where art Thou?" (Gen. 3:9).

Richards applied both questions to his listeners:

Before God, we, like Cain stand in a position of guilt, danger, and helplessness. The issue of that realization may well be the casting of one's self upon God for mercy. So it is with the second question, which like the first, comes again and again and again to the human soul. It is the logical completion of the first in so far as Christian faith is concerned, and oftentimes provides itself with the real answer to it. The position of the Christian's brother is always a revelation of the former's own state in the sight of God.[8]

Thus far, the sermon was a simple retelling of the Genesis story of two brothers. The application, however, was dramatic. In dealing with the first question, Richards pointed to the hearer's need for reconciliation with God. The climatic application was presented early in the sermon. The sequence of the sermon may be symbolic, but it is man's state in the sight of God that is important. The sermon listed numerous other ways in which the prophets and the apostles applied this. John, in his first letter, pointedly asked:

If a man says I love God, and hateth his brother, he is a liar, for he that loveth not his brother whom he hath seen, how can he love God, whom he hath not seen? (1 John 4:20).[9]

In a powerful insight, Dr. Richards moved to the specific from the general:

Where is thy brother in black? The facts require us to answer this question before the throne of God![10]

In Richards' view, the situation in the 1930s and early 1940s, dramatically and specifically raised questions in forms that gave cause for grave concern as well as for deepest shame. He detailed the evidence:

Our state's highest officials have used the racial issue to further their own political ends. Insulting and humiliating statements concerning the Negro have been made in public places and even in the Senate of the United States. I am not undertaking to discuss politics here. I mention these things in the pulpit, and I have no apology to make for doing so, because Christian principles and spiritual interests are at stake.[11]

Affirming that the African-American is indeed the brother of the Christian, Richards said:

> This "image of God in ebony" as Charles Lamb calls him, holds that place first of all by creation. Black and white and yellow are alike the handiwork of the Creator. Some, in the strictest Scriptural and theological sense, are believers in Christ as Lord and Saviour. They are members of His Church, and in the lives of many of them the unmistakable fruits of the Spirit are manifest. With the same right as we, they pray, Our Father, who art in Heaven, and by the same Adoption they are received into His family.[12]

The sermon moved, then, to answer the question, "Where is thy brother in black?" by saying, "He is in need." The list of needs escalated with injustice in pay, in employment, in education, and in medical care. Worst of all was abuse of every kind ranging from insults and humiliation to a lack of a vote at the polls.

> He is, in a physical sense here in America, 13,000,000 strong. He came as an unwilling guest, brought to our shores by force for profit. He is a neighbor to us all. It is the Negro maid and cook who contribute to the comforts of our homes, and despite our apparent scorn of the race, we entrust them again and again with the dearest possession of our hearts—our children![13]

One eloquent warning is affirmed. Said Richards:

> The Bible does not condemn the Negro to a subhuman status. Even if the white race is a privileged class, "unto whom much is given, much shall be required" (Luke 12:48). Did our Lord mean what he said? If so, our greater opportunities only mean that we must render a more truly Christian service. Take seriously the words of our Lord, "if thou bringest thy gift to the altar and there rememberest that thy brother has ought against thee, leave there thy gift at the altar and go thy way, and first, be reconciled to thy brother, and then come and offer thy gift" (Matt. 5:24).[14]

Richards concluded by affirming that the Bible does not condemn the African-American to a subhuman status, and that even if the white race is a privileged class, "unto whom much is given much shall be required." He asked, with passion and power, "Did our Lord mean what He said? If so, our greater opportunities only mean that we must render a more truly Christian service."[15] His plea:

"Take seriously the words of our Lord, if thou bringest thy gift to the altar, and there rememberest that thy brother has ought against thee, leave there thy gift at the altar and go thy way, first, be reconciled to thy brother and then come and offer thy gift." (Matthew 5:24) Has he aught against us today or not, this brother in black?[16]

Later, in the Columbia Seminary chapel, Richards used the relationship of Philemon and Onesimus to show the clear pattern of justice for all persons. He applied the words of Paul to Philemon as a pattern for relationships. Philemon, for Paul, was "no longer a servant, but a brother beloved" (Philem. 1:16).

Dr. J. Will Ormond, a 1943 graduate of Columbia Theological Seminary and pastor of Covenant Presbyterian Church in Tuscaloosa, Alabama, preached a similar sermon on this theme during the threat by Governor George Wallace to close the University of Alabama rather than admit an African-American student, Autherine Lucy. It was a very important and influential sermon and was supported by members of his congregation. Among them were faculty members of the university and members of the faculty and staff of a Presbyterian institution, Stillman College. Professor Albert C. Winn and Burt and Martha Vardeman, well known leaders in the Presbyterian Church, were influential members of Ormond's congregation. Richards whole-heartedly approved of Ormond's well-publicized sermon. It eloquently reflected the view and the spirit of Richards' prophetic efforts. The crisis in our nation, and the clear teaching of Scripture, Reformed Theology, and Presbyterian polity, led Richards and his former student, Ormond, to some clear convictions about God's will for justice in race relations. Prophetic attitudes and actions were the result. Ormond's sermon, like that of Richards', was published in the nation and throughout the world.

Many ministers, like Ormond, were sustained by Richards' example of strength and courage in a very challenging time for the Church. It was not enough for him to attend meetings of boards and commissions. He accepted the role of a prophet with courage and conviction. It was as essential to do so as breathing was to life. Beyond any expectation, this clear and courageous sermon to a relatively small group of clergy and laity reverberated throughout the city of Atlanta, Georgia, and around the world.

Thirty-nine years later, Delores L. Donnelly wrote:

On October 14, 1940, the words of a 38 year old rebel smashed down upon scornful remarks concerning Negroes made by the late Eugene Talmage, then Governor of Georgia. The words in his sermon, "Brothers in Black," came down hard on all those who believed the Negro to be inferior. This rebel, the Rev. J. McDowell Richards, President of Columbia Theological Seminary, slashed across the jugular veins of many "Christians" when he spoke for the black man. All knew where he stood. All knew his strong and bold position.[17]

Donnelly was right. Others agreed with Richards. In 1977, the Christian Council of Atlanta gave him the Charles Watt Award for his contribution to the improvement of the quality of life in that metropolitan area.

These reasoned and passionate words may not seem like much to the prophets of our age, but in 1941, they changed the attitudes of the predominately white church of Atlanta Presbytery and moved it forward toward racial justice in the Church and in the nation.

In addition to various appeals to the Church, Richards sought to influence the government "to do something" in a variety of situations. More than a decade before the Atlanta Manifesto, the national Commission on the Church and Minority Peoples began to research the situation in the lives of minority people in the United States. Richards was asked to join with them on October 1, 1943, at the height of World War II. Formed by the Federal Council of Churches, the commission's purpose was to aid the churches of the United States to understand the findings of science and how the teachings of Christianity related to the subject of race. It envisioned a detailed appraisal of attitudes and recommendations for new approaches. This outstanding committee was almost a "Who's Who" list of America's ablest scholars, clergy, and politicians, white and black. Most of all, a carefully formed program to change the minds and hearts of people was produced. In many ways, it was a well-developed approach.

In the beginning, Richards was positive and hopeful. He expressed enthusiastic support for the project in a letter to Bradford Abernethy, a Baptist minister from Columbia, Missouri, who was formerly secretary of the Commission to Study the Basis of a Just and Durable Peace. As time went on, however, Richards grew less positive and ultimately concluded, with much disappointment, that the commission was accomplishing little. He analyzed the problem in a few disparaging sentences:

> I felt at first that the attitude of the Church leaders who attended these conferences was decidedly encouraging. This was true both in the awareness of the situation, which was manifested, and the desire to take positive and constructive measures toward solutions. It was clear that churches and individuals were already doing much worthwhile work. At the same time, it seemed evident that no unified strategy has been developed and that those who are most concerned about the matter would welcome the development of such a strategy within the Christian Church.[18]

Richards then called for the development of strategy with specific details. Only after listening to the Church at large would any word have validity in the application of justice at that critical time. He urged consultation with scientists and scholars, but called for laying anew the spiritual foundation with which any hope of solving the problems of our minority peoples must ultimately rest. He noted sheepishly, "Those of us who are concerned about minority problems are themselves a minority within a minority, the Church."[19]

Furthermore, there was, in Richards' view, not much difference in the pattern of segregation between the attitudes of the North and the South. The major difference was in the legal approach in the South forbidding integration and, of course, intermarriage in a very few situations. Where the African-American was becoming a more visible minority in northern cities, the tendency to segregate and discriminate was increasingly evident. However, he saw, as demonstrated in his writing and teaching, that the South carried the burden of slavery history and of the existence of the Ku Klux Klan, with its cruel and abusive activities. What gave some substance to his argument were the tensions throughout the United States in housing, transportation, health care, education, and the standard of living that included pockets of poverty.

On the positive side, however, ten significant papers were prepared and studied. Various aspects of the Church and its relation to minority peoples were intensively researched. Anti-Semitism and anti-Catholic realities were analyzed. Most significant were topics discussed under the superb leadership of President Benjamin Mays of Morehouse College, Atlanta, Georgia. Central in that process were papers on themes such as "Negro Churchmen and the Race Question" and "The Church and the Oriental American."[20] The file ends with a reflection of conflict in a badly divided committee over a final paper on "Race and the Church."

On July 7, 1945, as World War II was nearing an end, Richards petitioned the Congress of the United States to provide the means to build houses and apartments for "the one third of Atlanta's population" which was in desperate need of housing. The vast majority of those in need were African-Americans. Through the efforts of many Atlanta officials, the first public housing in the United States was built at Techwood Homes. On July 10, 1945, Richards petitioned Mayor Hartsfield of Atlanta for more recreation facilities for blacks. He also responded supportively to a black minister who appealed for housing for black children who were orphaned and for the aged with no place to live. Unfortunately, more than Richards' "good wishes" in the project were needed to start building the next day. Ultimately, financing through public funds made it a reality.

On October 16, 1945, a similar fervent and reasoned appeal went to Grady Hospital asking that black doctors be used at the largest hospital in the city dealing with the indigent and the poor. All too slowly, his request was granted. A continuing exchange of correspondence took place with the administrative assistant to Mayor Hartsfield over a wide range of issues similar to those in 1945.

Perhaps the most significant action by Richards came in 1954 when the Supreme Court ruled that segregated schools were unconstitutional, and that legal segregation in education must end. There was a frenzy of political outrage in the South and in some large cities in the North. Vows of resisting to the death, threats to close the universities and colleges of the state systems, and, in essence, an escalation of a critically dangerous time arose in Georgia.

True to his pattern of "sweet reason," Richards worked for and with a strong biracial committee of the Atlanta Christian Council to do two things:

1. Admit that ministers and churches have failed to prepare our people for this inevitable change.
2. Unite in a fervent appeal for prayer, love for one another, and justice for all the people of the United States.[21]

This simple statement, similar to one Richards presented to the General Assembly of the Presbyterian Church (U.S.) a few weeks earlier, was hailed throughout the major churches of the United States as prophetic and persuasive. However, the response of those who disagreed was swift and at times quite angry. A July 13, 1954, letter from a public school teacher accused Richards of twisting the Scriptures, which, in the writer's view, "clearly taught segregation as the only way for us." The letter concluded, "Both races can go to Hell!"

The next day, July 14, 1954, a Presbyterian elder accused Richards and Dr. Stuart R. Oglesby of Atlanta's Central Presbyterian Church of "supporting this communistic civil rights program. You pop off as overeducated liberals, left wing visionaries, with no spiritual value." The writer's conclusion was that Presbyterian churches could best serve the cause of Christianity by continued segregation.

The momentum to abolish all public education continued with a frightening speed. That angry and emotional response, however, slowly began to wane as reason and conviction ultimately prevailed. Georgia politicians ready to close all the schools were puzzled by a growing concern among voters. Georgians of a wide variety concluded, "We need more education, not less."

The volatile and explosive atmosphere was frighteningly real, however. Church leaders of Atlanta asked Richards to head a committee of three persons to prepare a "Manifesto." It was a reasoned and yet passionate document. It warned of the damage school closings would do and the folly of believing that some private system could be put into place as a substitute. Most importantly, it eloquently appealed for justice.

The committee of Richards, Dr. Herman L. Turner of Covenant Presbyterian Church (UPUSA), and Rabbi David Marx of the temple met one Saturday morning with Editor Ralph McGill of the Atlanta *Journal-Constitution*. They presented a simple request that a statement urging that the schools not be closed, but rather strengthened, be published in the form of a paid advertisement. The threat to close the public schools if forced to integrate was described as unjust and, indeed, unchristian.

Editor Ralph McGill strongly agreed that Georgia's schools and colleges must be preserved. He had frequently and eloquently called for racial justice. Nonetheless, he stunned them, at first, by saying they could not purchase advertising space for the "Minister's Manifesto." "However," he went on, with growing excitement, "we will publish it as a news article on the front page of Sunday's edition." The "Call to Civil Obedience and Racial Good Will" appeared in the Atlanta *Journal-Constitution* on Sunday, November 3, 1957.

Eighty ministers signed, and I was one of them. Many others would have supported if there had been time to canvass the entire city. The manifesto did not claim to be a complete analysis of the racial crisis, and yet, it opened public dialog with a view that people of good will could effect change. In some ways, it also marked a significant step toward racial justice in the South.

The call read:

These are days of tremendous political and social tension throughout our entire world, but particularly in our nation and beloved Southland. The issues we face are not simple, nor can they be resolved over night. Because the questions, which confront us, are in many respects moral and spiritual as well as political, it is appropriate and necessary that men who occupy places of responsibility in the churches should not be silent concerning their convictions.

The signers of this statement are all ministers of the Gospel, but we speak also as citizens of Georgia and of the United States of America. We are all Southerners, either by birth or by choice, and speak as men who love the South, who seek to understand its problems and who are vitally concerned for its welfare. In preparing this statement we have acted as individuals, and represent no one but ourselves. At the same time we believe that the sentiments which we express are shared by a multitude of our fellow citizens, who are deeply troubled by our present situation and who know that hatred, defiance and violence are not the answer to our problems, but who have been without a voice and have found no way to make their influence effective.

In presenting our views for the consideration of others we can only speak in a spirit of deep humility and penitence for our own failures. We cannot claim that the problem of racial relationships has been solved, even in the churches we serve, and we are conscious that our own example in the matter of brotherhood and neighborliness has been all too imperfect. We do not pretend to know all the answers. We are of one mind, however, in believing that Christian people have an especial responsibility for the solution of our racial problems and that if, as Christians, we sincerely seek to understand and apply the teachings of our Lord and Master, we shall assuredly find the answer.

We do not believe that the South is more to blame for the difficulties which we face than in other areas of our nation. The presence of the Negro in America is the result of the infamous slave traffic—an evil for which the North was as much responsible as the South. We are also conscious that racial injustice and violence are not confined to our section and that racial problems have by no means been solved anywhere in the nation. Two wrongs, however, do not make a right. The failures of others are not a justification for our own shortcomings, nor can their unjust criticisms excuse us for a failure to do our duty in the sight of God. Our one concern must be to know and to do that which is right.

We believe that the difficulties before us have been greatly increased by extreme attitudes and statements on both sides. The use of the word "integration" in connection with our schools and other areas has been unfortunate, since to many that word has become synonymous with amalgamation. We do not believe in the amalgamation of the races, nor do we feel that right-thinking members of either race favor it. We do believe that all Americans, whether black or white, have a right to the full privileges of first class citizenship. To suggest that a recognition of the rights of Negroes to the full privileges of American citizenship, and to such necessary contacts as might follow would inevitably result in intermarriage is to cast as serious and unjustified an aspersion upon the white as upon the Negro race. Believing as we do in the desirability of preserving the integrity of both races through the free choice of both, we would emphasize the following principles which we hold to be of basic importance for our thought and conduct:

1. Freedom of speech must at all costs be preserved. "Truth is mighty and will prevail." No minister, editor, teacher, state employee, business man, or other citizen should be penalized for expressing himself freely, so long as he does so with due regard to the rights of others. Any position which cannot stand upon its own merits and which can only be maintained by silencing all who hold contrary opinions, is a position which cannot permanently endure.

2. As Americans and as Christians we have an obligation to obey the law. This does not mean that all loyal citizens need approve the 1954 decision of the Supreme Court with reference to segregation in the public schools. Those who feel that this decision was in error have every right to work for an alteration of the decree, either through a further change in the Supreme Court's interpretation of the law, or through an amendment to the Constitution of the United States. It does mean that we have no right to defy the Constitution of the United States. Assuredly that also means that resorts to violence and to economic reprisals as a means to avoid the granting of legal rights to other citizens are never justified.

3. The Public School System must not be destroyed. It is an institution essential to the preservation and development of our democracy. To sacrifice that system in order to avoid obedience to the decree of the Supreme Court would be to inflict tremendous loss upon multitudes of children whose whole lives would be impoverished as a result of such action. It would also mean the economic, intellectual and cultural impoverishment of our section, and would be a blow to the welfare of our nation as a whole.

4. Hatred and scorn for those of another race, or for those who hold a position different from our own, can never be justified. It is only as we approach our problems in a spirit of mutual respect, of charity, and of good will that we hope to understand one another, and to find the way to a cooperative solution of our problems. God is no respecter of persons. Every human personality is precious in His sight. No policy, which seeks to keep any man from developing fully every capacity of body, mind and spirit, can be justified in the light of Scripture. This is the message of the Hebrew prophets as it is of Christ and His disciples. We shall solve our difficulties when we learn to walk in obedience to the Golden Rule: "Therefore, all things, whatsoever you would that men should do to you, do ye even so to them, for this is the law and the prophets."

5. Communication between responsible leaders of the races must be maintained. One of the tragedies of our present situation is found in the fact that there is so little real discussion of the issues except within the separate racial groups. Under such circumstances it is inevitable that misunderstandings will continue and that suspicion and distrust will be encouraged. One of the reasons that extreme measures have been so often proposed or adopted by groups within both races is found in the fact that those who are most concerned have never faced the issues in a situation where there could be a free exchange of ideas.

We believe that willingness on the part of white leaders to talk with leaders of the Negro race, and to understand what those leaders are really seeking for their people is necessary and desirable. An expressed willingness on our part to recognize their needs, and to see that they are granted their full rights as American citizens, might well lead to a cooperative approach to the problem which would provide equal rights and yet maintain the integrity of both races upon a basis of mutual esteem and of free choice rather than of force.

6. Our difficulties cannot be solved in our own strength or in human wisdom. It is appropriate, therefore, that we approach the task in a spirit of humility, of penitence, and of prayer. It is necessary that we pray earnestly and consistently that God will give us wisdom to understand His will; that He will grant us the courage and faith to follow the guidance of His Spirit.

To such prayer and obedience we would dedicate ourselves and summon all men of good will.

Support for the preservation of the schools burgeoned with a rapid and astonishing escalation. Yes, all who signed the appeal received a few critical letters and a small number of phone calls disagreeing with the statement. However, those who came to me personally were few, and were usually calm and courteous in differing with the proposed integration of public education. In other words, some writers disagreed without being disagreeable. A few other ministers who signed the manifesto received threats and accusations of being "race mixing communists."

In contrast, however, many letters and phone calls of gratitude and support were received. Expressions of appreciation came in from people and places near and far. These messages expressed genuine satisfaction that at long last a clear and specific word was spoken for justice and reason. Since the "Minister's Manifesto" appeared on a Sunday morning, a number of persons spoke supportively to pastors after worship that day.

I understood at the time that Richards was the author of the "Minister's Manifesto" with suggestions and revisions from his colleagues. As manifestos go, it will seem mild to today's generation of prophets. Atlantans also know, today, that some schools have resegregated due to changing residential patterns of race in the areas around them. However, it seems the "Minister's Manifesto" was used of God and by the Church to take a forward step in peaceful and more just relations between races.

In my congregation, a dozen people thanked me for signing it. One good elder, a son of the South, wrote a letter defending segregation on Biblical grounds, but there was no hate or anger in his statement. He continued to be a faithful member of the congregation of which we were a part. A few letters from strangers came in on both sides. A retired teacher in a public school wrote accusing the manifesto signers of unintended consequences. In essence, the signers were accused of not using Scripture appealing for segregation. As a result, they said, "Your grand-daughters will marry Negroes. Furthermore, both races will go to Hell. Mulattos will take their place. This is the verdict of the Bible."

Another critic accused the ministers and especially Richards and Stuart R. Oglesby of espousing a communistic civil rights program in the name of the Southern Presbyterian Church. He made it specific by saying, "Your left wing visions are of no spiritual value. They divide the Church and impede progress. Presbyterian churches best serve the cause of Christianity by continued segregation."[22]

Richards answered letters for and against this appeal for justice for all people with courtesy and "sweet reason," based on the teaching of selected paragraphs from the Bible. Again and again, the case for a new day for all people was made without equivocation.

Ecumenics

James McDowell Richards was far more than an ecumenical Christian and minister in name only. He "talked the talk and walked the walk," as the saying goes. He was deeply involved in organizations representing the larger Church. He was a devoted and extremely useful participant in such groups as the Federal Council of Churches, the Atlanta Christian Council, and the World Alliance of Reformed Churches.

In the late 1930s and the early 1940s, Richards was one of five members of the important Executive Committee of the Federal Council of Churches. From 1942 to 1944, he served as vice president of the council. These positions took on importance not only because of Richards' ability, but also as the only Southerner with these assignments.

In the course of events for forty productive years, Richards was constantly involved in matters of the unity of the Church as the Body of Christ both locally and globally. Such unity of the Christian Church was "a given" for him from Presbyterian theology, polity, and scripture. Whether because of the confessional statements of the Church, the polity concepts which fashioned its government, or, most of all, the teaching of the Bible, they supported his commitment to the unity of believers in Christ's Church. Beyond any doubt, he believed we are "one in Christ."

When chosen as vice president of the Federal Council of Churches on June 17, 1941, he assumed responsibility for nominating PCUS ministers and members to various councils and committees of the Federal Council. He expended much time and energy in traveling to meetings in the pre-aviation mode, the train, and advising on the challenges the Church and the nation faced. As World War II spread from Germany throughout Europe and, ultimately, to most of the world, the issues of a just and lasting peace claimed much attention. As a vital part of his role, he regularly reported on this demanding but important task of representing the Presbyterian Church, U.S.

He wrote and spoke in detail on these and related issues to the General Assembly of the Presbyterian Church, U.S. He suggested preachers for the national radio broadcasts on Sunday mornings. During World War II, the choosing and credentialing of military chaplains from the Presbyterian Church was done through his recommendations. This activity was intense and important during the years of 1940–60. Once appointed and serving on active duty, he wrote long and thoughtful letters to those he knew, especially from Columbia Seminary.

Widely respected as a person who could bring people of varying views together, Richards led diverse groups in reaching solid theological and responsive conclusions to challenging issues. Having earned worldwide respect, he was asked on February 19, 1943, to take a leave of absence from Columbia's presidency and lead the new National Commission on Racial and Cultural Problems. To the great disappointment of the council board, but to the enormous relief of the seminary constituency, he declined. Before making his decision, he consulted with William M. Elliot Jr., chairman of the Board of Directors of Columbia Seminary. He wrote: "It may be that the Board of Directors would welcome the opportunity to be free of responsibility for the President for a year and, perhaps in some instances to be free of the President altogether."[23] This, obviously, was an excess of humility.

From personal experience, I know of Richards' commitment to the Christian Church in all its forms—local, national, and international. The first time I experienced personally the work of the Federal Council of Churches was at a meeting of its national board in Atlanta during my seminary days. Richards invited the three officers of the student government at Columbia Theological Seminary in 1942–43 to attend the meeting with him. Dr. Henry Pitts Van Dusen talked passionately with the three students on the need to reunite the Presbyterian Church as one denomination. An opposite view had been pressed in governing bodies with which I was familiar. The attendance at this important meeting in the heart of the Southeast drew national leaders of importance. The attendance from the Southeast, however, was disappointing.

As World War II confronted the nation with the critical need for a large military force, Richards facilitated service for many persons as military chaplains. So great was the need that the U.S. Navy was persuaded to choose as chaplains ministers with college and seminary degrees, but with no ordained experience as pastors. Four out of twenty members of the class of 1943 at Columbia Theological Seminary served as Navy chaplains and one with the Army. Others would have joined but failed the stringent physical exam. During the war, Richards personally arranged and led frequent seminars for chaplains at Columbia Seminary, beginning with lunch at thirty-five cents a plate.

However, for Richards, the greatest test of ecumenical participation was still the defense of the Federal Council. For thirty years, he was inundated with letters criticizing the council and its successor, the National Council of Churches. There was a constant need to respond to overtures from presbyteries to withdraw from it. His correspondence files are extensive in those days before the telephone seemed to be permanently attached to the ear and the mouth of leaders in every field. Neither had anyone heard of the fax machine or e-mail, though occasionally telegrams appear in these records.

Between 1945 and 1955, the criticism of the Federal Council grew in volume and sometimes in anger. Richards, appointed by the Presbyterian Church (U.S.) as a representative of the Church, often stood almost alone as the target of such attacks. Some of the elders who wrote, however, were among his closest friends and, by and large, they were courteous and respectful. They were convinced that the Presbyterian Church (U.S.) should withdraw immediately from the council. A few were much more volatile. The Richards Papers at the Presbyterian Historical Society (Montreat) have several hundred letters on this issue, and each one was carefully and courteously answered.

On November 17, 1945, Richards faced accusations that he was in a powerless minority of leadership in the Federal Council, that it was a hopeless task, and that he was in bad company. What hurt most was the conclusion of the writer that he was in it because "he loved the praise of man rather than the praise of the Master." The letter concluded: "Don't try to win those students at Columbia to your views even though one said you are a grand fellow!"[24]

Richards' response to a friend and an elder accusing him of being a fence straddler was calm and courteous:

> I favor remaining in the Federal Council because I believe all those who believe in Jesus Christ as Lord and Saviour are the children of God. I believe I should work with God's children to the best of my ability even if I believe they are mistaken.[25]

In response to another request that he get out of the council and urge the PCUS to do so, he wrote:

> I am definitely conservative theologically, but I am profoundly convinced that this is a day when the various branches of the Christian Church must learn to

understand one another better, and to work together to confront a world of staggering pagan forces.[26]

The issue of the council's views on business and economic practices took up almost as much time and discussion as that of race. Often the accusations included reports that a representative of the Federal Council testified on behalf of twenty-two million church members that the efforts to organize textile workers in a union had their support. Another charged that the council was clearly opposed to Christianity and favored communism and its atheistic, revolutionary strategy.

Peace with justice was a lifelong commitment for Richards, beginning with the "first step" effort of the National Council of Churches at its biennial meeting on February 16, 1942. An historic gathering was held with black ministers who were to become a part of the leadership of the national Church. Nor was it, many believe, a mere coincidence that Richards' sermon "Brothers in Black," preached as moderator of Atlanta Presbytery on October 14, 1940, was known by them all. After all, at least fifty thousand copies of the sermon were circulated throughout the world. Through that sermon, the eyes of many were opened to the real injustices suffered by African-Americans.

For example, on August 4, 1944, he chaired the complicated work of a commission dealing with international situations of conflict and argument. He was committed to this effort led by John Foster Dulles, who was the leader in developing the guiding principles called, "The Six Pillars for a Just and Durable Peace." Others who joined this extraordinary effort included Ernest Hocking, George Buttrick, John Bennett, Henry Sloan Coffin, Henry Luce, and Bishop Oxnam. Richards said in essence:

1. We must support various forms of "relief" for the post-war world, including Germany and Japan.
2. We should encourage and emphasize an effective foreign mission effort.
3. We should help create a new spirit of cooperation in our nation and the Church.
4. We should continue our efforts for racial relations with justice and peace.[27]

Much of Richards' views on these ecumenical councils can be summed up in his response to an invitation from the council in January 31, 1946, to be one of six to draft a statement of mission. He wrote:

It seems to me that what the Federal Council needs to stress most to the Churches at this time is the urgent need for a deepening of the spiritual life and loyalty to Jesus Christ. We cannot affect the emerging national or international order until our own life possesses a greater power than is now the case.[28]

This did not reduce Richards' commitment or his intense involvement in working for a just and durable peace. Too many meetings, too many hours, and too many words had involved him in these issues to distort this profound summons to devotion to that cause.

"We are ignored" was by far the common thread in the tapestry of complaints about the church's involvement in the council. Richards supposedly made such a remark to a friend, but assured such persons that he had never, in private or public, done so. Using the new name for the council, he addressed the full meeting of the National Council of Churches in the spring of 1951 saying:

> I am entirely committed to the position that our church should hold membership in the National Council of Churches and the World Council of Churches. This does not mean that I agree with those organizations at every point. As a matter of fact, I do not agree with every action taken by my own church, but that does not prevent me from being loyal to it. They are highly important to the life and witness of Protestant Christians and our Church can bear a far stronger witness to the faith in and through these organizations than it could possibly do outside them.[29]

Sometimes he responded to criticisms by saying that the largest item in the budget of the National Council was evangelism. This, today, is no longer true, but while serving on the council's Department of Evangelism for some years in the 1960s, I knew it to be the case.

Since "ecumenical" means much more than occasional gatherings of world wide groups, Richards supported with his presence and counsel such entities as the Christian Council of Atlanta, the Georgia Council of Churches, the Georgia Committee on Interracial Matters, the Inter-Seminary movement, and the National Student Christian Federation. All appear significantly, though briefly, in the Richards Papers. Two educational councils were begun in the Richards era. One, a consortium of major educational institutions in the Atlanta area, included the University Center in Georgia, began with Emory University, Georgia School of Technology, Agnes Scott College, the High Museum of Art, Oglethorpe College, and Columbia Theological Seminary. Today, in a consortium of twenty educational institutions, major additions include the University of Georgia, Atlanta University Center with five colleges, a seminary, and the Morehouse School of Medicine, Georgia Tech, Georgia State University, and Kennesaw College.

The most significant development for theological education, however, was without doubt, the Georgia Association of Pastoral Care. The only such clinical pastoral education program for seminary students and pastors in the South at that time, and one of two in the nation, it was initiated by the faculty of Columbia Seminary and that of the Candler School of Theology. Students, pastors, and counselors participated in varying forms of hospital chaplaincy and pastoral work under the intensive supervision of professors of pastoral care and counseling. The Georgia Association of Pastoral Care, in spite of some fierce opposition, ultimately developed curricula, trained supervisors, advocated the cause, and provided a tremendous resource for ministry. Ministers in hospitals and mental health facilities, and pastorates in varied settings, learned how to serve with integrity. With Professor Thomas H. McDill, Richards resolutely moved the program forward without yielding to the opposition of some traditional academic positions. In spite of occasional inept activities by a few counselors, the Georgia Association of Pastoral Care sustained a commitment to remain as a ministry of the Church.

In addition, the Christian Council of Atlanta was brought together initially by a half dozen ministers from the largest churches in Atlanta. It effectively survived indifference, uncertain mission, limited funding, and widely differing theological views. What is more, the Christian Council of Atlanta, in the twenty post-war years, did its important work as Atlanta quickly grew from a 250,000-population center with a number of small towns and counties to one of the most dynamic metropolitan entities in the United States. It has reached and passed the four million mark in population in seventeen counties and includes a variety of ethnic groups in varying communities. The core of the inner city is made up of great commercial buildings and many apartments and homes. It brings together the poor, the middle class, and the wealthy. Diverse religious entities are found in all parts of the city. A congregation of thirty worshippers, or one of thirty thousand, could use the places of worship. The level of education varies widely. Georgia State University, with the largest enrollment of any educational institution in the city, is in the heart of downtown Atlanta.

The summer of 1945 was a significant and extremely busy time for the leaders of the Christian Council. The Council focused on a variety of important and relevant issues ranging from social action programs to Sabbath observance. The positions formed were reflected in resolutions, communications to officials, and public statements. A call for justice cited a panorama of needs. The list included the lack of adequate housing for one-third of the Atlanta population, the absence of recreational facilities in the poorer sections of the city, the need for homes for the elderly of all races, the use of black doctors at the large municipal medical center, Grady Hospital, solutions to youth vandalism, and the Jewish-Christian relationships in Atlanta.

The most widely publicized resolutions were those on housing, recreational facilities, medical resources available to all, and youth vandalism. A specific instance of apparent brutality by a policeman was the beating of an African-American man in the view of a gathering crowd of outraged citizens. Similarly, a resolution on April 26, 1946, expressed concern about friction among races growing out of the housing crisis. While the city had good long-range plans for all its citizens in all parts of Atlanta, the council urged that:

> They press forward to implement them as rapidly as possible so that all of our citizens alike may have an opportunity to live and rear their children in comfortable homes and wholesome surroundings.[30]

Ernest Brewer, executive secretary to the office of mayor, and on behalf of Mayor Hartsfield,[31] replied in a letter to Richards:

> We are going to continue every effort to bring about a happy solution to this problem. If we succeed, it will be a precedent of which we all may be very proud. It will prove to our citizens, both white and black, that we can sit down together and work out satisfactorily even such a delicate problem as that of "encroachment."[32]

Whites were increasingly hostile toward the movement of black families to Atlanta from throughout the state and, indeed, the nation. The inevitable changing racial patterns and their need for housing challenged the entire metropolitan area. In November of 1946, Richards informed the council that Rev. M. L. King Sr.[33] asked to meet with the Committee on Race Relations to discuss the tension regarding the housing situation in Atlanta. Only Franklin Talmage, Richards, and Ernest Brewer from that committee were present. The entire membership of the Christian Council was invited for a subsequent discussion on November 18, 1946, and the invitation was properly and frantically urgent.

The pressures in West End area of Atlanta continued, and President Benjamin Mays of Morehouse College appealed for immediate attention to the growing racial tensions there. The mayor's office and the City Council then backed down from a tentative proposal to buy back houses bought by African-Americans in that area. All who had bought them owned them and had every right to live there. As the years went on, the white flight continued, and today West End is largely African-American in racial categories. A part of it, however, is a very expensive example of high-quality residential housing at its best. Some of the most outstanding African-Americans in Atlanta and in the nation live there.

The Christian Council of Atlanta had other agenda items of varying importance. They included statements on federal aid to parochial schools,[34] plans for the use of free radio time for devotionals, or thought for the day items. The United Church Women complained about a lack of support for their activities in various social action programs. Dr. Philip Weltner, president of Oglethorpe College and a Presbyterian elder, asked the council to deal with anti-Semitism in the relationship with David Marx, a much beloved rabbi, and a well-known Atlanta citizen. Weltner asked, "Why isn't Rabbi Marx a member of the Christian Council of Atlanta?"

Dr. Stuart Oglesby, pastor of Central Presbyterian Church, and Richards were asked to meet with Dr. Marx and invite him to speak to the council in observance of his fifty years of service as a rabbi in the tradition called Reformed Judaism. Jewish leaders were to be invited. He did speak, but warned the council that he did not support Zionism, the movement of Jews to Israel. He said with genuine chagrin, "We probably face more real difficulty by reason of differences among our Jewish friends than we do because of the differences between Jews and Christians."[35]

His successor, Rabbi Jacob Rothschild, a brilliant and more traditional Reformed Rabbi, favored Zionism. In his commitment to Judaism's worship and program, he had a long and significant influence in his congregation, the temple, and in the city. This was particularly so in the relationships between whites and blacks. He preached fervently and eloquently for racial justice. As a result, under the cover of darkness one night, the temple was bombed. Racial hate groups were suspected of committing this evil act.

The congregation included some of Atlanta's outstanding leaders, and the great majority of Atlantans were appalled that racism was so alive and vicious. Many Atlantans immediately rose to strongly support the repair and rebuilding of the temple. When the building was originally constructed, First Presbyterian Church offered its facilities for use by the temple congregation for worship on Friday evenings. As a permanent symbol of their gratitude, the temple congregation presented two magnificent silver urns to their neighbors and friends in that Christian church. A strong relationship was maintained through the years. The second offer for use of their facilities was gratefully declined, since the temple could still use a part of the building for worship in spite of the damage. Many individual Atlantans contributed to the rebuilding effort.

Melissa Faye Greene, in her book, *Praying For Sheetrock,* depicted her efforts to assist poor African-Americans in rural Georgia in building housing and other facilities. *The Temple Bombing* was a second literary success for her. It vividly and realistically pictured life in Atlanta, good and bad, and the impact of that evil act at the temple on Jews and Christians alike.

By far, the most widely publicized and most influential act of the Christian Council of Atlanta occurred in the decades after the Supreme Court ruled that public education must be available to all without regard to race. Schools could not remain separate, segregated by race. The frightening development of an imminent threat to close Georgia public schools and universities rather than desegregate was ominously growing. The real heroes of that time were the children and college students who not only integrated public restaurants with "sit-ins" and faced great abuse, but who also integrated schools and colleges with courage, persistence, and hope.

In tandem with the efforts of the Christian Council of Atlanta, churches, ecclesiastical governing bodies, women's groups, and congregations voted to prepare and publish a statement opposing Governor Ernest Vandiver's plan to close educational institutions rather than desegregate. It is this effort that is described in graphic detail in the section on racial justice, and which involved a statement by Richards and eighty ministers at that time.

The "Minister's Manifesto" may seem mild to many of us today, and critics say that our schools have segregated by race again. Perhaps so, but for the times, it was the right word at the right time from the right people.

What influences in Richards' life brought him to such courageous, though lonely actions? Why was he willing out of conscience to do what he thought was Christian and right, even though he was often alone in such actions? These traits are important in understanding the various aspects of his prophetic efforts. He was motivated by two main commitments: to the life of the mind and to the globalization of theological education.

It is impossible to understand, let alone interpret, the life and work of James McDowell Richards without a focus on his lifelong commitment to education. Here, in ways often ignored, he showed great openness to the educational experiences of his life from an early age, and his great commitment to educational leadership. He also was shaped by a study of the Bible, and especially the teachings of Jesus. Equally influential in Richards' career was his commitment to justice, openness to new situations and ideas, and a passionate commitment to do the will of God in his own life and the life of the world. His overseas experiences confirmed this.

With degrees from Davidson College, Princeton University, Oxford University, and Columbia Theological Seminary, the institution which he led for thirty-nine years, he sought the best in education for himself and for the students at Columbia Seminary. He was not always successful in the latter, but it was not because of a low aim. The lack of funds, the limited faculty, the smallness of the library, and the varied assortment of students produced by the Church were always working against achieving such a high goal. It is true, however, that hundreds of pastors, missionaries, and teachers passed through

Columbia under his presidency, twenty-five hundred in all. Some were known around the world, such as Peter Marshall of Washington, D.C. Some were pastors of our strongest churches, but in places far and near, large and small, most served in faithfulness outside the spotlight of publicity. They built the Church with devotion and commitment, even in extremely difficult places. They were shaped by the example of an admired and respected president. In his prophetic leadership, Richards again demonstrated a sincere commitment to the Church in varying settings and groups. Strong in Presbyterian polity and theology, he reached beyond those boundaries. The following three examples are representative of many:

1. The Atlanta Theological Association originally consisted of four institutions training ministers and located largely in Atlanta. A wide variety of institutions were included. The first members were the Interdenominational Theological Center, the Candler School of Theology of Emory University, Columbia Theological Seminary and Erskine Theological Seminary. Represented in these institutions was a cluster of ecclesiastical affiliations. Students from Presbyterian, Methodist, Baptist, Episcopalian, and Associate Reformed Presbyterian Churches from around the world were enrolled. What is more, in the largest private African-American institution in the United States, the Atlanta University Center, members of thirteen church bodies were united in a common mission. American, Asian, African, and Hispanic churches were represented by students and faculty and contributed greatly to these educational experiences. Most importantly, this led to an exchange of students and a sharing of faculty and library resources.

2. The University Center of Georgia began with Agnes Scott College, Emory University, Georgia School of Technology, the University of Georgia, and Columbia Theological Seminary. Today it includes twenty educational institutions including the largest private African-American institutions in the world and is an active educational community. Library books are circulated every day to any library in the center requesting them, facilitated by the resources of the electronic age with the latest technology. An exchange of lecturers and faculties is of great benefit, particularly for the smaller institutions. The presidents of these institutions meet quarterly for a sharing of experiences and dreams for the future.

3. The Georgia Association of Pastoral Care, initiated by Columbia Seminary and the Candler School of Theology, was initially the only one in the South. Essential to its existence and growth was the

support of Columbia's president and the appointment of Thomas H. McDill as professor of pastoral care and counseling in 1951. With strong opposition from other traditions in the curriculum, the concept of "learning by doing under supervision" ultimately proved itself as being as important to theological education as clinical experiences are to medical schools.

Of course, for years before this development, Columbia's requirements included fieldwork experiences in churches. Richards personally recommended scores of students for summer work with congregations and, in some instances, service in and with churches during the school year. It was useful to congregations and helpful to the students educationally and, to some degree, financially. It was, however, nowhere near the present system of supervised ministry experience in the crucial process of evaluation and the insights it produces. The experience impacts the churches, hospitals, and students.

To show the importance of it, as far back as 1942, President Ben R. Lacy of Union Theological Seminary in Richmond, Virginia, and President Richards consulted on a proposal from the military chaplaincy officials that the three-year program for the bachelor of divinity would be accelerated to eliminate the two summers of work in churches. They agreed to oppose this acceleration of any theological education program without this part of the curriculum, because the summer work had proven to be of such importance. Even more, to eliminate it would run the risk of sending "immature" ministers into the chaplaincy.[36] However, the practical approach does appear in Richards' reaction. He cautioned against a rigid response if the war should go on and on. In addition, he suggested that if the war ended in two years, the question would become moot.[37]

Moreover, the Georgia Association of Pastoral Care, in its ecumenical structures today, provides supervisors and settings in church, hospital, and international locations for "clinical experiences." Thomas H. McDill began the program of counseling practicums, and his successors have seen it grow in numbers and opportunities for students and pastors. The professor of supervised ministry at Columbia, Jasper N. Keith Jr., also directed a well-planned and administered course for students in all degree programs in various local church settings. Again, this is an example of reaching beyond the borders of Columbia to provide theological education in many fields.

A faithful participant in the Association of Theological Schools of the United States and Canada, President Richards also met with the presidents of Presbyterian Church in the U.S. theological schools for consultation and action to strengthen the role of theological education. These associations were a vital thing in the life of these presidents and their institutions. The personal and financial support by Columbia Seminary for ministers seeking further study in the important universities of the United States and Europe was rather unique among theological schools of the size and financial resources of Columbia. Richards wanted the windows of the mind to be opened to the world. Faith and the Church were "local," but ministry was strengthened if seen in a "global" context.

You cannot think "globally," however, without memories of America's involvement in World War II and the agonizing decisions facing Christians during that time. Dr. D. P. McGeachy, for many years pastor of Decatur Presbyterian Church, wrote in his retirement to Richards and raised serious questions of conscience about a statement from the Presbyterian Church (U.S.) entitled "Our Duty as Christian Citizens in Time of War."[38] McGeachy challenged the report, produced by a committee of which Richards was a member, as taking the "war method" for granted. He further questioned the concept in the statement that spoke of right attitudes, purified sins, and unceasing action. In the name of the Presbyterian Church (U.S.), the statement, "Our Duty as Christian Citizens in Time of War," claimed that it was our duty as Christians to do all we can to help in this struggle. Dr. McGeachy further charged that the report erroneously claimed that we may have come to believe that Christianity is not practical and cannot be put into operation in the kind of world in which we live. That, he said, is "exactly what we have come to believe." He deeply believed that "if, even in the midst of war, the Church were to step out in the way of love, it would work!"

Again, Richards' response is one of conciliation, respect, and openness. He wrote:

> Your letter was read with care and with respect, for, although I am compelled to differ with some of the statements which you make, they could not be lightly dismissed. I wish I could talk with you about them . . . I agree that we could have prevented World War II, but I do not believe that the Church can stop the war today. If so, it would still mean, as far as I can see, that Hitler and the philosophy that he represents would be dominant in the major portion of Europe. Do you believe that this situation, with the fate which it would involve for the Jews and for millions of other subject people and with the assurance that the youth of those countries who would be educated and indoctrinated would be less of an evil than the war itself? For my own part, I do not believe so.[39]

While a chaplain in the U.S. Navy stationed on the island of Guam, I received numerous letters from Richards largely pastoral in nature. In them, one of the most powerful concerns was the nature of the peace in the post-war world. Richards believed deeply that the Church and Columbia Seminary should reach out to former enemies with assistance and reconciliation. Exchange of students was one way of approaching that need. As he had received refugee students from Europe during the war, he hoped for student exchanges in both directions.

For Richards, too, the most significant aspect of this reaching out to the whole Church can be seen in the early years of the 1980s. Richards' last speech to any gathering that I know about was at a meeting of representatives of the Synod of the Southeast and of the twelve southeastern presbyteries who were considering the vote on the Plan of Reunion with the United Presbyterian Church in the United States of America (UPCUSA). He sat in a chair and listened intently while the denomination's moderator, J. Randolph Taylor, spoke of details of the plan. Unable to stand due to poor health, Richards spoke eloquently and passionately for ten minutes in favor of reunion. He concluded by saying, "This is God's will for God's people at God's time."

All but one of the presbyteries in the synod voted in favor of reunion. It was, indeed, an affirmation of his influence in the action on this issue, and a demonstration of his feeling that the Church is one.

One final question remains. Did he allow himself and his reputation to be used by people who wanted to buttress a cause or an agency? He confessed, once, that he was weary of constantly defending one such agency. The answer: Yes, he was occasionally unfairly used.

In summary, James McDowell Richards was a deeply committed Christian, a gifted minister, and a good husband and father. In his career, he carried enormous responsibilities on campus and into the whole world. He was conservative in theology, liberal in matters of race, ecumenism, and social issues, compassionate in ministering to "the least of these." In his role as a prophet, Richards, by any measurement, found what it means to be faithful to Christ in both faith and practice in his time and place.

Epilogue

COLUMBIA THEOLOGICAL SEMINARY HAS A MISSION TODAY in the Church and the world that is as important as any in its history. With considerable resources in faculty, facilities, and students, it faces challenging opportunities in Church and society. The life and work of James McDowell Richards has provided a basis for a new era that calls for effective ministers for a new world. The grace of God sustained him in his faithfulness to the mission of that day. Thanks be to God!

The last chapter of Richards' life was spent in the Presbyterian Home in Summerville, South Carolina. There he received the special care he needed, and there on August 10, 1986, a great and good man ended his earthly life. His ministry of teaching, preaching, counseling, and administering enriched the life of the Church and nourished the lives of hundreds of people at home and abroad. As those who knew him sorted out memories and experiences and gave thanks for him, his impact on the Church and the world was recalled. Expressions of gratitude for his life and work came in from around the world. Indeed, immense appreciation was a common thread in them all.

Though a man of many gifts, he was adept at relating to individuals in diverse groups. Those who listened to his sermons and addresses remembered with clarity and appreciation the important ideas he used and the applications of them he effectively made. His delivery was quiet and never flamboyant. His message was almost always powerful and relevant. His deep commitment to life and work was apparent. He had the capacity to inform and convince. His knowledge of Scripture and literature, and the gift of language, characterized his sermons. He demonstrated the love of learning.

Richards was not only scholarly and brilliant, but also adept in relating intellectually to persons from diverse and unique groups. His addresses, sermons, and articles were thoughtful and persuasive. Whether in the pulpit, a classroom, or in one of the Church's governing bodies, he had the ability to inform and convince. Careful preparation, research, knowledge of

Scripture, and the gift of language characterized his work. Growing up in the family of a professor of Bible at Davidson College, he developed an appetite for intellectual stimulus and nourishment. He was an example of the love of learning.

To know President Richards for almost fifty years, to listen to his sermons, addresses, lectures and conversations, and, most of all, to read his extensive correspondence and other written materials, is to be impressed with his integrity. He valued education, and he related with kindness and respect to persons of differing opinions and views. Most of all, to observe his firm commitment to Jesus Christ as a disciple and servant, and his commitment as a minister of Christ in the Presbyterian Church, was to recognize a unique human being. He was a great listener and a diplomatic critic, but he remained faithful to his commitments and to his love for God and God's people.

Though a recipient of superb education in the United States, he had the advantage of study and travel in Europe from 1923 to 1926, at a crucial time in the world's history. A liberal arts education at Davidson College, graduate study at Princeton University, the Rhodes Scholar program at Christ College,[1] Oxford University, and a theological degree from Columbia Theological Seminary all gave Richards a foundation in literature, theology, and Bible. Best of all, it gave him a lifelong thirst for knowledge. What was equally dramatic in shaping patterns of ministry for him was his extensive travel in Europe during the period of study at Oxford University in England. France, Germany, and Italy all exposed him to culture and to history. He visited every museum, climbed every mountain, and saw firsthand the aftermath of World War I in each of these countries. He was stunned to find that even in 1924, the German family with whom he lived for four weeks was only doing business with non-German currencies.[2] Perhaps Richards' lifelong pattern of a very frugal use of money was fixed in that period.

Four years in a parish in the mountains of North Georgia, and a year in a strong ministry in Thomasville, Georgia, brought him back to the diverse realities of the world and the pastorate. He remarked in a conversation late in his life that the committee seeking a president for Columbia Seminary came to him in 1931, after having been turned down by twenty-three others. The other candidates thought the problems at the seminary were too great. Unless he accepted their call, Columbia Seminary would be closed. The appeal worked, for he could not imagine a Church without an educated ministry and without a seminary in the fast growing southeastern United States.

This conviction was produced, not by a provincial attitude, but by a commitment to the essential nature of theological education. A key aspect of his concern for educating ministers was reflected in a meditation at the memorial service for Felix Bayard Gear, his colleague as professor of theology. Richards said of him:

As a teacher, Professor Gear was outstanding. He was not always popular because he worked his students hard, required of them that they think, and sometimes thrust them into depths they did not want to enter. He challenged them to reach out for a greater intellectual grasp of the truths of Christian doctrine, and how to bring those truths to bear upon the life of the 20th Century world and church.[3]

The windows looking out upon life in the real world were, therefore, opened wide.

Richards was intensely involved in the churches, committees, and boards of the Presbyterian Church and related ecumenical entities. President of Columbia for thirty-nine years, chairman of the Davidson College Board for twenty-seven years, chairman of the Board of Church Extension of the Presbyterian Church in the U.S., and active in synod and presbytery, he never withdrew from his feeling of responsibility in the Church.

His regular preaching, teaching, and writing for congregations and publications immersed him in congregational life, as well as that of the governing bodies of the Presbyterian Church, U.S. He planned and spoke at numerous convocations over the years, such as in Tampa, Florida, and the Montreat Minister's Forum. He was frequently invited to preach at youth conferences, and once was asked to prepare materials for a unit entitled "Toward a Christian America" for fifteen- through seventeen-year-olds. It was used in programs at youth fellowship meetings. He said, somewhat sheepishly, that writing for teenagers was the hardest assignment he ever had. What would he think today!

At the invitation of President John A. Mackay of Princeton Theological Seminary, Richards joined a founding board of twenty-six of the most outstanding theologians in the United States in publishing *Theology Today*. His suggestions for areas of thought to be utilized in its articles were impressive:

A. The Nature of God
B. The Nature of Man
C. The Nature and Validity of the Christian Revelation
D. The Ecumenical Movement
E. The Relevance of the Christian Faith to the Problems of Our World[4]

With the Association of Theological Schools, Richards led Columbia Seminary through the regular accreditation reviews and listened to the analysis and recommendations with great care and thought. For example, one recommendation made for Columbia and for many such institutions called for a program that exposed students to the culture of the world around them nationally and internationally. Gradually, this was done. The exchange of professors and students between institutions in Britain, Hungary, Korea, and

China are examples. Richards also brought faculty to the campus from Europe, Australia, and Scotland. These actions were extremely important in opening the campus to the realities of the world.

Perhaps Richards' characteristic regard for scholarship is reflected in his great appreciation for learning and teaching. The professors whom he had experienced as a student greatly influenced him. Once he was asked by a columnist in the *Atlanta Constitution*, the Rev. Dr. Louie D. Newton, to name the teacher in Columbia Seminary who had rendered the greatest service. After much research and many disclaimers that he might not choose the right one, he suggested James Henley Thornwell as the most "illustrious of all the men who had taught at Columbia Seminary." One can only wonder how those who were his colleagues there at the time regarded this. The case was made for Thornwell by these items:

1. Thornwell was elected moderator of the Presbyterian Church in 1847 at the age of thirty-four.
2. He so impressed a group of scholars in a discussion of philosophy at a dinner in New York City, that the historian, Bancroft, sent him a copy of Aristotle with this inscription on the flyleaf: "A Testimonial of regard to the Reverend J. H. Thornwell. The most learned of the land." Dr. Henry Ward Beecher wrote of him, "By common fame, Dr. Thornwell was the most brilliant minister in the old school Presbyterian Church and the most brilliant debater in the General Assembly."
3. Thornwell's real love was teaching rather than writing, but in spite of this, his collected writings comprise nine volumes which still constitute a valuable contribution to the thought of the Christian Church.[5]

Clearly, Richard himself followed that intellectual and theological commitment in his ministry.

Richards' heritage was always a source of much gratitude for those who lived and served before him. It is a varied and impressive "clan." Reunions in Liberty Hill, South Carolina, included worship, feasting, talking, and his favorite sport, baseball. He played catcher, a good position to prepare him for a seminary presidency since he was often a recipient of many questions and attacks. Mrs. Richards and their three children have all pursued education with appreciation and success. He was continually appreciative of the influence of his home on his life and work. As a student at Oxford, England, he wrote on Christmas, 1923, of how much he regretted being away from home and how much he missed his family.[6]

Richards enjoyed the support of church members, the elders, the women of the Church, and his ministerial colleagues. The Church and Richards had respect for each other even when they disagreed. The feeling of a close partnership in mission and ministry held them together.

In his retirement, the churches of the Atlanta area and beyond happily utilized his services as preacher, counselor, and interim pastor. For example, in a report to the session of the Bethesda Presbyterian Church, Camden, South Carolina, he began by saying:

> These six months of service in your church have been one of the happy experiences of my life. You have received me with a warmth and a responsiveness which I have not deserved . . . I feel, and shall always feel, that I am truly a member of the Bethesda Family.

His integrity, however, led him to raise some questions about such things as "inactive members," "the lack of cooperation between the session and deaconate," and "the deficit in offerings." His conclusion is one of praise and affirmation, but he also strongly pleads for even greater faithfulness.[7]

The people of God in the churches who shared life with him as pastor, and, above all, as seminary president, were a source of strength, wisdom, and challenge for President Richards.

While none of the above is exaggeration, no one is perfect. Were there flaws in approach and personality that appear in the life and ministry of a gifted faithful servant of Jesus Christ? Inhibited by my own indebtedness to James McDowell Richards, I would have to think hard to come up with anything major or extensive. What about his patience with and acceptance of students, faculty, and ministers throughout the Church? His confidence in a few was obviously misplaced. He, as did seminary presidents for years, received many requests for recommendations. He always gave priority to Columbia graduates. At times, he seemed to lean over backwards to give some of them the benefit of the doubt. He defended his practices, however, once saying, "I have never consciously recommended anyone for a Church where I believe he was not qualified for it, and I do not intend to do so."[8]

A description, frank and candid, was sent in response to a request for an evaluation of a graduate: "As a student here, Mr. ——— did about average work in his classes and showed somewhat more than average promise as a preacher. He is aggressive and not lacking in self-confidence. He is perhaps a little inclined to hot-headedness and I do not think that his judgment in all matters is particularly sound. However, I do not question the sincerity of his Christian character and motives."[9]

He could be firm, of course, in matters both large and small. For example, one student kept a dog in his room on campus in clear violation of campus life policies. One cold winter day, he decided to wash the dog in the main floor men's rest room. This event took place on a weekend when the students and faculty were away. However, Richards came up the hill from the president's house and, as he entered Campbell Hall, heard the strange sounds of water splashing, a student whistling a merry tune, and a dog barking its protests! He turned, opened the door, and faced the guilty perpetrator with obvious irritation at such a violation of campus rules.

The student remarked, "I'll be through in a minute, Dr. Richards, and I'll get my dog out of here and you'll never know I've been here on this freezing, cold day!"

President Richards icily replied, "See that you do!"

The next morning, without being summoned, the student visited the president in his office, and the conversation went immediately to the point: "I'm sorry, Dr. Richards, I know I upset you sometimes, but I'm sorry. I promise to do better."

President Richards responded, "Well, Mr. ———, we have learned that you are different from the other students. You seem to have a little more of the animal in you than they."

More seriously, in attempting to be scrupulously fair, Richards would recommend students to churches as pastors, even though there were some difficulties and, sometimes, very serious problems, in their lives. To his credit, he was frank with the churches about these matters, but in the days when ministers were in short supply, graduates could easily get a call. Sometimes those recommended turned out to be disasters. Some, however, grew into effective servants of the Church. Fortunately, the disasters were a rare occurrence.

What was most difficult for President Richards was the change in governance for educational institutions such as a seminary. For years, he appointed faculty, approved curriculum, planned the budget, and all of the while sought gifts for the institution. In the last half of his presidency, the collegial system became the pattern. Faculty participated in appointments and planned curriculum with increasing authority. The multiplication of numbers of faculty, students, and, of course, meetings and committees ultimately changed the life of the institution in graphic ways. Though it was not easy for him, to his credit and to the benefit of all who followed, Columbia gradually moved to a more collegial and consultative system.

For example, once, three young and valuable faculty members came to ask for a joint committee of administration and faculty. The scope of their task would include most important decisions in academic matters and, especially, faculty appointments. He listened with growing impatience, looked out the office window, and his face reddened a bit. After a long silence, he replied, "I don't see what is wrong with the present system of appointment, for all of you are here today because of it! I didn't do so badly, did I?"[10]

Indeed, President James McDowell Richards did well.

Notes

Prologue

1. James Kilpatrick, *New York Times*, Sunday, 11 June 2000.
2. Jack Welch and John A. Byrne, *Jack: Straight From the Gut* (New York, N.Y.: Warner Books Incorporated, 2001), 1.
3. Richards' sister, Mrs. Jane Leighton Liston, provided a complete genealogy of more that two hundred relatives of Richards.
4. Report to the faculty and Board of Directors, 28 March 1966, Richards Papers, Presbyterian Historical Society, Montreat, N.C.
5. Richards, sermon, "The Inevitable Choice," ed. Ferguson Wood, *Living Echoes* (1943): 11.

Chapter One

1. T. Erskine Clarke, introduction to *As I Remember It: Columbia Theological Seminary 1932–1971*, by J. McDowell Richards (Columbia, S.C.: CTS Press, 1985), 2.
2. Richards to his father, Charles Malone Richards, Richards Papers.
3. James McDowell to Charles Malone Richards, 22 January 1895, Richards Papers.
4. "Liberty Hill Church Centennial," *Camden News* (21 August 1951), 1.
5. Charles Malone Richards' life spanned from February 1, 1871 to December 25, 1964.
6. *Davidson Update* (10 October 1938): 2.
7. Gillespie to Richards, 2 March 1946, citing Thornwell Jacob's autobiography, Richards Papers.
8. This name is also used by Richards' children for him.
9. A full discussion of this issue is found in chapter 6, on Richards' role as presbyter.
10. With a goal of $75,000, the campaign produced $89,915.36.
11. Richards to Charles Malone Richards, 4 May 1943, Richards Papers.
12. Ibid., 5 November 1943.
13. Ibid., 5 August 1943.
14. Turner to Richards, 5 August 1943, Richards Papers.
15. Huie to Richards, 28 December 1964, Richards Papers.
16. *Charlotte Observer* (26 December 1964): 3.
17. Walter L. Lingle, *Memories of Davidson College* (Richmond, Va.: John Knox Press, 1947), 47.
18. Richards to his sister, Mrs. J. C. Bailey, 9 December 1936, Richards Papers. Her letter enclosed a check to Columbia Seminary designated for the president's salary.
19. Richards to his sister, Mary Richards, 13 April 1938, Richards Papers.

20. Richards to Mr. and Mrs. John C. Bailey, 4 November 1949, Richards Papers.

21. Richards to First Presbyterian Church, Thomasville, Ga., 31 December 1945, Richards Papers.

22. Richards to Cola Barr Stamper, 9 February 1944, Richards Papers.

23. Letter, Richards Papers.

24. Richards to First Presbyterian Church, Thomasville, Ga., 11 February 1947, Richards Papers.

25. Richards to Binns, 7 October 1955, Richards Papers.

26. Richards to Roberts, 1 September 1954, copy.

27. Richards to Roberts, 21 December 1955, Richards Papers.

28. Delores L. Donnelly, "He Clanged No Cymbals, Sounded No Trumpets," *Atlanta Constitution* (2 May 1979): 5.

29. Richards to Roberts, 21 December 1955, Richards Papers.

30. Colossians 4:7 (KJV).

31. Ibid.

32. J. Phillips Noble, sermon, "Discovering the Key to a Transformed Life," First Scots Church, Charleston, S.C., 9 May 1982.

33. Mrs. J. Holmes Smith to Richards, 13 December 1940, Richards Papers.

34. Richards to FPC, Winston Salem, N.C., 17 December 1940, Richards Papers.

35. Richards, 18 December 1940, Richards Papers.

36. Richards to Salters, Richards Papers.

37. Richards Papers.

38. Richards to Moffatt, 2 February 1965, Richards Papers.

39. Ibid.

40. Richards Papers.

41. Donnelly, "Sounded No Trumpets," 5.

42. Ibid.

43. Richards Papers.

44. Ibid.

45. Richards to Young, 20 December 1960, Richards Papers.

46. Gault to Richards, 11 October 1969, Richards Papers.

47. Richards to Gault, 14 October 1969, Richards Papers.

48. Expressed to faculty, 25 August, 1970.

49. Richards to prospective donors, 25 August 1970, Richards Papers.

50. Gordon to Richards, Richards Papers.

51. Richards to student, 8 September 1964, Richards Papers.

52. Richards to Charles Malone Richards, Richards Papers. The faculty invited Dr. Richards' father, Professor Charles Malone Richards of Davidson College, to give three chapel talks on "A Minister's Family Life," "Prayer Life," and "Use of the Bible." The honorarium included tickets to the Tech-Navy football game.

53. There are no prayers before football games today, except in rare instances. Neither are prayers offered in public gatherings asked "in Christ's name."

54. Richards to executive, 15 January 1943, Richards Papers.

55. Richards to graduate, 17 December 1954, Richards Papers.

56. Ibid.

57. Harrison to Huie, 5 July 1948, Richards Papers.

58. Miller to Richards, 2 April 1944, Richards Papers.

59. Miller to Richards, Richards Papers.

60. One of the Marys is Richards' sister, and the other her friend, Mary Black.

61. Richards' Diary, October 1923–March 1924, Richards Papers.

62. Interviewer from the *Atlanta Constitution*. Richards spoke of the twenty years since his "Brother in Black" sermon. He contrasted the issue then as being equal treatment and equal facilities, but in 1940 it was integration of the races.

Chapter Two

1. T. M. Cornfield in *The Academic Mysteryhouse, the Man, the Campus, and Their New Search for Meaning*, by Robert Merrill Holmes, (Nashville, Tenn.: Abingdon Press, 1970), v.

2. The effort to secure the original chapel for the historic site in Columbia, South Carolina, failed in the face of other more urgent and critical needs to survive as a resource for the Presbyterian Church. It was given to Winthrop College. However, the Women's Club of Columbia has originated and supported the effort to make that entire city block once used by Columbia Seminary a registered historic site. The building and the property have been restored and maintained. The club's generous support and productive effort resulted in a splendid historic site focusing on Woodrow Wilson's heritage through his family. Wilson's father and uncle taught at Columbia Seminary from 1828 to 1927 when it was located in Columbia, South Carolina.

3. The official seal of Columbia Seminary included a motto: "Poimenes and didaskolos," which is translated, "pastors and teachers."

4. One of the battles around Atlanta in the Civil War was fought in this area. Bullets, cannon balls, and other debris from the battle have been found in significant amounts by archeologists.

5. Emeritus professor of Christian theology, McGill University, Montreal, Canada.

6. Douglas John Hall, "Stewardship as a Missional Discipline," *Journal For Preachers* (Advent, 1998): 19–27.

7. More in-depth discussions of this view may be found in three works by Douglas John Hall, *The Steward: A Biblical Symbol Come of Age* (New York: Friendship Press, 1982); *Imagine God: Dominion as Stewardship* (New York: Friendship Press, 1984); and *Stewardship of Life in the Kingdom of Death* (New York: Friendship Press, 1985).

8. 4 June 1930, Richards Papers.

9. Patrick Dwight Miller and C. Darby Fulton were two of the twenty-three people asked to assume the presidency.

10. Richards, *As I Remember It*, 60.

11. The General Assembly during this decade first rejected the idea of merger of the seminaries, and then in 1938, approved it. The merger failed to receive approval by the synods who owned and controlled the seminaries. It is enormously helpful to the health of the Church in the "New South" that Columbia remained in the heart of this dynamic region, the southeastern United States.

12. Richards, inaugural address, Columbia Theological Seminary, 1933.

13. Ibid.

14. Richards to Campbell, 6 September 1932, Richards Papers.

15. Campbell to Richards, 11 October 1932, Richards Papers.

16. The great generosity of one of Atlanta's most devoted Presbyterian elders led Mr. Campbell in later years to establish foundations which were, and still are, a great power for good in the Church and community. Of course, one of his earliest gifts enabled the seminary to move to Decatur, Georgia, from Columbia, South Carolina. The first building, Campbell Hall, was named for his mother, Virginia Orme Campbell. Mr. Campbell's father died when he was four years old, and Mr. Campbell and his mother

were devoted to each other. Campbell Hall was the center of seminary life until 1950, and was used for offices, classrooms, library, chapel, and dining hall. The fourth floor also provided rooms for single students, although Simons-Law Hall was the dormitory for the majority of students.

17. Richards to Campbell, 21 December 1932, Richards Papers.

18. In 1929, Leila Russell wrote to President Gillespie suggesting that the seminary chapel in Columbia, South Carolina, be moved to the new campus. Even though it had "hallowed memories" and Woodrow Wilson, as a seventeen-year-old, made a profession of faith there, the money could not be found to do it. However, in the 1980s, the Historical Society of Columbia, South Carolina, moved it to its original location. An entire city block is designated as an historic site and preserves the original building of Columbia Seminary as well as the chapel.

19. Campbell to Richards, 27 January 1934, Richards Papers.

20. Campell to Lindsey Hopkins, 29 January 1934, Richards Papers.

21. Campbell to Richards, 1 February 1933, Richards Papers. Mr. Campbell suggested and, perhaps, directed President Richards to go to the churches of the constituency and tell the story.

22. Richards to Campbell, 29 January 1934, Richards Papers.

23. Ibid., 20 May 1933.

24. Tenney, address, 4 February 1934.

25. Plan of Government, 1936.

26. Ibid.

27. In the collegial system, the president leads consultations with faculty, administrative staff, trustees, and when appropriate, student leaders.

28. McSween to Richards, 9 April 1936, Richards Papers.

29. Ibid., 27 April 1936.

30. Memorial bulletin, "John Bulow Campbell, Esq., 1870–1940," 28 June 1940, Richards Papers.

31. Ibid., 18.

32. Ladd to Richards, 22 July 1941, Richards Papers.

33. President Richards' first budget in 1932 was supposedly $30,000, but he never had more than $20,000 in hand. In 1940, the total budget was $26,732.

34. The role of the president was beginning to change with delegation of decisions to faculty and administrative staff. The greatest changes were to come during the last twenty years of Richards' presidency, but already the Plan of Government was studied and revised during the 1940s.

35. Winston Churchill was elected again as prime minister in 1951, and in the four-year term sought valiantly to keep war from breaking out with Soviet Russia.

36. The simple cottage at Warm Springs, Georgia, designed by Richards' brother-in-law, Henry J. Toombs, is well-maintained today, and often visited by tourists and Roosevelt scholars. It is deceptively plain with small rooms and sparse furnishings. One ordinary dial phone by the small bed in Roosevelt's bedroom is the only visible instrument of communication with the world in the cottage. No doubt there were others used by the secret service persons who guarded the president and his staff.

37. William Childs Robinson, sermon, 7 April 1945, *Christian Observer* (2 May 1945): 3.

38. Franklin D. Roosevelt to Robinson, 11 April 1945, shortly before the end of the war in Europe, Richards Papers.

39. This phrase is no longer in the vows ministers take when ordained and installed.

40. Board of Directors, meeting minutes, October 1940.

41. Metropolitan Atlanta has seen explosive growth. The population reached one million by the 1960s, and today has a population of four million people.

42. Churchill's warning was sounded in an address at Westminster College in Fulton, Missouri.

43. Today, with "at-large trustees" elected by the board, lay members are often in the majority.

44. Plan of Government, spring meeting, 1950.

45. Richards admits, however, that he doesn't agree with all of it. Cf. Letter, 5 June 1945, *A Conservative Introduction to the Old Testament.*

46. Actually, Professor Cartledge did his study for the Ph.D. in the field of textual criticism which, unlike higher criticism, seeks to determine the earliest and most accurate texts of Biblical material, which, of course, were copies of the original manuscripts.

47. The reference here refers to the theological and ecclesiastical commitments required by the *Book of Church Order* at that time.

48. Plan of Government (1936).

49. Richards to Charles Malone Richards, 10 December 1944, Richards Papers.

50. Review by Cresap and Associates.

51. Ibid.

52. J. McDowell Richards, "The Crisis of Our Times," report to Board of Directors, Columbia Theological Seminary (20 March 1954): 43.

53. In the last decade of his presidency, Richards would say "men and women." It meant breaking a lifelong habit, of course.

54. J. McDowell Richards, article, Richards Papers.

55. Richards Papers.

56. There were from time to time strong criticisms from more conservative church ministers and laypersons. These were usually about faculty or Richards' positions on racial justice and in ecumenical bodies.

57. Richards took great satisfaction in a record of "no deficits."

58. The Presbyterian Church (U.S.) first ordained a female, Rachel Henderlite, on May 12, 1965. She was a graduate of Austin Presbyterian Theological Seminary.

59. The curriculum is described in general terms with areas and required hours: Hebrew, 15; Greek, 15; biblical studies, 18; theology, 24; church history, 17; preaching, 6; Christian education, 4; pastoral work, 4; psychology, 6; apologetics, 4; hymnology, 3; evangelism, 4; speech, 3; and electives, 27. Among the electives, the most frequently selected were English Bible, systematic theology, and pastoral counseling.

60. P. D. Miller, address, 25 October 1958. To the completion of his service, Richards gave priority to a balanced budget. Even when the Board of Directors approved an increase, he had to be persuaded that the members would help secure the necessary funds for the total budget.

61. Consultation on Churches Uniting (COCU) is an organization in consultation with various denominations seeking an ecumenical organization for the whole Christian Church.

62. United Presbyterian Church in the United States of America (UPCUSA).

63. Richards, president's report to the Board of Directors of Columbia Theological Seminary, 11 November 1969, Richards Papers.

64. Today, all students who have completed a four-year bachelor's degree in colleges and universities will receive the master of divinity for satisfactory work in the seminary course of study. This is true for all institutions that are members of the Association of Theological Schools for the United States and Canada.

65. Richards, president's report to the Board of Directors of Columbia Theological Seminary, 20 April 1971, Richards Papers.

66. Such gifts are now called "grants from mission dollars."

67. The gift was to be in the form of an annuity and would go to Columbia Seminary at the donor's death.

68. Letter to Richards, 1963 or 1964, Richards Papers.

69. Watson to Richards, 20 October 1965, Richards Papers.

70. Winn to Richards, 10 September 1960, Richards Papers.

71. Richards to Reeves, 10 November 1964, Richards Papers. The book referred to, *Christian Doctrine* (1968), was used in the Covenant Life curriculum of the Presbyterian Church (U.S.), and has been circulated around the world as an excellent summary of Reformed Theology. A revised edition is now in print. Guthrie received an honorarium of $300 for the first edition and much, much more for the revised one!

72. Richards' relationship to students is further discussed in chapter four, regarding his role as pastor.

73. Bailey to Richards, 3 May 1970, Richards Papers.

74. Albert S. Winn, pamphlet, "Spiritual Resources and Disciplines," 19 March 1969, Richards Papers.

75. The analysis of unfair attacks on Columbia Seminary was addressed to the Board of Directors, board minutes, 28 September 1970, Richards Papers.

76. Presbyterian Churchmen United was formed by ministers and sessions of the Presbyterian Church (U.S.) and existed for a relatively short period leading up to the formation of the Presbyterian Church in America. John E. Richards of Macon, Georgia, served as executive secretary. Other groups with similar criticisms have continued.

77. Wallace to Richards, 29 September 1970, Richards Papers.

78. Ibid.

79. J. Millen Darnell, president, World Mission Chairmen's Association, to Richards, 21 March 1970, Richards Papers.

Chapter Three

1. Acts 20:27 (RSV). It was a part of Paul's eloquent farewell address to the elders of the Ephesus church as he departed on a hazardous journey to Jerusalem.

2. Several chapel talks in the last five years of his presidency were based on brief notes. Since the service was only thirty minutes, the talks were no more than ten or fifteen minutes.

3. Richards, "Men Perplexed by a Changing World," *Presbyterian Survey* (February 1964): 6.

4. Richards, "The Relevance of the Gospel," Richards Papers.

5. Based on a quotation from F. W. Boreham of England. It also appears in a sermon preached by Richards in First Presbyterian Church Staunton, Virginia, on January 8, 1956, at a celebration of the one hundredth anniversary of the birth of President Woodrow Wilson in Staunton, entitled "Woodrow Wilson—The Christian and the Churchman."

6. The collection of sermons, Richards Papers.

7. Richards defined that truth as one that includes the Christian gospel and the Presbyterian heritage. The collection of sermons, Richards Papers.

8. The collection of sermons, Richards Papers.

9. Chapter 6, "Prophet," provides a detailed discussion of this very widely read sermon.

10. Richards, "Brothers in Black," Atlanta Presbytery, 14 October 1940.

11. Richards always affirmed the authority of Scripture as interpreted by the Holy Spirit.

12. Richards often taught this book in Columbia's curriculum early in his presidency.

13. Richards, "Is There Any Word from the Lord for Today?," Richards Papers.

14. Ibid.

15. George Buttrick, *Jesus Came Preaching* (New York: Charles Scribner's Sons, 1931), 89.

16. Ibid.

17. Richards, "Preaching and the Issues of Today," 25 October 1966, Erskine Theological Seminary, Due West, S.C.

18. Ministers and elders from Florida, Georgia, and South Carolina attended the 1974 Synod of the Southeast in Spartanburg, South Carolina.

19. Richards, "A Benediction," 1974 Synod of the Southeast, Richards Papers.

20. Richards, sermon, "Principle or Profit," Richards Papers.

21. Ibid.

22. Ibid.

23. Richards, sermon, "The Christian Sabbath in Contemporary Society," Richards Papers.

24. Richards, "Christian Education and Evangelism," Richards Papers.

25. Richards affirmed that God used the uneducated in the formal sense, but suggested that many bizarre and dangerous heresies are perpetuated by the uneducated.

26. "Church triumphant" refers to those in heaven.

27. Richards, Davidson College Church, 1952, Richards Papers.

28. Ibid.

29. Richards, "The God of History," Richards Papers.

30. This sermon reflects quite clearly Richards' view of the church and Davidson College.

31. Richards, memorial sermon for Mrs. J. Holmes Smith, 15 May 1978, Richards Papers.

32. Shields to Richards, 27 May 1978, Richards Papers.

33. Richards, memorial sermon for Patrick Dwight Miller, 5 July 1974, Richards Papers.

34. Ibid.

35. Richards, memorial sermon for Eugene T. Wilson, 23 May 1978, Richards Papers.

36. Willis to Richards, 20 June 1959, Richards Papers.

37. Wardlaw to Richards, 17 September 1969, Richards Papers.

38. Boyd displayed an admirable spirit in his actions when the minister, on leave to serve in the military chaplaincy, returned and wanted to assume the pastorate there. Boyd sought another call without complaint and acted with honor and grace.

39. Fry Jr. to Richards, 25 November 1948, Richards Papers. Richards, with typical frugality, presented expenses involved in the amount of ten dollars.

40. An example of Richards' frugality and willingness to serve the churches is that he received very little in the way of honoria and expense reimbursement. This Holy Week program offered $250 from which he paid travel, hotel, and meal expense. Little would remain after those deductions.

41. Funk to Richards, 17 April 1944, Richards Papers.

42. Station WSB asked Dr. Charles A. Sheldon, the organist-choirmaster of First Presbyterian Church of Atlanta, to play organ music to fill in gaps in programming. He reported to me once that he sometimes played for three hours without more than a brief break once or twice in that time.

43. The theme could be summarized by the statement, "The true Christian cannot be a person of pride."

44. Richards to Hudson, 12 January 1944, Richards Papers.

45. Mr. and Mrs. George F. Nixon to Richards, 10 January 1944, Richards Papers.
46. Dr. and Mrs. D. P. McGeachy Sr. to Richards, 22 December 1946, Richards Papers.
47. Richards, "In the Hands of God," 3 October 1948, Richards Papers.

Chapter Four
1. MacNair to J. Davison Philips, 10 September 1977, Richards Papers.
2. MacNair to Richards, 14 June 1947, Richards Papers.
3. Richards to pastor, 5 October 1954, Richards Papers.
4. Letter to Richards, 13 August 1943, Richards Papers.
5. Richards, president's report to the Board of Directors of Columbia Theological Seminary, 8 May 1962, Richards Papers.
6. Richards to researcher, 30 September 1946, Richards Papers.
7. Richards to Boyd, 1 July 1949, Richards Papers.
8. He served Central Presbyterian Church, Atlanta, Ga., 1930–58.
9. Lecture, 26 July 1978, Richards Papers.
10. Minister to Richards, Richards Papers.
11. Richards to Dugger, 6 May 1948, Richards Papers.
12. Ibid.
13. Minister to Richards, 30 May 1940, Richards Papers.
14. Minister to Richards, 30 April 1964, Richards Papers.
15. Leith to Richards, 2 August 1943 Richards Papers.
16. After ordination, they were recipients of his encouragement in their careers. Equally important, Leith sent them synopses of current theological research and made recommendations of many to churches seeking pastors.
17. Richards Papers.
18. Richards to pastor, Richards Papers.
19. Minister to Richards, Richards Papers.
20. Mathes to Richards, 16 April 1969, Richards Papers.
21. Pastor to Richards, 1 May 1947, Richards Papers.
22. Minister to Richards, 10 April 1956, Richards Papers.
23. Richards to pastor, 1 May 1947, Richards Papers.
24. Reference to this citation from one of Crane's books appears in an address to the faculty in the fall of 1953.
25. Richards understood that a letter can ventilate frustration, but also that frustration of this kind is not unusual in the pastorate. Pastor to Richards, Richards Papers.
26. Letter to Richards, Richards Papers.
27. Richards letter, 10 April 1956, Richards Papers.
28. Richards to minister, 1 December 1945, Richards Papers.
29. Wardlaw to Richards, 15 January 1948, Richards Papers.
30. Richards letter, 28 January 1947, Richards Papers.
31. Ibid.
32. Letter, 14 December 1960, Richards Papers.
33. Harrington to Richards, 17 March 1964, Richards Papers.
34. Ibid., 1 May 1966.
35. An example of this rescue effort was a provision of $250 per month for a minister exhausted by pressures and problems at this time to study at Columbia Seminary and, hopefully, to heal. Letter, 30 April 1964, Richards Papers.
36. Smith Jr. to Richards, 30 January 1963, Richards Papers.
37. Richards to Smith Jr., 14 February 1964, Richards Papers.

38. Carter to Richards, 18 March 1970, Richards Papers.
39. Minister to Richards, 26 May 1970, Richards Papers.
40. Nam Chin Cha to Richards, 2 January 1964, Richards Papers.
41. Ibid.
42. Richards to Nam Chin Cha, 2 February 1964, Richards Papers.
43. Glasure to Richards, 23 May 1944, Richards Papers.
44. Minister to Richards, 24 January 1953, Richards Papers.
45. Richards to Dr. and Mrs. Boyce, 1 December 1943, Richards Papers.
46. Boyce to Richards, 10 January 1944, Richards Papers.
47. Richards to Montgomery, Richards Papers.
48. Richards to Malcolm and Sally Bullock, 9 October 1965, Richards Papers.
49. Richards to missionaries, 1 December 1955, Richards Papers.
50. Swetnam to Richards, 30 January 1949, Richards Papers.
51. Moore to Mrs. Eugene L. Daniel, 6 April 1943, Richards Papers.
52. Eugene L. Daniel Jr., *In the Presence of Mine Enemies: An American Chaplain in World War II German Prison of War Camps* (Attleboro, Mass.: Colonial Lithograph, Inc., 1985), 20.
53. Richards Papers.
54. The one-year course in Christian education included both educational and biblical units.
55. Richards to Arbuthnot, 1 December 1940, Richards Papers.

Chapter Five

1. It was later known as the Committee on Christian Relations.
2. The excellent collection of Richards' essays, articles, and sermons, "Change and the Changeless," published by the faculty at the time of his retirement, provides not only this list, but comments on the settings of many of them.
3. Walter W. Van Kirk to Richards, 14 January 1943, Richards Papers.
4. Ibid.
5. Richards to Westcott, 14 January 1947, Richards Papers.
6. That meeting of the General Assembly met in First Presbyterian Church, Atlanta, Georgia.
7. Humphrey to Richards, 2 June 1948, Richards Papers.
8. Richards to family, 23 September 1955, Richards Papers.
9. The official title of the denomination was the Presbyterian Church, U.S.; however, it was largely Southern in its membership.
10. This statement was used throughout the Church in the United States and in areas overseas as an official statement of mission for the board.
11. Those who signed this evaluation included eight of the most useful leaders of the entire Church.
12. Richards gradually began to move from masculine words about ministers and elders, but his habit never ended completely.
13. Seven single-spaced pages presented a balanced and honest position. Richards dealt with twelve aspects of the disunity in the Church and the biblical case for unity.
14. Moderator's letter to the Presbyterian Church (U.S.), 16 July 1964, Richards Papers.
15. A significant address delivered on 11 November 1968. He was asked to present a formal analysis of the state of the seminary by the board and the faculty.
16. Ibid.

17. Ibid.
18. Ibid.
19. Ibid.
20. Ibid.
21. Ibid.
22. Richards, report to the Board of Directors of Columbia Theological Seminary, 20 October 1970, Richards Papers.
23. Ibid.
24. Ibid.
25. Richards Papers; author's personal files.
26. Richards, report to the supporting synods, 28 October 1970, Richards Papers.
27. Coblenz to the Covenant Fellowship of Presbyterians, 5 January 1971, Richards Papers.
28. Richards, report to the Board of Directors of Columbia Theological Seminary, regarding Columbia Seminary and segregation, 25 October 1963, Richards Papers.
29. Professor Thomson served Columbia Theological Seminary for several years as a visiting professor of New Testament.
30. Richards to Thomson, 3 February 1970, Richards Papers.

Chapter Six
1. Richards, *As I Remember It*, 7.
2. Richards Diary, 19 October 1923, Richards Papers.
3. The term "Negro" was the choice of the Civil Rights leaders of the time, including Martin Luther King Jr. Today, "African-American" is the preferred title.
4. Moderators serve for terms, usually for one meeting and during the intervening months until the next meeting.
5. Richards, *As I Remember It*, 76.
6. Ibid.
7. Richards, "Brothers in Black," Atlanta Presbytery, 14 October 1940.
8. Ibid.
9. Ibid.
10. Ibid., 10.
11. Ibid., 3.
12. Ibid., 4.
13. Ibid.
14. Ibid.
15. Ibid., 10.
16. Ibid., 11.
17. Delores L. Donnelly, "A Modern Prophet," 4 May 1979, *Atlanta Constitution*.
18. Richards to Abernethy, 5 October 1943, Richards Papers.
19. Richards to Abernethy, director of Commission on the Church and Minority People, 6 April 1944, Richards Papers.
20. Unfortunately, during World War II the war mobilization refused permission for travel to the meeting to deal with this issue, since travel was largely restricted to the military.
21. Richards Papers.
22. Although some individuals wrote more critical accusations in letters than they would affirm face to face, they were passionate and dead serious in their commitments. Richards Papers.

23. Richards to Elliott Jr., 24 April 1943, Richards Papers.
24. Letter to Richards, 19 February 1943, Richards Papers.
25. Richards to elder, 20 January 1947, Richards Papers.
26. Richards to critic, 11 March 1947, Richards Papers.
27. Richards Papers.
28. Richards to Federal Council, 31 January 1946, Richards Papers.
29. Richards, manuscript, 2 April 1951, Richards Papers.
30. Minutes, Atlanta Christian Council, 26 April 1946, Richards Papers.
31. Hartsfield was famous for his slogan at that time, "Atlanta, a City too busy to hate."
32. Brewer to Richards, 5 October 1946, Richards Papers.
33. The Rev. M. L. King Sr. was the father of the famous Civil Rights leader, Martin Luther King Jr.
34. The council was opposed.
35. David Marx, Richards Papers.
36. Lacy Jr. to Richards, 20 May 1943, Richards Papers.
37. Richards to Lacy Jr., 24 May 1943, Richards Papers.
38. McGeachy to Richards, 18 April 1943, Richards Papers.
39. Richards to McGeachy, 29 April 1943, Richards Papers.

Epilogue
1. Richards was the first Rhodes Scholar chosen from the South along with William Stubbs of Emory University.
2. Richards Diary, April 1924, Richards Papers.
3. Richards, meditation, memorial service for Gear, Richards Papers.
4. Richards to Mackay, 10 June 1943, Richards Papers. These suggestions were in response to the constitution of the new publication *Theology Today*, and Mackay's request for a response from each board member.
5. Richards Papers.
6. Richards Diary, 25 December 1923, Richards Papers.
7. Richards, report to the session, undated, Richards Papers.
8. Richards to Board of Directors, Columbia Theological Seminary, 29 January 1943, Richards Papers.
9. Richards, letter to a church, 21 April 1951, Richards Papers.
10. Reported by one of the three professors involved.

Selected Bibliography

Buttrick, George. *Jesus Came Preaching*. New York: Charles Scribner's Sons, 1931.

Charlotte Observer (26 December 1964): 3.

Clarke, T. Erskine. In *As I Remember It: Columbia Theological Seminary 1932–1971*. Columbia, S.C.: CTS Press, 1985.

Cornfield, T. M. In *The Academic Mysteryhouse, the Man, the Campus, and Their New Search for Meaning*. Nashville, Tenn.: Abingdon Press, 1970.

Daniel, Eugene L., Jr. *In the Presence of Mine Enemies: An American Chaplain in World War II German Prison of War Camps*. Attleboro, Mass.: Colonial Lithograph, Inc., 1985.

Davidson Update (10 October 1938): 2.

Donnelly, Delores L. "He Clanged No Cymbals, Sounded No Trumpets." *Atlanta Constitution* (2 May 1979): 5.

———. "A Modern Prophet." *Atlanta Constitution* (4 May 1979).

Hall, Douglas John. "Stewardship as a Missional Discipline." *Journal For Preachers* (Advent, 1998): 19–27.

Kilpatrick, James. *New York Times* (Sunday, 11 June 2000).

"Liberty Hill Church Centennial." *Camden News* (21 August 1951).

Lingle, Walter L. *Memories of Davidson College*. Richmond, Va.: John Knox Press, 1947.

Noble, J. Phillips. "Discovering the Key to a Transformed Life." First Scots Church, Charleston, S.C. (9 May 1982).

Richards, J. McDowell. "Brothers in Black." Atlanta Presbytery (14 October 1940).

———. "The Crisis of Our Times." Columbia Theological Seminary (20 March 1954).

———. "The Inevitable Choice." Edited by Ferguson Wood. *Living Echoes* (1943): 11.

———. "Perplexed by a Changing World." *Presbyterian Survey* (February 1964): 6.

———. "Preaching and the Issues of Today." Erskine Theological Seminary, Due West, S.C. (25 October 1966).

Richards Papers. Presbyterian Historical Society, Montreat, N.C.

Robinson, William Childs. Sermon (7 April 1945). *Christian Observer* (2 May 1945): 3.

Welch, Jack and John A. Byrne. *Jack: Straight From the Gut*. New York: Warner Books Incorporated, 2001.

Selected bibliography

Index

Aberdeen, Scotland, 73
Abernethy, Bradford, 164
Abingdon Presbytery, 75
"The Academic Mysteryhouse,"
 31
Achenbach, G. H., 154
Administrative Council, 147
Agnes Scott College, 9, 62, 67,
 69, 79, 138, 144, 155, 175, 180
Albright, William, 46
Alexander, John M., 143, 146
Alumni Association, 18, 73, 80
American Association of
 Theological Schools, 39
American Theological Society, 45
Amite, La., 132
Amsterdam Holland, 105
Andalusia, Ala., 102, 114
Anderson, Marion, 52
Annapolis (Naval Academy), 35
Arbuthnot, Charles B., Jr., 135
Area Laboratory School, 101
"Articles, Essays, and Sermons
 by James McDowell
 Richards," 86
Associate Reformed
 Presbyterian Church, 96, 180
Association of Theological
 Schools, 61
Association of Theological
 Schools of the United States
 and Canada, 181
Atlanta, Ga., 9, 26, 32–34, 37–41,
 44, 49, 51, 54, 61, 66, 80, 84,
 87, 89, 97–98, 100, 124, 135,
 153, 163, 165–66, 170, 172,
 175–78, 180
Atlanta Art Association, 138, 144
Atlanta Christian Council, 139,
 166, 171
Atlanta *Journal-Constitution*, 37,
 97–98, 159, 167
Atlanta Manifesto, 164

Atlanta Presbytery, 39, 41, 80,
 86, 97, 138, 140, 158–60, 164,
 174
Atlanta Public Library, 62
Atlanta Theological Association,
 61, 139, 144, 180
Atlanta University Center, 175,
 180
Atlee, Clement, 19, 49
Auburn, Ala., 116
Auburn University, 26
Augusta, Ga., 91, 102
Austin, Tex., 32
Austin Seminary, 6, 48
Bailey, Donald B., 73–74
Bailey, John C., Jr., 8, 10
Baptist Church, 180
Barth, Karl, 77, 105
Battle of Waterloo, 95
"Beer Hall Putsch," 158
Beethoven, 86
Bennett, John, 174
Benton, Wilson, 71
Bethesda Presbyterian Church,
 105
Bethlehem, 82
Binns, J., 11
Birmingham, Ala., 112
Black, Mary, **28**
Blackwelder, Oscar F., 41
Board of Church Extension, 99,
 138–39
Board of Cooperators, 139
Board of Directors, 63–64, 68,
 73, 98, 172
Board of World Missions, 76–77,
 129–30, 138–39, 146–47
Bonn, Germany, 29
Book of Church Order, 78, 115
Book of Order, 52, 139
Book of Remembrance, 18
Boreham, F. W., 81
Boyce, James R., 129–30

Boyce, Mrs. James R., 129
Boyd, William H., 102, 110
Brantley, J. T., 34
Brewer, Ernest, 177
"Brothers in Black," 86, 124–25,
 138, 140, 158–60, 163, 174
Brown, Aubrey N., 146
Bullock, Malcolm, 130
Bullock, Sally, 130
Buttrick, George, 90, 174
Cairns, David, 74
"A Call to Civil Obedience and
 Racial Good Will," 86, 167
Calvin, John, 89
Calvinism, 19, 75, 89, 136
Calvinist, 150
Cambridge University, 31
Camden, S.C., 105
Camden News, 4
Campbell, John Bulow, 32, 34,
 36–39, 42–44
Campbell Hall, 21, 51, 107, 111
Camp Chaffee, Ark., 11
Candidates Committee, 129, 147
Candler School of Theology, 34,
 61–62, 139, 144, 176, 180
Capek, Milio, 45
Carmichael, O. C., 69
Carrollton Presbyterian Church,
 145
Carter, George D., 125–26
Cartledge, Samuel A., 52–53, 73
Catholic Church, 144
Cedartown, Ga., 23
Central Presbyterian Church,
 166, 178
Central Presbyterian Church
 (Newark, N.J.), 127
Central Presbyterian Church of
 Atlanta, 9, 36, 81, 89, 97, 111
Central's Sunday Worship, 98
Cha, Nam Chin, 127
Chamblin, Knox, 71

"Change and the Changeless," 80, 86

Chaplains Corps, 132

Charleston, S.C., 89

Charleston, W.Va., 2

Charleston Bible Society, 89

Charles Watt Award, 164

Charlottesville, Va., 34

Cherokee Indian, 74

Chicago Cubs, 26

Chopin, Frederick, 82

Christ Church College, Oxford University, 14, 20, 28, 78–79

Christian Beacon, 7, 143

"The Christian Church in a World at War," 86, 141

Christian Council, 98, 177

Christian Council of Atlanta, 136, 164, 175–76, 178–79

"Christian Education and Evangelism," 93

Christian Observer, 47

"The Christian Sabbath," 92

"The Christian Sabbath in Contemporary Society," 92

"The Christ of Bethlehem is the Hope of the World," 84

"The Church and Its Ministry," 86

Church and Society Board, 98

"The Church and the Oriental American," 165

"The Church and the World Today," 80, 84

Churches of Christ in America, 141

Churchill, Winston, 19, 46, 49

Church of Scotland, 61, 76, 118

Citronelle, Ala., 132

City Council, 177

Civil War, 32

Clarksville, Ga., 78

Clearwater, Fla., 9, 101

Cleveland, Ohio, 141

Clinton, William Jefferson, 97

Coblenz, Paul, 153

Coffin, Henry Sloan, 174

College Religious Emphasis Weeks, 81

Colossae, 15

Columbia Drive, 32, 35, 64

Columbia Friendship Circle of Presbyterian Women, 96

Columbia Theological Seminary, 2–3, 5–8, 10, 14–22, 24, 27–28, 31–44, 46–49, 51–61, 63–78, 80, 83, 89, 96–100, 102, 105, 108–110, 112–118, 120, 123, 125–27, 129–31, 134–35, 137–39, 144, 147, 150–56, 158–59, 163, 172–73, 175–76, 179–82, **56**

Columbia Theological Seminary Day, 39

"Columbia Theological Seminary—Its Present and Future," 149

Columbia, Mo., 164

Columbia, S.C., 32–34, 39, 110

Commission on the Church and Minority Peoples, 164

Commission on the Minister and His Work, 116

Commission to Study the Basis of a Just and Durable Peace, 141, 164

Committee of Women's Work, 96

Committee on a Just and Durable Peace, 30

Committee on Candidates, 139

Committee on Race Relations, 177

Committee on Refugee Theological Scholars, 45

Committee on Sabbath Observance, 142

Committee on Social and Moral Welfare, 138

Committee on the Study of Theological Education in the United States and Canada, 61

Community Life Committee, 111

Concerned Presbyterians, 18, 150, 152

"A Condemnation of Mob Violence," 86

Confederate States, 32

Conference for Women, 101

Confessing Our Faith, 104

Confession of Faith, 62, 70

Congress, 143, 165

The Consequences of Unbelief, 104

A Conservative Introduction to the Old Testament, 53

Constituting Convention, 139

Constitution of the United States, 169

Consultation on Churches Uniting (COCU), 65

Conway, S.C., 122

Cornfield, T. M., 31

Cottingham, Yorkshire, England, 11

Council Executive Committee, 143

Courts and Company, 38

Cousar, R. W. 20, 146

Covenant Fellowship of Presbyterians, 153

Covenant Life Curriculum, 73

Covenant Presbyterian Church (UPUSA), 102, 163, 167

Crane, William E., 121

Cresap and Associates, 57

"The Crisis in Missions," 76

"The Crisis of Our Times," 59

"The Crystal," 85

Cunningham, John R., 83, 146

Dalton, Ga., 143

Daniel, Eugene L., 132–34

Daniel, Mrs. Eugene L., 132–33

Darnell, J. Millen, 77

Darwin, Charles, 82

Davidson, N.C., 4, 10

Davidson Church, 8, 94–95

Davidson College, 4, 8–9, 14, 20, 24, 27–29, 41, 78–80, 82–84, 94–95, 138, 179

Davidson College Church, 96

Davis, Martha Murphy, 66

Daytona Beach, Fla., 103

Daytona Beach Presbyterian Church, 103

Decatur, Ga., 32–35, 43–44, 51, 64, 74, 97, 109, 129, 155

Decatur Presbyterian Church, 25, 32, 96, 182

Declaration of Independence, 83

DeKalb County, 155

Dekalb County Library, 62

Deland, Fla., 108

Dendy, Henry B., 146

Department of Evangelism, 175

Detroit Tigers, 26

Dickson, Bonneau H., 35, 112

"Discontent," 92

Dixon, Joe, 109

Dobbs Room, 68

"The Doctrine of the Inner Life," 74

Donnelly, Delores L., 12, 19, 163–64

Druid Hills Presbyterian Church, 135

Dugger, Oscar, 114

Dugger, Mrs. Oscar, 114

Duke Medical Center, 119

Duke University, 26, 87

Dulles, John Foster, 141, 144, 174

Edinburgh, Scotland, 41, 76, 98, 155

Editorial Council, 138

Edris, Paul, 103

Eisenhower, Dwight, 58

Elliot, William M., Jr., 172

Emory University, 62, 138, 144, 175, 180
Enoree Presbytery, 53
Episcopalian Church, 180
Erskine Theological Seminary, 24, 61, 90, 139, 144, 180
Evans, William, 41
"The Everlasting Mercy," 84
Executive Committee, 54, 141, 171
Executive Committee Federal Council of Churches of Christ in America, 138
Executive Committee on Negro Work, 139
Faith and Missions, 104
Faith and the Law, 104
The Faith of Abraham, 104
"The Faith of a Soldier," 47
Farmville Presbyterian Church, 125
Faulkner, L. E., 143
Federal Council, 141, 143, 146, 172–74
Federal Council of Churches, 7, 9, 21–22, 52, 136, 138, 143–44, 164, 171–72
Fellowship of Concern, 152
First Baptist Church, 115
First Presbyterian Church, 9–10, 17, 35, 41, 50, 69, 102, 124, 178
First Presbyterian Church, Savannah, 126
First Presbyterian Church of Atlanta, 22, 34, 103–4
First Presbyterian Church of Thomasville, Ga., 79
Food Service, 16
Fort McPherson, 80, 103
Fort Ord, Calif., 12
Foster, John S., 41
Frac, Ixta, Mexico, 129
Free Church Seminary, 41
Fry, Thomas A., Jr., 103
Fulton, S. H., 145
Funk, D. H., 103
Future Shock, 90
Gailey, James H., 46
Gainesville, Fla., 24
Gammon Theological Seminary, 62
Gardner, William V., 146
Gault, Horace J., 23
Gear, 20
General Assemblies, 21
General Assembly, 2, 5–6, 12, 16, 34, 42, 48, 61–62, 65, 75, 119, 136–39, 141, 144–45, 157, 166

General Assembly Committees, 38
General Assembly Council, 138
General Assembly of the Presbyterian Church (U.S.), 126
General Board, 139
Geneva, Switzerland, 135, 139
George Washington University, 69
Georgia Association of Pastoral Care, 176, 180–81
Georgia Committee on Interracial Matters, 175
Georgia Council of Churches, 175
Georgia Council on Human Relations, 139
Georgia Institute of Technology, 26, 62, 87, 144, 175
Georgia School of Technology, 175, 180
Georgia State University, 175–76
Georgia Tech University. *See* Georgia Institute of Technology
German Panzer Unit, 133
Gillespie, G. T., 146
Gillespie, Richard T., Jr., 33–34
Gillespie, Richard T., III, 5
Gladstone, 82
Glasure, Alton, 128
"God's Commandment for His People," 86
Golden Rule, 169
Gordon, U. S., 24
Goulding, Thomas, 32, 137
Grady Hospital, 165, 176
Great Depression, 63
Green, 20
Green, James B., 41, 96
Green, Lillian Clinkscales, 96
Greene, Melissa Faye, 178
Greenville, S.C., 42
Guthrie, Shirley, 73
Gutzke, Manford George, 41
Hall, Douglas John, 33
Hamburg, Germany, 82
Hamilton, Butterfly, 20
Hammarskjold, Dag, 74
"Happiness," 83
Harper, Norman, 71
Harrington, W. Frank, 124–25
Harrison, C. Virginia, 20, 27, 35, 52, 110
Hart, Abel McIver, 73
Hartsfield (mayor), 165–66, 177
Harvard University, 94
Hay, John, 48

Hays, 3
Helen, Ga., 78
Henderson, Plato, 110
High Museum of Art, 175
Hinesville, Ga., 124
Hitler, Adolf, 44, 46, 158, 182
Hocking, Ernest, 174
Holmes, Oliver Wendell, 82
Holmes, Robert Merrill, 31
Holston Presbytery, 75
"The Holy Spirit and the Church," 86
Homrighausen, E. G., 46, 69
Honea Path, S.C., 127
Hope, Ark., 97
Hopkins, Lindsey, 38
Hough, W. R., 53
"The Hound of Heaven," 95
Houston, Tex., 69
Howe, Ruell, 119
Hromadka, 46
Hudson, W. H., 104
Hugo, Victor, 95
Huie, Wade P., 8, 27
The Humility of Faith, 104
Humphrey, Ewing S., 144
Hunter, A. M., 73
Ibsen, 29
In the Presence of Mine Enemies, 133
Independent Presbyterian Church, 118–119
Inman Drive, 21, 32
Interdenominational Theological Center, 61, 139, 144, 180
Inter-Seminary movement, 175
Investment Committee, 22, 43
Iverson, Daniel, 146
Jackson, Miss., 53
Jacksonville, Fla., 111
Jim Crow, 158
John Birch Society, 124
Johns Hopkins University, 46
Johnson, Lyndon Baines, 71–72
Johnson C. Smith Theological Seminary, 61
Kehre, Harriett, 41
Keith, Jasper N., Jr., 181
Kennedy, John F., 71
Kennesaw College, 175
Kerr, E. D., 52–53
Kerr, Hugh, 46
Keyes, Kenneth, 150–52
King, Charles L., 69, 87
King, Martin Luther, Jr., 177
King College, 69
King Committee, 69
Kirk Road, 32
Kline, C. Benton, Jr., 67

Knight, Mary Evelyn, 79
Korean War, 55, 132
Kraemer, Charles E., 146
Kualien, Taiwan, 130
Ku Klux Klan, 165
Labour Party, 49
Lacy, Ben R., 181
Ladd, W. P., 45
Lamb, Charles, 162
Lanier, Sydney, 85
Lapsley, R. A., Jr., 146
Laramie, 74
Laurinburg, N.C., 145
Leith, John Haddon, 20, 44, 111, 116–17
Lenin, Vladimir, 158
Lexington, Ga., 32, 137
Liberty Hill, S.C., 2–3, 25
Liberty Hill Church, 2, 4–5
Life, 155
The Life of Faith, 104
Lincoln, Abraham, 82
Lingle, Walter L., 9
Linton, Thomas Dwight, 75–77
Liston, Jane Leighton Richards, **13**
Liston, Jane Leighton, 8
Liston, Robert T. L., 69, **13**
Liverpool, England, 82
London, England, 82
The Lone Ranger, 74
Long, George William, Jr., 52
"The Lord God Omnipotent Reigneth," 84
Lord's Prayer, 101
Loring, Eduard N., 66
Los Angeles, Calif., 41
Louisville, Ky., 32
Louisville Presbyterian Theological Seminary, 6, 42, 48, 39, 72, 74
Love, J. Erskine, Jr., 109
Lowell, James Russell, 95
Luce, Henry, 174
Lucy, Autherine, 163
Lunenburg, Germany, 50–51
Lyons, J. Sprole, 34
MacArthur, Douglas W., 58
Mackay, 46
MacNair, Arch L., 108
Magdalen College, 29
Main Street, 50
Makemie, 2
Malone, 2
"Manifesto," 166
Marshall, Peter, 83, 180
Marshall Plan, 47, 50
Martindale, Charles O'Neale, 53
Marx, David, 167, 178

Masefield, John, 84
Mathes, Frank Alfred, 18, 118–19
Mays, Benjamin, 165, 177
McCain, James Ross, 69, 146
McCallie, J. P., 146
McCallie School, 20, 28, 78
McClure, Charles G., 146
McCorkle, William, 87
McDill, Thomas H., 119–20, 176, 181
McDowell, James, 3
McDowells, 2
McElroy, W. T., 146
McGeachy, D. P., 105, 182
McGeachy, Mrs. D. P., 105
McGill, Ralph, 167
McIntire, Carl, 7, 143
McLaughlin, Henry Woods, 40
McPheeters, 20
McSween, John, 42
"The Meaning of Christmas," 80–81, 104
Memphis, Tenn., 27
Mendelssohn, Felix, 82
"Men Perplexed by a Changing World," 80
Meridian, Miss., 26
Meridian Presbytery, 34
Methodist Church, 124, 180
Michelangelo, 1, 29
Middle Ages, 94
Miller, Patrick Dwight, 19, 28, 63, 99–100, 125, 135
Milton, Ben, 25
Minister's Annuity Fund, 68
"Minister's Manifesto," 167, 170, 179
Missionary Drive, 32
Mission Haven, 54, 65, 131
Mississippi Central Railroad, 143
Mississippi River, 1
Moffatt, A. S., 18
Montgomery, Robert N., 130
Montreat, 115
Montreat, N.C., 11, 28, 71, 93
Montreat College, 72
Montreat Conference Center, 81, 87, 131
Montreat Presbyterian Church, 71–72
Moore, Ira, 130
Moore, Mrs. Ira, 130
Moore, Robert R., 132–33
Morecraft, Joseph C., III, 73, 75–77
Morehouse College, 165, 177
Morehouse School of Medicine, 175

Moses, 99
Muezens, 29
Munich, Germany, 158
Murrow, Edward R., 81
Nacoochee, Ga., 78
Napoleon, 82, 95
Nashville, Tenn., 48, 116, 125
National Arts Club, 141
National Commission on Racial and Cultural Problems, 172
National Council of Churches, 120, 136, 139, 142, 153, 173–75
National Student Christian Federation, 175
"Negro Churchmen and the Race Question," 165
Newark, N.J., 127
New College, 98
New Orleans, La., 16, 97, 109, 145
New Testament, 14, 24, 52–53, 73, 76, 78, 151
New York, N.Y., 111
Nix, John Arthur, Jr., 9
Nix, Mary Makemie Richards, 3, 9, 13. *See also* Richards, Mary Makemie
Nix, Thomas Makemie, 9
Nixon, George, 104
Nixon, George, Mrs., 104
Noble, J. Phillips, 15
North Augusta, S.C., 124
North Augusta Presbyterian Church, 124
The Obedience of Faith, 104
Obermeister of Lunenburg, 51
Oglesby, Stuart R., 111, 166, 171, 178
Oglesby, Stuart R., Jr., 81, 97–98
Oglethorpe College, 175, 178
Oglethorpe University, 5
Oldsmobile, 18
Old Testament, 52–53, 76, 78, 151
"The Open Door," 66
Orlando, Fla., 145
Ormond, 20
Ormond, J. Will, 44, 163
"Our Duty as Christian Citizens in Time of War," 182
Our Lord, An Affirmation of the Deity of Christ, 41
Oxford, England, 84
Oxford University, 11–12, 93, 135, 157–58, 179, **28, 159**
Oxnam, Bishop, 174
"The Pale Horse," 48
Panama, 48
Paris, France, 29

A Pastoral Communication on the Issues before the Church, 147

Patrick, Joseph E., Mrs., 129

Peace Memorial Presbyterian Church, 101

The Peace of the Believer, 104

Peachtree Presbyterian Church of Atlanta, 100, 109, 124

Pearl Harbor, 45–46

Perrin, Frances McDowell, 3

Pew, J. Howard, 22

Phi Beta Kappa, 28

Philadelphia, Pa., 139

Philips, J. Davison, 44, 152

Philips, Katherine Wright, 134

Pilgrim's Progress, 98

Plan of Government, 40, 52, 54, 61–62, 137

Plan of Reunion, 65, 183

Pompeii, Italy, 29

"A Prayer of Invocation," 86

Praying For Sheetrock, 178

"Preaching and the Issues of Today," 90

Presbyterian Church, 2–3, 5, 9, 21, 30, 32–33, 38, 46, 55, 61–62, 65, 69, 73, 82, 89, 98, 105, 107, 115, 137, 140, 143, 145, 148–49, 163, 172, 180–81

Presbyterian Church, U.S. (PCUS), 4–5, 7, 12, 14, 16, 32, 34, 44, 48–49, 52, 61–63, 66, 70–72, 75, 77, 96, 99, 111, 119, 124, 128–29, 132, 136–39, 141, 145, 147–50, 152–154, 157, 166, 172–73, 182

Presbyterian Church (U.S.A.), 157

Presbyterian Church in America (PCA), 65, 70, 154

Presbyterian Church in the United States (PCUSA), 5, 64, 136, 141–42, 152–53, 171, 173

Presbyterian Churchmen United, 75

Presbyterian College, 100

Presbyterian Education Educational Association of the South, 139

Presbyterian Historical Society (Montreat), 173

Presbyterian Home, 13–14, 78

Presbyterian Hour, 81, 103

Presbyterian Ministers Fund, 139

Presbyterian Program of Progress, 146

Presbyterian Survey, 80

Presbyterian World Alliance, 136

Presbytery of Atlanta, 136–37

Presbytery of Savannah, 119

President's Report, 64

Prince Edward County, Va., 125

Princeton Theological Seminary, 45–46, 69

Princeton University, 14, 20, 28, 78, 94, 179

"Principle or Profit," 91

"Program of Progress," 145

The Proof of Faith, 104

Protestant Hour, 81, 83

Protestant Radio Center, 139

Public School System, 169

Rabun Gap, Ga., 78

Rabun Gap Nacoochie School, 79

"Race and the Church," 165

The Range Rider, 74

Red Springs, N.C., 103

Reeves, Thomas J., 73

"Reflections on Armistice Day," 86

Reformed Church of America, 89, 150

Reformed Judaism, 178

Reformed Theological Seminary, 65

Reformed Theology, 73, 117, 134, 163

"The Relevance of the Gospel," 80, 86

"Renewal of the Spiritual Life of the Church," 87

Reserve Officer Corps, 132

Rhodes Scholar, 12, 28, 84, 135, 157

Rhodes Scholarship, 25

Rice, J. Sherrard, 87

Richards, 2, 28

Richards, Charles, 81, 114

Richards, Charles Malone, 2–5, 7–9

Richards, Charles Malone, II, 9, 11–12, 18

Richards, Emily Malone, 9

Richards, Evelyn, 13–14, 18, 20–21, 25, 28, **13**

Richards, Evelyn Knight, 9–10

Richards, James McDowell, Jr., 9

Richards, Jane Leighton, 2

Richards, Jane Leighton McDowell, 3

Richards, John Edwards, 2

Richards, John G., Jr., 2

Richards, John Gardiner, 2

Richards, Makemie, 81

Richards, Mary Evelyn (grandchild), 9

Richards, Mary Evelyn, 9

Richards, Mary James, 4, **28**

Richards, Mary Jane, 8

Richards, Mary Makemie, 9–12. *See also* Nix, Mary Makemie Richards

Richards, Michael McDowell, 9–12

Richards, Paul, 26

Richards, Steven Malone, 9

Richards Center, 68

Richardson, John R., 146

Richards Papers, 3, 23, 36, 79, 101, 107, 173, 175

Richmond, Va., 32, 38–41, 48, 116–17, 181

Righton, 2

Riviere, William T., 36–37

Robbins, Clyde D., 155

Roberts, A. A., 11–12

Robinson, Laurence Beaver, 127

Robinson, William Childs, 41, 47, 73

Robinson Lectures, 90

Romadka (professor), 45

Roman Catholic Church, 143

Rome, Ga., 104

Rome, Italy, 29

Roosevelt, Franklin D., 47–48, 81

Rotary Club, 51, 80, 84

Rothschild, Jacob, 178

The Ruins, 95

Rural Institute, 40

Salters, Rex, 17

San Antonio, Tex., 135

Savannah, Ga., 118, 126, 149

Savannah Presbytery, 118, 126

Second Presbyterian Church, 2

"The Seekers," 85

Seminary Board, 43

Seminary Bursar, 110

Seminary Endowment, 53

Seoul, S. Korea, 55

"Service of Celebration and Praise in Gratitude to God for Stuart R. Oglesby Jr.," 98

Sheldon, Charles A., 41

Shields, Jane Smith, 97

Shrewsbury, 82

Sibley, Celestine, 97

Simons-Law Hall, 16, 51, 54

The Sinfulness of Man, 104

"The Six Pillars for a Just and Durable Peace," 174

Sizoo, Joseph R., 69

Smith, 2

Smith, Egbert T., 41

Smith, J. Hoge, Jr., 125

Smith, J. Holmes, 130